A Sigh of Relief

COAST-TO-COAST ACCLAIM FOR THIS BESTSELLING CLASSIC

"A profusely and clearly illustrated book . . . designed to help parents overcome their own panic, and their child's panic, and handle the emergencies at hand."
—NEWSDAY

"Well designed and carefully organized for use by parents, baby-sitters or anyone else responsible for children's well being . . . . Every household should have a copy (or two) of **A SIGH OF RELIEF** within reach." —B. DALTON NEWSLETTER

"It's a godsend . . . . The handbook contains fast, basic instruction, wonderfully clear illustrations, a good, convenient index, and plenty of information on safety, toys, equipment and just about anything a parent might need to know . . . . This handbook is just what the doctor ordered . . . . Along with the text, the illustration and design of the book are exceptionally attractive. And that's one reason why parents will love it . . . . This kind of guide can, literally, be a lifesaver." —CALIFORNIA TIMES

"Parents can breathe a sigh of relief as long as they have (this) childhood emergency book . . . . This book is designed so that you can take care of any emergency in a matter of seconds . . . . Filled an enormous void." —THE HOUSTON POST

"This book is a first-of-its-kind." —RESEARCH INSTITUTE OF AMERICA

"Parents who have raised children without this large format, illustrated guide will wonder how they ever got along before . . . . Comprehensive and clearly written, it has hundreds of step-by-step instructions for just about every imaginable misfortune . . . . Simple diagrams should inspire confidence in the lay person called upon to administer first aid . . . . An indispensable book to have at the ready." —PUBLISHERS WEEKLY

"A unique, easy-to-use handbook for childhood emergencies . . . . This book should help parents learn how to react calmly — and breathe a sigh of relief." —NEWSWEEK

"(This) profusely illustrated, easy-to-read first-aid handbook could save a child's life . . . a terrific backup until help arrives." —THE BOSTON HERALD AMERICAN

" . . . a welcome addition to the family library." —FORT WORTH STAR-TELEGRAM

"**A SIGH OF RELIEF** is an important handbook, and long overdue on every family's shelf."
—QUALITY PAPERBACK BOOK CLUB REVIEW

"This handbook will be an asset in any home, institution or classroom."
—INTERNATIONAL READING ASSOCIATION — "SIGNAL"

"Fortunately, a new book has been published that should provide valuable help to parents, teachers and even baby-sitters." —U.S. DEPARTMENT OF HEALTH, EDUCATION AND WELFARE MAGAZINE

" . . . the first easy-to-use comprehensive handbook on childhood emergencies . . . . It's a sane, straight-forward book that can guide panicky parents — or baby-sitters — safely through a crisis with its full-page illustrations, simple instructions and a thumb index for extra-quick reference."
—FAMILY CIRCLE MAGAZINE

"This is exactly the kind of book I wish I'd had handy when my own children entered the toddler age of exploration." —KING FEATURES SYNDICATION

"An authoritative and graphically exciting first-aid manual . . . . This is one reference book that every parent will want to keep within easy reach." —EXPECTING MAGAZINE

"Wherever there is a child, there should be a copy of **A SIGH OF RELIEF**. It is a unique book . . . . While it has been developed for lay people, it can also be used by the health professional both as an emergency care management resource and as a strongly recommended reading reference for parents. **A SIGH OF RELIEF** has a foolproof system that provides quick access to the information needed. This book is an important contribution to child safety . . . innovative and comprehensive approach to accident management . . . . Everyone dealing with children should have a copy of **A SIGH OF RELIEF**."
—THE AMERICAN JOURNAL OF MATERNAL CHILD NURSING

"This book ought to be in every home with or without children . . . . No book on the market today is quite like this and we feel it ought to be in the hands of every baby-sitter, every expectant mother, grandparent, teachers, scout leaders — anyone." —STARS & STRIPES MAGAZINE

"Unusually helpful . . . . Though mainly designed for use by parents, most of the book will prove equally useful for teachers . . . . A copy of this book belongs in every Christian school, preferably in every Christian school classroom." —CHRISTIAN EDUCATORS JOURNAL

"(**A SIGH OF RELIEF** is an) excellent first-aid handbook for childhood emergencies. The format includes large print, well-detailed illustrations and quick reference — all aimed at reducing panic and speeding recovery."
—MOTHER'S MANUAL

"The best of its kind . . . . **A SIGH OF RELIEF** does for first aid what Sesame Street did for pre-schoolers. With simple, but dramatic graphics, it demonstrates clearly basic tools of survival . . . . One idea which is as simple and brilliant as the paper clip and should be widely adopted by other publishers is the printing of the index on the outside back cover of the book." —THE BALTIMORE NEWS AMERICAN

FROM UNSOLICITED LETTERS

"**A SIGH OF RELIEF** is the best book I have found concerning this topic and recommend it highly to parents."
—CHRISTINE BRIGHT, R.N.
Buffalo, N.Y.

"I have just discovered **A SIGH OF RELIEF** . . . and it is EXCELLENT. I have read it from cover to cover. After teaching Pediatric Emergency Care for 20 years I am delighted to see a book I can recommend — and **will** recommend — to parents and baby-sitters and teachers . . . . Good for you!"
—ELIZABETH S. HILLMAN, M.D.
Director of Ambulatory Education,
Janeway Child Health Centre, Newfoundland, Canada

"I recommend your handbook highly to all my patients' parents. Thank you for caring."
—PAULA REITER, R.N.
Pediatric Nurse Practitioner
Long Beach, California

A Sigh of Relief

the first-aid
handbook
for
childhood
emergencies

·

Revised Edition

Created, Designed & Produced
by
Martin I. Green

BANTAM BOOKS
TORONTO·NEW YORK·LONDON·SYDNEY·AUCKLAND

A Sigh of Relief

the first-aid
handbook
for
childhood
emergencies

A Bantam Book/September 1977
8 printings through 1983
Bantam Revised Edition/July 1984
12 printings through 1988
Bantam Revised Edition/September 1989

Published simultaneously in the United States and Canada.

Bantam books are published by Bantam Books, a division of Bantam Doubleday Dell Publishing Group, Inc. Its trademark, consisting of the words "Bantam Books" and the portrayal of a rooster, is registered in the United States Patent Office and in other countries. Marca Registrada. Bantam Books, 666 Fifth Avenue, New York 10103.

This edition published by arrangement with Martin I. Green and Berkshire Studio.
Printed in The United States of America
DW 0 9

Credits

Created, Designed & Produced by — MARTIN I. GREEN
Edited by — ROSS FIRESTONE
Illustrator & Associate Designer — BOBBI BONGARD
Research Coordinator — BERNICE CIRINCIONE
Research Associates — CIA ELKIN
— MARY SIPP GREEN
— ADELE MANDEL PUHN, M.S.

Proofreader — CIA ELKIN
Editorial Assistant — BERNICE CIRINCIONE
Medical Consultant — KENNETH JAY SOLOMON, M.D.
Assistant Designer — MARY SIPP GREEN
Mechanical Art — CANDY SEYLER

I am forever indebted to the following for their extraordinary support and encouragement: Michael J. Albano, Seymour Z. Baum, Martha Donovan, Gail Firestone, Robert Goldoff, Bruce Geller, William Gold, Leslie Kamerling, Adele Mandel Puhn, Ben Schawinsky and Anna D. Sipp.

Many thanks to Paul A. Cirincione and Herbert H. Sipp for their invaluable participation in the production of the first edition of A SIGH OF RELIEF.

Thanks, too, to the following for their contributions to the first edition: Frank Bongard, Alan Douglas, Steve Futterman, Lee Goldstein, Robert Moses, Harvey Rottenberg and Service Art Studio.

Finally I would like to express my very special appreciation to Brad Miner, whose enthusiasm, integrity and tireless efforts made this edition happen.

MIG

Berkshire Studio

WEST STOCKBRIDGE, MASSACHUSETTS 01266

Acknowledgments

We are most grateful to the following for providing us with information, for making their facilities available to us, and for reviewing and commenting on the manuscript during its various phases.

Commander George D. Armstrong, MPH, RPH
Office of Biometrics & Epidemiology
National Center for Drugs & Biologics
Rockville, Maryland

John C. Bernhartsen
United States Coast Guard
Washington, D.C.

C.P. Dail
Director of First Aid Programs
American Red Cross
National Headquarters
Washington, D.C.

Alan R. Dimick, M.D.
Director of Burn Center
University of Alabama
Birmingham, Alabama

Stephen Kaufman, M.D., F.A.C.E.P.
Director, Emergency Services
Columbia Memorial Hospital
Hudson, New York

LCDR William R. Ladd
United States Coast Guard
Washington, D.C.

Kenneth S. Lampe, Ph.D.
American Medical Association
Chicago, Illinois

National Safety Council
Chicago, Illinois

Gary Oderda, Pharm.D.
Director
Maryland Poison Center
Baltimore, Maryland

Don Sleeper
Assistant Director of First Aid Programs
American Red Cross
National Headquarters
Washington, D.C.

John B. Sullivan Jr., M.D.
Arizona Poison Control Center
University of Arizona
Tucson, Arizona

Joseph A. Wallick, MPH
American Red Cross
Santa Clara Valley Chapter
San Jose, California

We wish to thank the American Academy of Pediatrics, American Diabetes Association, American Lung Association, and the U.S. Consumer Product Safety Commission for information provided.

We are also indebted to the Boston Children's Medical Center in Boston, Massachusetts and the National Clearinghouse For Poison Control Centers in Bethesda, Maryland, for their participation in the first edition.

FOR
MY PARENTS ANNE AND BEN GREEN,
MARY,
OUR SON JARED
AND
ALL CHILDREN EVERYWHERE

Contents

Preface

By Vincent L. Tofany
Past President, National Safety Council

A Sigh Of Relief is an interesting contribution to the literature on child safety. I hope it will be carefully read and widely used.

The book is divided into two parts. The first deals with the prevention of childhood accidents, and the second with the action required after an accident has taken place. Prevention is, of course, the single most important element in child safety. When successful, it makes emergency measures unnecessary.

There are few mysteries in accident prevention. The preparations, practices and required actions are usually, if not always, simple, obvious and based upon common sense. But as many writers have pointed out, common sense is an uncommon commodity and the obvious is often overlooked, so it is always useful to have these basic preventive measures brought to our attention.

And sometimes common sense is not enough. In the more than 60 years that the organized voluntary safety movement has been in existence in the United States, it has developed and tested a great variety of preventive techniques applicable to all ages and activities. The authors of this book have made extensive use of this body of work as collated and disseminated by the National Safety Council, the clearinghouse for safety information.

As every safety worker knows, no matter how ardently prevention may be advocated, there will always be failures in prevention which may lead to accidental injuries. It is entirely appropriate, then, that the second part of **A Sigh of Relief** goes on to treat emergency management—"first aid" is perhaps the better known term. The emergency management section of this book has an original and, I believe, useful format designed to supply parents and other responsible adults with the needed information in quickly retrievable, highly graphic form.

Without question, parents who take seriously what they read here will be better able to protect their children from harm. And children reared by safety-minded parents will themselves grow up even more alert and informed about safety than their parents were.

For more information on child safety write:

National Safety Council
Child Safety Program
444 North Michigan Avenue
Chicago, Illinois 60611

Introduction

By Kenneth Jay Solomon, M.D.

Over the past few decades medicine has made remarkable progress in such difficult areas as cancer and leukemia survival and the prevention and treatment of infectious diseases. We have reached something like a 20 percent improvement in the overall mortality rate. Yet accidents still account for the greatest proportion of childhood deaths. There is even some indication that the death toll is increasing for certain groups of youngsters, most notably those between five and 14. What is responsible for these sad facts, and what can we do to give our children more adequate protection?

As a parent and pediatrician, I feel the main problem is that adults are so poorly prepared for the steps that must be taken in an emergency. I have been faced countless times with distraught, bewildered parents whose best intentions failed to aid their children because they didn't know what to do. The basic information was not readily available to them in a truly usable form.

Prevention remains our best defense against childhood accidents, but we must also know how to respond quickly and appropriately to any emergency situation if it arises. Nothing is more tragic than an emergency made worse by a parent's impulsive but misguided efforts to help the child. Hippocrates articulated the principle when he said, "First, do no harm."

This book has been carefully designed and organized for use by parents, baby-sitters and other laymen responsible for children's well-being. The unique indexing system on the back cover provides immediate access to guidance on how to handle just about any medical emergency your youngster may encounter. Each first-aid procedure is presented in easy to follow instructions printed in large type and is supported by clarifying step-by-step illustrations.

I suggest you read through the entire emergency section as soon as possible so you will have some familiarity with the recommended procedures before you ever need to use them. Remember that the basic purpose of first aid is to preserve the child's life and prevent further physical and psychological injury until help arrives. It is never a substitute for professional medical care. Since prevention is always preferable to cure, I also suggest you carefully study the opening section on preventions for the helpful guidance it has to offer. Keep the book in an accessible place known to everyone in your family.

To my knowledge, up to the present moment there has never been a handbook for parents that treated both the prevention and management of childhood emergencies. I am delighted that such a book now exists.

A WORD ABOUT THIS REVISED EDITION

A Sigh of Relief was first published in 1977. Since then, it has gone through eight large printings in the United States and been published in Japan, France, Italy, Yugoslavia, Germany, Mexico, Israel and other countries.

This new edition updates the original manuscript by incorporating the latest research in the management of childhood emergencies. After extensive review by a full range of medical experts, many procedures have been revised or expanded and a dozen new procedures added. These additions include state of the art techniques for treating major injuries as well as common mishaps like splinters and blisters. Although such mishaps are certainly not life-threatening, they are so pervasive that it was judged advisable to extend the scope of the book to accommodate them. All these revisions make **A Sigh of Relief**, in my opinion, even more indispensable than it was initially.

Part One

Preventions
Reducing the Odds

Parents, Children & Accidents

Accidents are by far the most common type of childhood emergency, the biggest single threat in the first 15 years of a youngster's life. Children are more likely than adults to have serious accidents because they are not only the victims but often the unconscious perpetrators. It is ironic that the major contributing factors are also some of the most basic, desirable and enjoyable characteristics of childhood itself.

During infancy the child's environment is severely limited, and it is relatively easy for parents to control its potential dangers. But as every parent learns, this phase soon ends as the baby begins to crawl and then to walk. This new mobility expands the child's world and exposes him to a greatly increased risk of injury. Yet it is normal for children to explore their new environment, to want to understand and master it with their newly developed abilities and almost limitless energy. What often places them in situations of high risk is, of course, their inexperience.

At the beginning, when your child is young and completely vulnerable, you can protect him from harm by staying physically close. But the developmental process begun at birth is designed to produce a self-sufficient, independent individual at maturity, and the child's environment must necessarily soon expand beyond the point where you can (or should) be physically present every moment of the day.

Fortunately, at about the same time the youngster's world expands, he begins to understand and respond to language. It is usually at this point that the admonition "No!" begins to be used around the home with increasing, sometimes maddening, regularity. The child's ability to respond to simple instructions is what makes it possible for you to protect him from a distance. It also enables you to begin his safety training.

Safety training involves three major steps:
- **Defining** the limits of safe behavior for the large number of threatening situations the child may be expected to encounter.
- **Teaching** these limits patiently until he understands and accepts them.
- **Reinforcing** these limits whenever he forgets or ignores them.

Consistency is an important factor in this process. It is easier for a child to follow a simple unchanging rule than one which may be altered by parental mood or whim. Restrictions that come and go according to special circumstance present younger children with confusing distinctions and subtleties that may be beyond their scope. The more clear and simple the rule, the more likely the child to abide by it.

Restrictions appropriate at one point in a child's life may become unrealistic and unnecessary only a few months later. A parent must try to strike the fine balance between the youngster's need for reasonable protection from danger and the comparable need for diversity of experience and the freedom to explore.

This is one of the most difficult responsibilities of parenthood, because the balance shifts constantly as the child's judgment and abilities improve. As the years pass, the need for parental guidance slowly decreases until, finally, the child is autonomous. As this scenario unfolds, you must be able to loosen the limitations imposed upon your child, relaxing them gradually as he demonstrates ever increasing maturity.

Yet accidents will still sometimes happen because of the child's natural tendency to test all limits. Boys and girls are aware of their ongoing physical development and constantly try to master new physical skills. Moreover, parents usually prize their child's achievements, and the youngster is encouraged by this approval to stretch out for new accomplishments.

The child's healthy development also requires a secure and loving environment in which he occupies an important place. To be truly effective, safety training and the discipline that comes with it should always be offered in the spirit of concern, acceptance and love. We must strive to show our children that while we may not approve of certain things **they do,** we do not disapprove of **them.**

In some households, one or both parents is particularly, even morbidly, fearful for the child's safety and tends to become overly protective. Not infrequently, a parent will have difficulty acknowledging a youngster's improved abilities, to the extent of inhibiting his normal pursuit of experience. The children of neurotically fearful parents are often insecure and profoundly lacking in confidence. Of course we should protect our children from **unreasonably** dangerous situations which have considerable potential for serious injury. Yet it is through systematic exposure to new and demanding experiences that we provide the stimulation and environmental richness essential to their ongoing development. We should want to encourage our sons and daughters to operate somewhere near the limits of their capacities without either exposing them to unreasonable danger or smothering them with our own unreasonable fears.

Home Safety

Every parent wants to give his child a safe home, a place to live and grow free of foreseeable danger. Your efforts here have a double benefit: they protect your youngster from physical harm and also establish a consciousness about safety he will take out into the world with him wherever he goes.

This chapter discusses the most prevalent kinds of home accidents and the ways they can be prevented. (Drowning, certainly one of the major hazards, is treated on pages 56 - 63 of the chapter on **Water Safety**.) You'll also find here room-by-room suggestions about the special dangers inherent in each different area of your home.

Remember that hazards change according to a child's age and development. Safety training is a continuing process with different requirements for each stage of childhood. Parents must not only recognize present dangers around the home but anticipate the ones to come.

Remember also that the moods and circumstances of your family have an important influence on your child's safety. Accidents are most likely to occur:

● When children are so hungry or thirsty they are ready to eat or drink anything. Many poisonings take place just before mealtime.
● When children and mothers are tired, usually before it's time for a nap, in late afternoon or before bedtime.
● When children are overactive or rushed and don't allow enough time to do things carefully.
● When mothers are pregnant or ill and not able to supervise their children with their usual patience and care.
● When parents quarrel or are under emotional stress and aren't paying adequate attention to the child. The child may react in rebellious or hazardous ways.
● When the family routine is upset by moves, long trips or vacations.
● When baby-sitters or other less-experienced people are supervising the child.

SUFFOCATION

Because of their inexperience and relative helplessness, infants are particularly susceptible to accidental suffocation. Parents of younger children must stay constantly on the alert to this danger and learn to take the following precautions:

● Keep plastic bags out of your child's reach. Never use them as waterproof sheets or toys. They should be knotted and thrown away immediately.
● Don't give a younger child soft pillows and other bedclothes which might interfere with his breathing. Tuck the bottom sheet smoothly under the mattress and keep the top sheet loose enough to let him move about freely.

● Never leave your infant unattended with a feeding bottle propped up in his mouth.
● If you have a refrigerator or freezer stored away in your basement or garage, remove the door so your child can't be trapped inside.
● Keep storage areas uncluttered and never pile things so high they could cave in on the child.
● Put ropes, cords and long scarves where young children can't get to them.
● To prevent choking, don't let your youngster run with food in his mouth or engage in horseplay at mealtime. Make sure he doesn't put small toys and other objects in his mouth.

FALLS

Falling accidents are a major cause of serious injury to children of every age. Here's what you can do to keep them to a minimum:

● Make sure your floors aren't slippery. Don't wax them to too high a finish. Wipe up spilled liquids immediately.

● Check that all carpets and scatter rugs are anchored firmly in place.

● Install nonskid rubber mats or abrasive treads inside bathtubs and showers. Use nonskid bath mats to keep your child from slipping when he steps out.

● Don't leave toys and other objects lying around the floors. Toys should be put away promptly after each use so they won't be tripped over and broken.

● Whenever you put your baby in his crib, be sure to raise the sides to their fullest height and lock them in position.

● All rooms and hallways should be lit adequately.

● Doorways and halls should be free of obstructions.

● Never leave your infant alone in a baby carrier you've placed on a table, counter, couch or chair. Stay within arm's reach and be sure to fasten his safety belt to keep him from slipping out.

● Make sure stairways remain uncluttered and in good repair. Major hazards include loose or missing handrails, loose carpeting, worn treads, poor lighting, stairs of unequal height and unanchored scatter rugs at the top of the landing. For younger children, install safety gates at the top and bottom of the stairways. Keep the stairs free of objects that don't belong there, and don't let your youngster run, sit or play on them.

● Check that all balconies and high porches are in good condition and protected with strong railings.

● Open windows from the top, not the bottom, and fit them with screens with child-proof latches. Don't let your child sit on windowsills or lean against the screens.

● Make sure your child's skirts and pants aren't too long and that shoes aren't too large or left untied. Never let a youngster dress up in a sash, scarf or cape that trails on the floor behind him.

● Keep your child away from tabletops and other high surfaces. Don't let a toddler try to climb into his highchair by himself. Make sure to fasten the safety harness. Bunk beds are safe only for older children.

● Discourage roughhousing, bravado and wild play inside the home.

POISONING

Most poisoning accidents take place in the home and involve children under five eating or drinking toxic substances carelessly left within their reach. Almost every room in the house contains common substances that can poison a child if he ingests them:

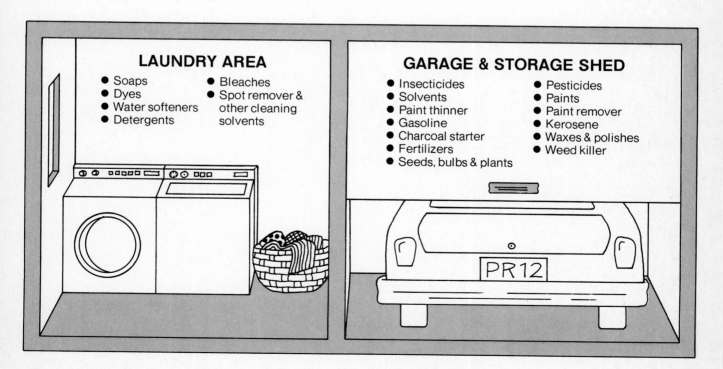

LAUNDRY AREA
● Soaps
● Dyes
● Water softeners
● Detergents
● Bleaches
● Spot remover & other cleaning solvents

GARAGE & STORAGE SHED
● Insecticides
● Solvents
● Paint thinner
● Gasoline
● Charcoal starter
● Fertilizers
● Seeds, bulbs & plants
● Pesticides
● Paints
● Paint remover
● Kerosene
● Waxes & polishes
● Weed killer

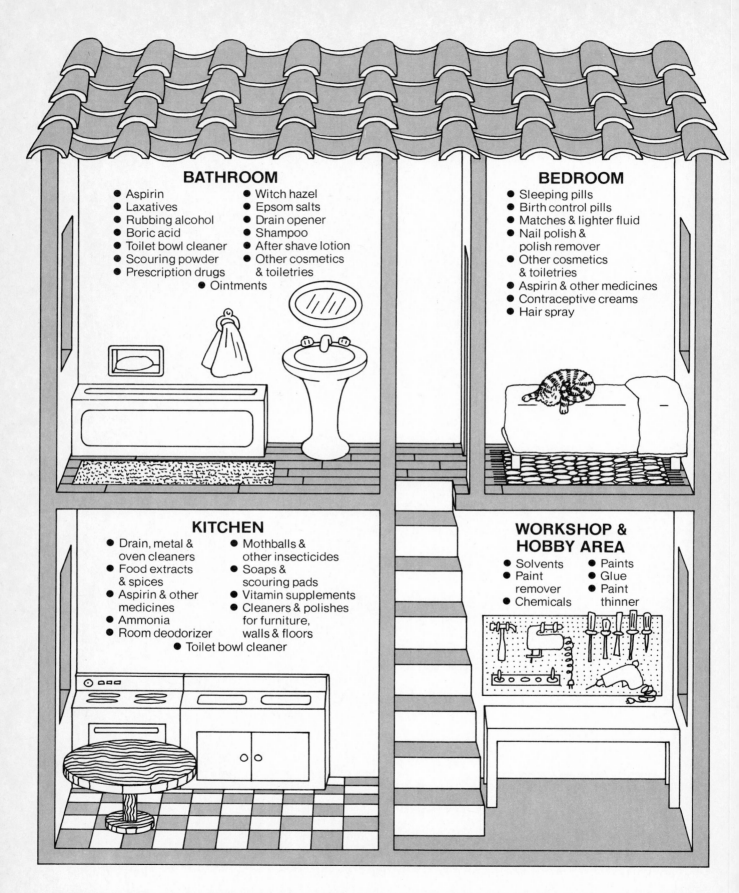

BATHROOM

- Aspirin
- Laxatives
- Rubbing alcohol
- Boric acid
- Toilet bowl cleaner
- Scouring powder
- Prescription drugs
- Witch hazel
- Epsom salts
- Drain opener
- Shampoo
- After shave lotion
- Other cosmetics & toiletries
- Ointments

BEDROOM

- Sleeping pills
- Birth control pills
- Matches & lighter fluid
- Nail polish & polish remover
- Other cosmetics & toiletries
- Aspirin & other medicines
- Contraceptive creams
- Hair spray

KITCHEN

- Drain, metal & oven cleaners
- Food extracts & spices
- Aspirin & other medicines
- Ammonia
- Room deodorizer
- Mothballs & other insecticides
- Soaps & scouring pads
- Vitamin supplements
- Cleaners & polishes for furniture, walls & floors
- Toilet bowl cleaner

WORKSHOP & HOBBY AREA

- Solvents
- Paint remover
- Chemicals
- Paints
- Glue
- Paint thinner

All these substances should be kept stored where a child can't get to them, well beyond his reach and preferably under lock and key. To prevent any possible confusion, store them separately from food and other things your child might seek out, and never keep them in soda bottles, milk cartons, coffee cans or other familiar containers. Each substance should be labeled clearly and tightly covered or capped with a child-proof lid. And never leave handbags or briefcases lying around; they may hold some of the same dangerous substances found elsewhere in the home.

The severity of a childhood poisoning may depend on the speed with which you can obtain expert emergency information and treatment. Get the telephone number of your local Poison Control Center from the phone book and write it down in the space provided on page 264. In case of an emergency, the Center will give you immediate instructions on what to do. You might also prepare yourself by having on hand the various recommended antidotes: syrup of ipecac, Epsom salts and activated charcoal. In case you are unable to reach your Center for some reason, see **POISONING**, pages 226-241, in our emergency first-aid section.

FIRE AND BURNS

Fire poses a serious threat to everyone in your home as well as your children. Here are some basic measures to minimize the risk of injury:
- Be sure the electrical wiring in your home is sound.
- Never overload the circuits. Be cautious about using extension cords and multiple sockets.
- Frequently examine electric heaters, cooking equipment and other appliances to make sure they are still in good operating condition. Replace frayed cords and broken or loose plugs.
- Oily cloths and flammable liquids should be stored away from heat in closed metal containers. Rubbish should be discarded promptly.
- Be careful when you smoke.
- Use a fire screen in front of your fireplace.
- Put fire extinguishers in your kitchen and on each floor of your house.
- Install smoke detectors in rooms and hallways.
- If you live in an apartment building, make sure everyone in your family knows the proper evacuation procedures.
- If you live in a house with more than one story, install fire ladders in the upper rooms.
- Plan escape routes in advance and practice them frequently with your household. Include a meeting place outside the home where your family can assemble and be counted.

You can also protect your child against fire and burns by giving him the supervision his age requires, teaching him to avoid foreseeable hazards and taking care not to imperil him through your own carelessness.
- Make sure he understands that fires can burn and that he is to stay away from stoves, heaters, open flames, hot liquids, matches and lit cigarettes.

- Be particularly careful when you're cooking. Use the back burners whenever possible, and always turn pot handles to the rear so your child can't brush up against them or grab them. Keep highchairs away from the stove.

- At mealtime, keep hot food and drink near the center of the table where a youngster can't get at them. Never pass hot food over his head.

- Teach your child to take extreme care when turning on a hot-water faucet, particularly in the shower or bath.

- Unplug electric appliances when they're not being used. When this isn't practical, make sure the cords are well out of a young child's reach so he can't chew them or pull the appliance down.

- Block off unused electrical outlets with special plugs made for this purpose, or with heavy electrical tape. Teach your youngster never to stick keys, pins or other metal objects into an outlet.

- When you disconnect an extension cord from an appliance, don't leave it plugged into the wall. Your child could burn or shock himself badly if he puts it in his mouth or touches it with wet hands.

- Don't let your child use a radio, television set or other appliance around water.

- Check that all electrical toys are listed by the Underwriters Laboratory (UL) and inspect them frequently for frayed wires and loose or broken plugs.

- Teach your child what to do in a fire emergency and review it with him frequently. As soon as he's old enough, make sure he knows how to summon aid from the fire department.

GUNS

If you have guns at home, be sure to keep them unloaded and take special care to lock them safely out of your youngster's reach. Ammunition should also be locked away but in a separate storage area. Guns should always be treated as if they were loaded and never pointed at anyone.

Home Safety Tips

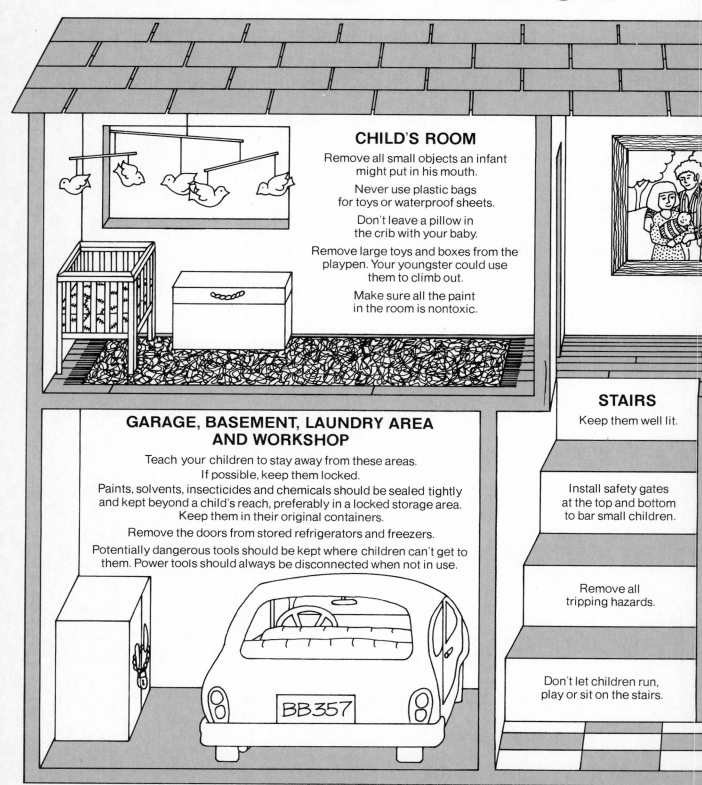

CHILD'S ROOM

Remove all small objects an infant might put in his mouth.

Never use plastic bags for toys or waterproof sheets.

Don't leave a pillow in the crib with your baby.

Remove large toys and boxes from the playpen. Your youngster could use them to climb out.

Make sure all the paint in the room is nontoxic.

GARAGE, BASEMENT, LAUNDRY AREA AND WORKSHOP

Teach your children to stay away from these areas. If possible, keep them locked.

Paints, solvents, insecticides and chemicals should be sealed tightly and kept beyond a child's reach, preferably in a locked storage area. Keep them in their original containers.

Remove the doors from stored refrigerators and freezers.

Potentially dangerous tools should be kept where children can't get to them. Power tools should always be disconnected when not in use.

STAIRS

Keep them well lit.

Install safety gates at the top and bottom to bar small children.

Remove all tripping hazards.

Don't let children run, play or sit on the stairs.

BB357

BATHROOM

Never leave an infant or
young child alone in a tub.

If possible, lock medicine and toiletry cabinets.
Open shelves should be high enough so your
child can't get to them. Discard old
prescription medicines.

Keep the toilet cover closed.
Keep electrical appliances away from water.

Install rubber mats or abrasive treads
inside tub or shower.
Use nonskid bath mats.

Keep the door closed so your
toddler won't wander in.

SOME GENERAL TIPS

Cover unused electrical outlets with
heavy electrical tape or special plugs.

Keep children from leaning against
window screens or playing on windowsills and other high places.

Make sure to unplug an extension cord
from the outlet when you remove it
from the appliance.

Never leave an infant or
young child at home by himself.

KITCHEN

Turn pot handles toward
the back of the stove.

Household cleaners, chemicals,
bleaches and other dangerous
substances should be stored
high up and under lock and key.

Make sure knives and other dangerous
utensils stay out of reach.

Keep electrical appliances
away from water and unplugged
when not in use.

Don't place a highchair near
the stove or around such busy areas
as doorways and refrigerators.

Infant Equipment

Not all infant equipment on the market is safely designed and constructed. Here's what to look for when you shop for a crib, carriage or the like, along with some pointers about how to use them safely:

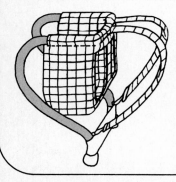

BABY CARRIERS

- The base should be wide and sturdy. Supporting devices must fasten securely to keep the carrier from collapsing.
- Check that the carrier comes with safety belts to hold the child in place.
- Attach rough-surfaced adhesive strips to the bottom to prevent it from slipping when you set it down.

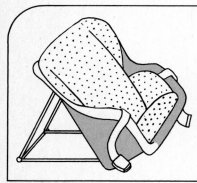

BABY WALKERS

- Make sure the walker is stable and won't tip over easily. The wheel base should be longer and wider than the frame. Small, flimsy wheels or a narrow base may cause the child to fall when he leans, reaches, runs or tries to get over thresholds and rugs. Help the child past such obstacles and remove throw rugs from his path.
- Check that coiled springs and hinges are encased in protective covers. Many older style walkers are made with X frames which can catch a child's fingers. Locking devices and fasteners should be free of sharp edges and points.
- The seat should be made of unbreakable plastic or sturdy fabric with heavy-duty stitching and large, rugged snaps.

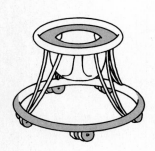

BACKPACKS

- Select the carrier appropriate to your youngster's size and weight. Make sure it is deep enough to support his back and comes equipped with safety belts.
- Leg openings should be small enough to keep the child from slipping out but large enough not to chafe his legs.
- Check for sturdy materials, strong stitching and large, heavy-duty snaps. The metal frame near his face should be cushioned with soft padding.
- Make sure the joints fasten securely and can't accidentally close on the child. Look out for points, sharp edges and rough surfaces.

CRIBS

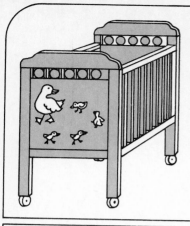

- Check that the slats aren't so widely spaced that your infant can slip his head or body through them. The law in the United States is they can't be more than 2-3/8 inches apart.
- Bumper pads should extend around the entire crib and tie into place with at least six ties.
- Make sure the mattress fits snugly. If you can get two fingers between the mattress and the sides of the crib, it's too small.
- Look for a substantial distance between the top of the side rail and the mattress support. When your child is eventually able to stand, lower the mattress to the bottom position and lock the side rail at maximum height. You will also have to remove bumper pads, large boxes and toys, and anything else he could use to climb out. If the side is less than 3/4 of the child's height, the crib is too small for him and should no longer be used.

HIGHCHAIRS

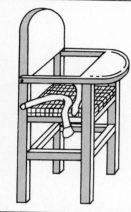

- The chair should have a wide base to keep it stable and come equipped with a safety belt that attaches to the frame, not to the tray. Be sure to fasten the belt whenever you put your child in the chair.
- Always make sure the tray is properly latched on both sides. Don't use it as a restraining device; that's what the safety belt is for.
- Make sure the latching mechanism and the rest of the chair are free of sharp edges and points.

PLAYPENS

- Check that the slats are narrow enough to keep your child from slipping his head or body through them. They shouldn't be more than 2-3/8 inches apart. (If you have an old playpen with wide slats, interweave sheeting between them and fasten securely.)
- The weave in mesh netting should be so small that it can't catch the buttons on the baby's clothes. Large openings also make easy toeholds for climbing and could possibly strangle him should he catch his head in them.
- Make sure the floor support is sturdy enough not to collapse when your child jumps on it.
- Hinges and latches should fasten securely so they won't catch his fingers.
- Install a foam pad on the bottom of the pen. The material is long-lasting and won't mildew.

STROLLERS

- Make sure the backrest is firm and nearly vertical and that the seat is firm and flat. If there is a canopy, it should clear the child's head and allow room for growth.
- Check that there are seat belts to keep the child from falling out and a brake that locks securely. Brakes on both wheels provide extra safety.
- Avoid strollers with points, sharp edges or scissors-like folding mechanisms. Latches should be out of the child's reach and must fasten securely.
- If the stroller adjusts to a reclining position, be sure it won't tip over backwards when the baby lies down.

Toy Safety

Look for sharp edges, points and splinters which can cut, scratch or puncture.

Metal toys with unfinished slots, holes and edges can cause razor-sharp cuts.

Don't let your child play with lead soldiers or other toys made with lead.

Check that the toy isn't too heavy for the child.

Projectile toys should only be used by responsible children over 8.

Unsafe: Poorly constructed dolls and animals stuffed with small loose pellets that will fall out when the seams tear open.

Overly loud toys may damage your child's hearing. Caps should never be fired close to the ear.

Make sure that riding toys are stable and well-balanced.

Cloth toys should be labeled "Flame Resistant," "Flame Retardant" or "Nonflammable." Don't buy dolls with cellulose hair and other cellulose toys.

**BEWARE!
UNSAFE TOYS
Children Not Allowed**

All children love toys, and the playthings we give our sons and daughters benefit them a number of important ways. Toys teach them to focus their attention, aid their intellectual, psychological and aesthetic growth, help them develop adult skills and, of course, provide them with fun and entertainment. Unfortunately, not all these toys are safe, nor are the ways they are sometimes used.

Parents could prevent toy-related injuries more effectively if they were always caused by unsafe toys alone. There's no question that entirely too many toys **are** unsafe and account for a large portion of childhood accidents, yet other factors are usually also involved. Reputable toy manufacturers try to make their products as safe as possible, but they have to assume that parents will choose the appropriate toys for their children and give them adequate supervision. What finally determines the risk during play is a combination of the particular toy, child and circumstances and what you do (or fail to do) to protect your youngster from harm.

UNSAFE TOYS

A toy is inherently unsafe if its design or materials are defective or if there are flaws in its manufacture. Before buying a toy for your child, examine it carefully for its injury potential, looking for quality design, materials and construction throughout:

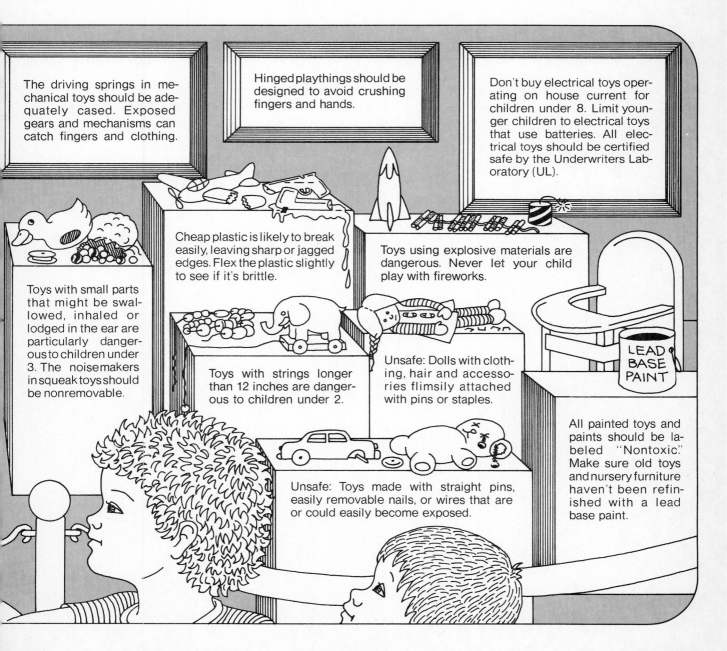

The driving springs in mechanical toys should be adequately cased. Exposed gears and mechanisms can catch fingers and clothing.

Hinged playthings should be designed to avoid crushing fingers and hands.

Don't buy electrical toys operating on house current for children under 8. Limit younger children to electrical toys that use batteries. All electrical toys should be certified safe by the Underwriters Laboratory (UL).

Cheap plastic is likely to break easily, leaving sharp or jagged edges. Flex the plastic slightly to see if it's brittle.

Toys using explosive materials are dangerous. Never let your child play with fireworks.

Toys with small parts that might be swallowed, inhaled or lodged in the ear are particularly dangerous to children under 3. The noisemakers in squeak toys should be nonremovable.

Toys with strings longer than 12 inches are dangerous to children under 2.

Unsafe: Dolls with clothing, hair and accessories flimsily attached with pins or staples.

LEAD BASE PAINT

Unsafe: Toys made with straight pins, easily removable nails, or wires that are or could easily become exposed.

All painted toys and paints should be labeled "Nontoxic." Make sure old toys and nursery furniture haven't been refinished with a lead base paint.

TOYS TOO OLD FOR YOUR CHILD

Toys appropriate for older children may be hazardous and frustrating for a younger child because of his inability to use them properly. Children themselves purchase 1/3 of all toys sold, so it's particularly important to teach them which playthings are—and are not—suitable for their age.

● When selecting a toy for your child, keep in mind his age, abilities, interests and limitations. Make a point of checking the manufacturer's age recommendations. Such warnings as "Not Suitable For Children Under 3 Years" are generally sound and intended to protect the younger child from toys that have small parts, break relatively easily, or for some other reason aren't safe for youngsters under the given age.

● When buying toys for older children, consider the risks to their younger brothers and sisters. Young children are always curious about the toys of their older siblings, and since they are usually unaware of the dangers, they can be seriously hurt if allowed to play with them. Teach your older children to keep their toys away from the younger kids around the house. Store toys separately for children of different ages.

BROKEN TOYS

Even reasonably well-made toys may break eventually, leaving jagged or sharp edges and points. Some apparently safe toys use hazardous prongs and knife-like points in their inner construction, which become exposed when the toy is broken.

● Select toys likely to withstand being frequently pushed, pulled at and dropped. Children like to explore how their toys are put together, and a toy should be sturdy enough to withstand their probing. Even when it breaks, it should still remain safe. Tug gently at attached parts to test their strength. Flex plastic toys slightly to see if they are brittle and likely to break easily.

● To minimize breaking (and to keep them from being tripped over), make sure that toys are put away soon after they've been played with. Indoor toys shouldn't be left outdoors, where they can be damaged by moisture and rust.

● Check your child's toys regularly to make sure they are still safe for continued use. Broken toys and children's furniture should be repaired promptly. Use only lead-free paints to restore the finish. If the toy can't be fixed, discard it.

PLAYING SAFELY

Some toy-related injuries have less to do with any defect in the toy itself than with the way it is used. Parents sometimes forget their children's inexperience and neglect the preventive measures that would keep them out of harm's way.

● Give your child the supervision and guidance his age requires:

• Children up to the age of 2 require extremely close—almost constant—supervision. By the time they are toddlers they can be taught not to walk or run with things in their mouths.

• 2 to 4 year olds are most susceptible to toy-related injuries and continue to require close supervision. This is particularly the case with boys. From this age on, they are statistically more likely than girls to have accidents. Safety training in the proper use of toys should be actively undertaken throughout these years.

• 4 to 6 year olds should be able to demonstrate more of an understanding of toy hazards and exhibit good safety practices at play. Safety training should continue.

• 6 to 8 year olds are now in school and playing further away from the direct supervision of their parents. Make sure your child has internalized the principles of safe play.

• 8 to 12 year olds may (or may not) be mature enough to play with some of the questionably safe toys they may want. Before letting your child play with chemistry sets, projectile toys, sharp tools and other potentially hazardous playthings, be certain he knows how to use them safely. Parental supervision may still be required.

● Keep an eye on your child's playmates and the way they play together. An accident may happen because a friend hasn't learned the potential dangers of a toy.

● When your youngster gets a new toy, read over the instructions with him and make sure you both understand them. Teach him the proper use of the toy, explaining the hazards which may result from its misuse. Take the time to help him develop the necessary skills.

● A toy must be given the play space it requires. Outdoor toys should only be used outdoors. Projectile toys are particularly dangerous in inadequate space.

● Check the chapter on **Bicycle Safety** for the proper use of two-wheel bikes. Your child should know the following basic safety rules for such sidewalk vehicles as coaster wagons, skateboards, roller skates, scooters and tricycles:

• Always be careful of other people, and go slowly enough to stop suddenly if you have to.

• Never fool around or show off.

• Only play on sidewalks that aren't crowded.

• Don't hold packages in your arms while you ride. Leave your arms and hands free for balancing.

• Look carefully both ways before crossing a driveway.

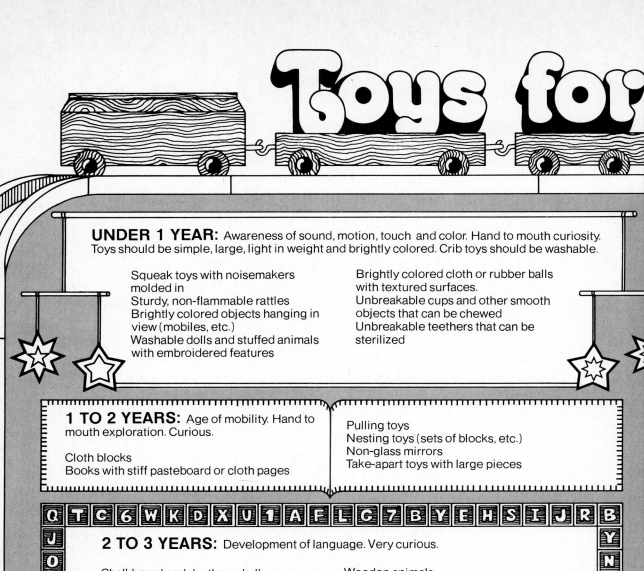

Toys for

UNDER 1 YEAR: Awareness of sound, motion, touch and color. Hand to mouth curiosity. Toys should be simple, large, light in weight and brightly colored. Crib toys should be washable.

Squeak toys with noisemakers molded in
Sturdy, non-flammable rattles
Brightly colored objects hanging in view (mobiles, etc.)
Washable dolls and stuffed animals with embroidered features

Brightly colored cloth or rubber balls with textured surfaces.
Unbreakable cups and other smooth objects that can be chewed
Unbreakable teethers that can be sterilized

1 TO 2 YEARS: Age of mobility. Hand to mouth exploration. Curious.

Cloth blocks
Books with stiff pasteboard or cloth pages

Pulling toys
Nesting toys (sets of blocks, etc.)
Non-glass mirrors
Take-apart toys with large pieces

2 TO 3 YEARS: Development of language. Very curious.

Chalkboard and dustless chalk
Low rocking horse
Simple musical instruments
Simple jigsaw puzzles with large pieces
Lotto-type matching games

Wooden animals
Blocks with numbers and letters
Toys that stimulate color, size and shape identification

3 TO 4 YEARS: Vigorous physical activity. Imagination and imitation.

Manipulative toys
Sturdy trucks and non-electric trains
Toy telephone
Metal tea set
Dolls with simple wrap-around clothing
Large wooden stringing beads
Construction sets with easily connecting large pieces
Jigsaw puzzles with large pieces

Simple musical instruments
Counting frame with large beads
Pegboard
Large crayons
Rugged key-wound or friction-operated toys
Blunt scissors
Lacing cards
Simple card and board games

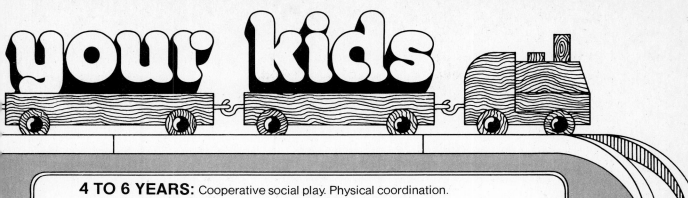

your kids

4 TO 6 YEARS: Cooperative social play. Physical coordination.

Blocks of various geometric shapes
Picture books
Pail and shovel
Hand and finger puppets
Watercolor paints
Modeling clay
Simple kaleidoscope
Key-wound or friction-operated toys
Cut-out paper dolls

Magnetic numbers and letters
Felt board
More advanced construction toys
Kites
Stencils
Activity books
More demanding board and card games
Simple musical instruments

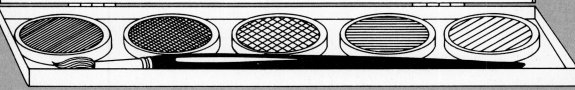

6 TO 8 YEARS: Independent play. Physical and intellectual interests.

Kites
Boats and planes not driven by gasoline engines
Puppets and puppet theater
More complicated jigsaw puzzles
Games requiring some reading
Well-constructed, lightweight tool sets
Dolls and doll equipment

Equipment for playing store, bank, filling station, etc.
Magnets, magnifiers and sets demonstrating simple principles of science
Flower press
Simple musical instruments

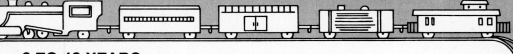

8 TO 12 YEARS: Arts, crafts, building and science interests.

Construction models of boats, planes and cars
Hobby material for coin and stamp collecting, etc.
Arts and crafts kits and materials

Electric trains and other electrical toys certified safe by the Underwriters Laboratory (UL)
Chemistry and other science sets
Bikes and sidewalk vehicles

School Safety

By the time your child goes off to school, he is feeling a new independence and is no longer as subject to your direct supervision. The school will take on some of the responsibility for overseeing his safety, but it is crucial that you reinforce the safety lessons he learns there and show him how to protect himself from potential dangers between school and home.

GETTING TO AND FROM SCHOOL

If your child walks all or part of the way to school, map out the safest possible route, the one that exposes him to the least traffic, fewest intersections and avoids such hazards as construction sites. Emphasize that he is to follow this route and this route only, explaining why it is the safest and pointing out the hazards that do exist along the way. Make sure he understands never to hitchhike or accept rides from strangers. He should also understand the following rules of pedestrian safety. They are probably his single best protection against accidental injury.

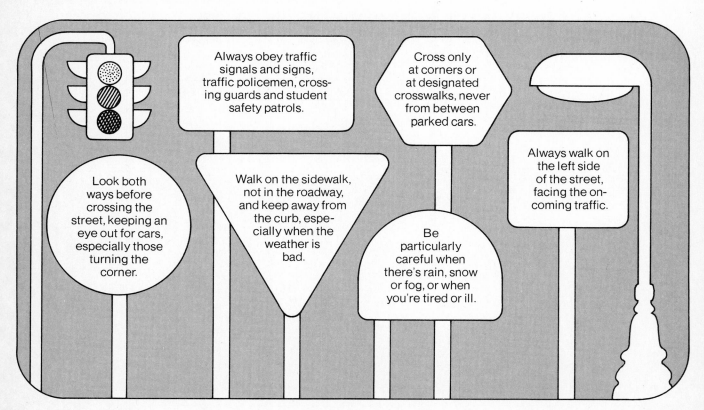

Always obey traffic signals and signs, traffic policemen, crossing guards and student safety patrols.

Cross only at corners or at designated crosswalks, never from between parked cars.

Look both ways before crossing the street, keeping an eye out for cars, especially those turning the corner.

Walk on the sidewalk, not in the roadway, and keep away from the curb, especially when the weather is bad.

Be particularly careful when there's rain, snow or fog, or when you're tired or ill.

Always walk on the left side of the street, facing the on-coming traffic.

If your youngster uses the school bus, make sure he allows himself enough time to get to the bus stop without rushing. While waiting for the bus, he should stay away from the edge of the road. If he has to cross the road to enter the bus, tell him to wait until the driver or crossing guard signals that the way is clear.

Here are some other precautions he should follow once he's gotten on board:

● Take your seat promptly and stay there until you reach your destination.

● Always obey the driver, student monitor or school safety patrolman.

● Never distract the driver or engage in horseplay.

● Don't stick your head or hands out the window or throw anything into the street.

● Make sure you know how to use the emergency exit.

If your child uses public transportation, go along with him the first few times to make certain he knows the way. He should always carry some form of personal identification, and enough money to call home in case he gets lost.

If you drive him to school yourself, make a point of dropping him off directly in front of the entrance so he doesn't have to cross the street. Stopping on the other side of the street needlessly exposes him to traffic and may encourage him to cross in the middle of the block.

IN SCHOOL

The classroom is probably the safest place in school because of the teacher's presence, but much of the school day is spent moving from classroom to classroom to gymnasium to cafeteria. Every school sets up safety rules to insure the safe movement of large numbers of children, and you should encourage your child to learn and obey them. It's likely that many of these precautions will be the same ones you use at home, so your youngster will already be familiar with them. But make sure he is also aware of the following basics that apply specifically to the school situation:

● Walk, do not run, in the school corridors.

● Never engage in horseplay.

● When using busy stairways, keep to the right and hold on to the handrails. Take one step at a time. Never jump down the stairs or slide down the railings.

Tell your child to pay particular attention to the teacher's directions in woodwork and metal shop, science and photography labs, and the art and home economics rooms. Hand and power tools, kilns, stoves, chemicals and other specialized equipment can be extremely dangerous if not used in accordance with these established safety procedures:

● Always wear safety glasses when using such equipment as power saws, grinders and lathes.

● Remove rings, wristwatches, bracelets and cumbersome buckles when working around machinery. Make sure to keep neckties, scarves, loose clothing and long hair away from moving parts.

● Never remove or tamper with the safety features of a machine.

● No running or horseplay. They are particularly dangerous here.

● Keep work areas and aisles free of tripping hazards.

● Know the location and use of cutoff switches, fire extinguishers, fire blankets and other emergency devices.

Schools are particularly concerned about fire prevention. Make sure your child has a good understanding of the following safety measures:

● Never bring matches to school.

● Only use stoves, Bunsen burners and the like under a teacher's supervision.

● Always follow the teacher's directions during fire drills.

● Know how to respond quickly and correctly to the fire alarm.

● Report fires immediately to a teacher or other adult.

● Know how to use fire alarm boxes and how to telephone the fire department.

Car Safety

Automobile accidents pose the single most serious threat to your child's safety. The following preventive measures will offer a great deal of protection:

● Make sure your car stays in good operating condition.

● Take all the necessary precautions when you drive. Obey the rules of the road and stay alert for any unexpected emergencies.

● Always keep the doors locked (when you're parked as well as when you're in motion). Install child-proof safety locks on the rear doors.

● Teach your child to enter and leave the car on the passenger side only and to be careful not to catch his fingers when the door is closing.

● Don't allow him to stand on the seat or climb around when the car is in motion.

● Make sure he doesn't stick his head, hands or anything else outside the window.

● Don't allow yelling, horseplay or other distractions when you drive. If your child needs attention, pull safely off the road, then tend to him.

● Never allow him to play with the car controls, even when you're parked.

● Be sure to have on hand a first-aid kit, a flashlight with fresh batteries and emergency flares.

● On long trips, provide quiet games to keep your youngster occupied, and stop at least every two hours so he can stretch his legs. Try not to travel too far in one day.

● Never leave children alone in a car for even a few minutes.

● Have the right kind of safety restraint for your child and always remember to use it.

This last point about safety restraints requires some further discussion because their importance is often overlooked. More than half the children seriously injured or killed in car accidents were not wearing safety harnesses or belts or protected by safety seats. It's simply not enough to hold your child in your arms while the car is in motion. Any sudden stop will tear him away from you and subject him to the full force of a collision.

Nor do all the safety devices on the market protect him adequately. Perhaps the worst offenders are children's car seats which merely hook loosely over the back of the regular seat. When purchasing a safety restraint for your child, check that it meets or exceeds current government standards and make certain it's the appropriate model for your child's size and age.

No safety device can offer protection if it isn't used, so be sure to place your child in the restraint for even the shortest trips. Teach him to request this protection when he's driving with someone else. If an adult safety belt is the only thing available, a small pillow should be placed between the belt and the child to serve as padding.

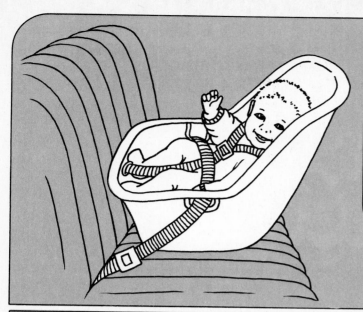

FROM NEWBORN TO ABOUT 20 POUNDS

Use a well-padded, firmly constructed infant seat that secures to the car structure with a seat belt. The seat should be designed to stay parallel to the regular seat and preferably face backwards. Car beds are unsafe.

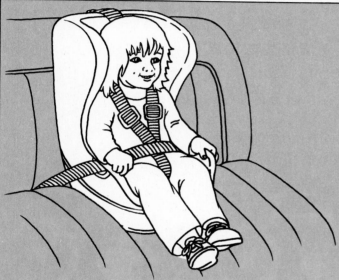

FROM 20 TO ABOUT 50 POUNDS

A well-padded safety seat will provide protection from head-on, side and rear collisions. Make certain it is designed to be secured in place with an adult lap belt. Check that all the areas your child's head may touch are lined with padding and that there are no sharp or pointed edges anywhere on the seat. Reject models made with toy steering wheels. To protect the upper part of the body, the seat should incorporate an impact shield or restraining belts at least 1-1/2 inches wide. Also look for features that protect against whiplash injury.

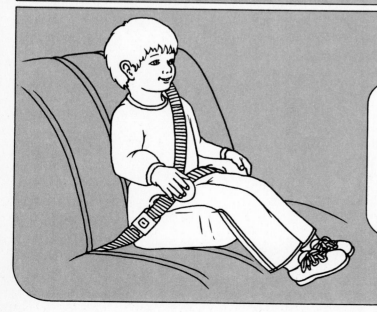

OLDER AND LARGER CHILDREN

When your child outgrows the safety seat, install a lap belt that buckles firmly against his hips (not over his abdomen). If necessary, place a hard cushion under him to keep the belt low enough and allow him to see out the window. If the child is more than 4-1/2 feet tall, also use a shoulder harness. A 3-point lap and shoulder belt offers maximum protection.

Bicycle Safety

Bicycles are a wonderful source of exercise and fun, but they are not without their dangers. Too many children are injured and killed from falls and collisions that could have been avoided through proper preventive care. This chapter discusses the most common causes of childhood bike injuries and shows you how to work with your youngster to keep him safe from harm.

THE RIGHT SIZE BIKE

Bicycles are expensive, and parents sometimes buy them too large so their children can use them longer. Yet overly large bikes are one of the major causes of bicycle-related injuries. About one out of three youngsters involved in bicycle accidents was driving a bike with blocks on the pedals. When choosing a bicycle for your son or daughter, keep in mind these general guidelines about bike size and age:

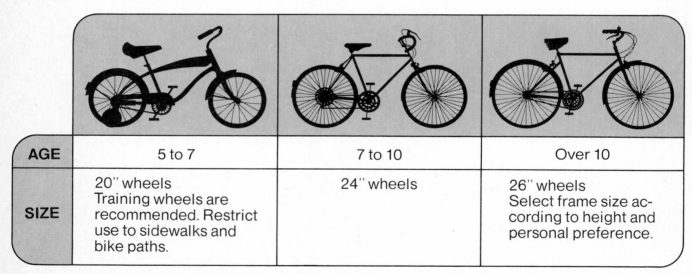

AGE	5 to 7	7 to 10	Over 10
SIZE	20" wheels Training wheels are recommended. Restrict use to sidewalks and bike paths.	24" wheels	26" wheels Select frame size according to height and personal preference.

Bikes for beginners and young drivers should be equipped with coaster brakes rather than hand brakes, which require better coordination. Don't buy a beginner a high-rise bike; they are hard to balance.

These guidelines are rather broad, and you should go on to take a more detailed look at how the bike fits the child. To make absolutely sure it's the right size, take your youngster along to the store with you. When the two of you have narrowed down your selection, have him sit on the bike with his hands on the handlebar grips and the arch of one foot on the lower pedal, then use this illustration to check the fit:

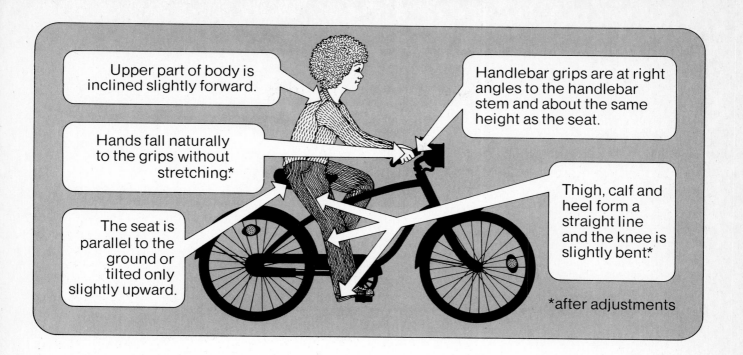

Upper part of body is inclined slightly forward.

Hands fall naturally to the grips without stretching*

The seat is parallel to the ground or tilted only slightly upward.

Handlebar grips are at right angles to the handlebar stem and about the same height as the seat.

Thigh, calf and heel form a straight line and the knee is slightly bent*

*after adjustments

EQUIPMENT AND OPERATING CONDITION

Many of the bicycles involved in accidents have some mechanical defect or aren't properly equipped, and these include new bikes as well as old. Make sure your child's bike has all the equipment it needs to be used safely, and periodically check it out to see whether it's still in good operating condition. Here's what to look for:

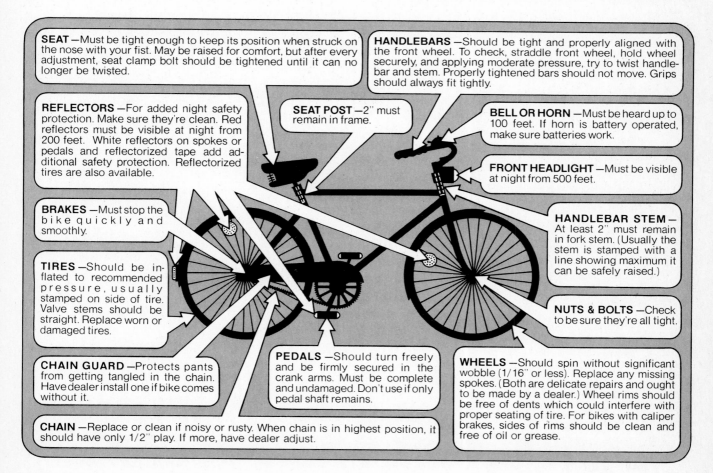

SEAT—Must be tight enough to keep its position when struck on the nose with your fist. May be raised for comfort, but after every adjustment, seat clamp bolt should be tightened until it can no longer be twisted.

HANDLEBARS—Should be tight and properly aligned with the front wheel. To check, straddle front wheel, hold wheel securely, and applying moderate pressure, try to twist handlebar and stem. Properly tightened bars should not move. Grips should always fit tightly.

REFLECTORS—For added night safety protection. Make sure they're clean. Red reflectors must be visible at night from 200 feet. White reflectors on spokes or pedals and reflectorized tape add additional safety protection. Reflectorized tires are also available.

SEAT POST—2" must remain in frame.

BELL OR HORN—Must be heard up to 100 feet. If horn is battery operated, make sure batteries work.

FRONT HEADLIGHT—Must be visible at night from 500 feet.

BRAKES—Must stop the bike quickly and smoothly.

HANDLEBAR STEM—At least 2" must remain in fork stem. (Usually the stem is stamped with a line showing maximum it can be safely raised.)

TIRES—Should be inflated to recommended pressure, usually stamped on side of tire. Valve stems should be straight. Replace worn or damaged tires.

NUTS & BOLTS—Check to be sure they're all tight.

CHAIN GUARD—Protects pants from getting tangled in the chain. Have dealer install one if bike comes without it.

PEDALS—Should turn freely and be firmly secured in the crank arms. Must be complete and undamaged. Don't use if only pedal shaft remains.

WHEELS—Should spin without significant wobble (1/16" or less). Replace any missing spokes. (Both are delicate repairs and ought to be made by a dealer.) Wheel rims should be free of dents which could interfere with proper seating of tire. For bikes with caliper brakes, sides of rims should be clean and free of oil or grease.

CHAIN—Replace or clean if noisy or rusty. When chain is in highest position, it should have only 1/2" play. If more, have dealer adjust.

BICYCLE SKILLS

It may not take your son or daughter more than a few hours to learn how to remain upright, steer and stop, but there is more to driving a bike than hopping on and pedaling away. And the cyclist is a **driver,** not just a rider. "Rider" suggests the passive role of someone only "along for the ride" and perpetuates the attitude that the bicycle is a toy. It isn't.

Most injuries to beginners come from falls. As your youngster gains experience and confidence, he'll fall a lot less, but boys and girls who have been driving for less than 2 years—typically, children about 6 to 8—are subject to a great many falling accidents. These can be minimized by enrolling your child in one of the bicycle training programs designed to teach basic driving skills. In many communities these courses are offered by the police, the "Y" and other such organizations as part of their youth activities programs.

If such a course isn't available in your neighborhood, you can conduct your own. It will take a certain amount of effort but will give your child valuable protection and provide an enjoyable afternoon or two in the process. Youngsters are always eager to demonstrate their mastery of new skills, so it shouldn't be hard to get yours involved. And by all means have some fun with it. Make it a game to be enjoyed rather than an ordeal to be endured.

Here are nine exercises or games that will check out the basic bicycle skills your child needs to master. Space has been provided to mark off each skill as it is demonstrated. Keep in mind that these games indicate the child's control of the bike but do not prepare him to drive in traffic. We'll get to that afterward.

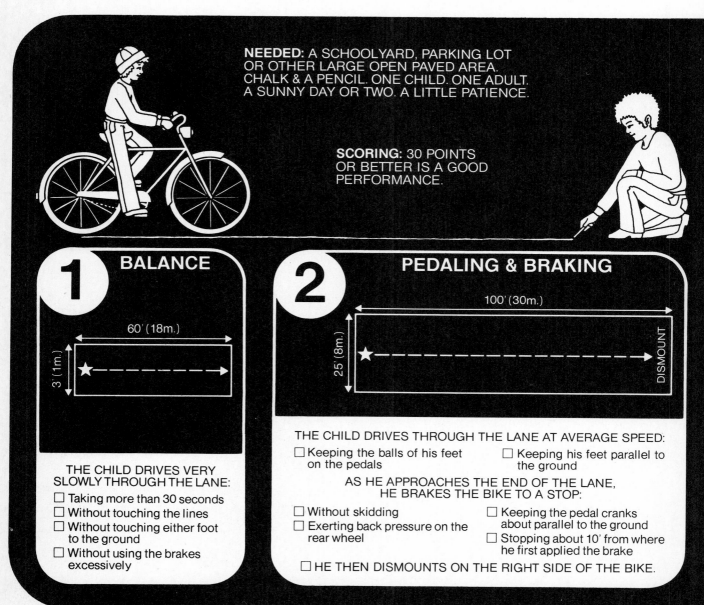

NEEDED: A SCHOOLYARD, PARKING LOT OR OTHER LARGE OPEN PAVED AREA. CHALK & A PENCIL. ONE CHILD. ONE ADULT. A SUNNY DAY OR TWO. A LITTLE PATIENCE.

SCORING: 30 POINTS OR BETTER IS A GOOD PERFORMANCE.

1 BALANCE

60′ (18m.)

3′ (1m.)

THE CHILD DRIVES VERY SLOWLY THROUGH THE LANE:

☐ Taking more than 30 seconds
☐ Without touching the lines
☐ Without touching either foot to the ground
☐ Without using the brakes excessively

2 PEDALING & BRAKING

100′ (30m.)

25′ (8m.)

DISMOUNT

THE CHILD DRIVES THROUGH THE LANE AT AVERAGE SPEED:

☐ Keeping the balls of his feet on the pedals
☐ Keeping his feet parallel to the ground

AS HE APPROACHES THE END OF THE LANE, HE BRAKES THE BIKE TO A STOP:

☐ Without skidding
☐ Exerting back pressure on the rear wheel
☐ Keeping the pedal cranks about parallel to the ground
☐ Stopping about 10′ from where he first applied the brake

☐ HE THEN DISMOUNTS ON THE RIGHT SIDE OF THE BIKE.

3 STRAIGHT LINE

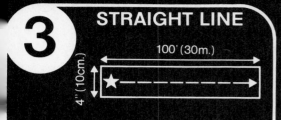

THE CHILD DRIVES THROUGH THE LANE:

☐ Without undue exertion
☐ Without touching the lines
☐ Without touching either foot to the ground
☐ Without skidding when he stops

4 SINGLE OBSTACLE COURSE

FROM A MOVING START, THE CHILD DRIVES THROUGH THE COURSE, WEAVING IN & OUT AMONG THE SQUARES:

☐ Without touching either foot to the ground
☐ Without skidding
☐ Without using the brakes excessively
☐ Without undue exertion

5 DOUBLE OBSTACLE ZIGZAG COURSE

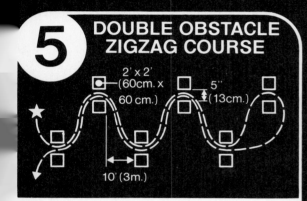

FROM A MOVING START, THE CHILD DRIVES THROUGH THE COURSE, ZIGZAGGING BETWEEN THE SQUARES, THEN RETURNS THROUGH THE COURSE FROM THE OPPOSITE DIRECTION:

☐ Without touching the lines
☐ Without touching either foot to the ground
☐ Without skidding the rear wheel
☐ Without using the brakes excessively

6 FIGURE 8 BALANCE & STEERING

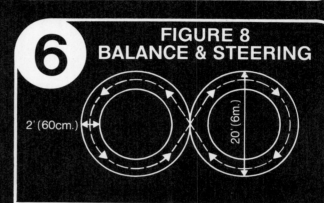

FROM A MOVING START, THE CHILD STEERS THROUGH THE COURSE SLOWLY:

☐ Taking more than 45 seconds
☐ Making smooth & easy turns
☐ Keeping both hands on the handlebars
☐ Without undue exertion
☐ Without touching either foot to the ground
☐ Without touching the lines
☐ Without using the brakes excessively

7 TURNING AROUND

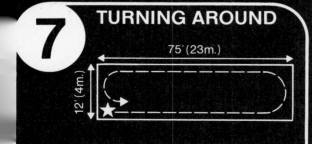

THE CHILD DRIVES DOWN 1 SIDE OF THE LANE, TURNS AROUND, DRIVES BACK & TURNS AROUND AGAIN:

☐ Without touching the lines
☐ Making smooth & easy turns
☐ Without touching either foot to the ground
☐ Without excessive braking

8 EMERGENCY STOP & TURN

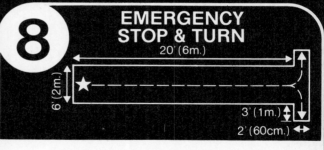

THE CHILD DRIVES DOWN THE LANE, MAKES A RIGHT TURN & STOPS, THEN DRIVES DOWN THE LANE AGAIN, MAKES A LEFT TURN & STOPS:

☐ Without touching any lines
☐ Without skidding
☐ Without touching either foot to the ground until the bike has stopped

DRIVING IN TRAFFIC

For the older child, a bicycle is not just a plaything but an important means of transportation used to visit friends, go to school, run errands, etc. As he moves from the relative safety of sidewalk and driveway out into the traffic of the street, there is a dramatically increased risk of injury from collisions with fixed objects, other bicycles, and automobiles and trucks. Since a bicycle offers no protection at all, the cyclist is the most exposed and vulnerable element in the traffic flow, and even a minor collision can have serious results.

Make certain your youngster develops a sensible attitude about using his bike in traffic and has a good understanding of traffic rules and regulations. A bicycle is considered a vehicle by law and is subject to all the traffic regulations that apply to cars and other motor vehicles. Every cyclist is expected to know these laws as well as the special regulations for bikes. You can obtain a copy of these rules at the Registry of Motor Vehicles in your community. The importance of sticking to them may be judged by the fact that 80 percent of the bicyclists killed or injured in traffic accidents were violating traffic laws at the time.

It's particularly important your child take the following precautions whenever he drives in traffic:

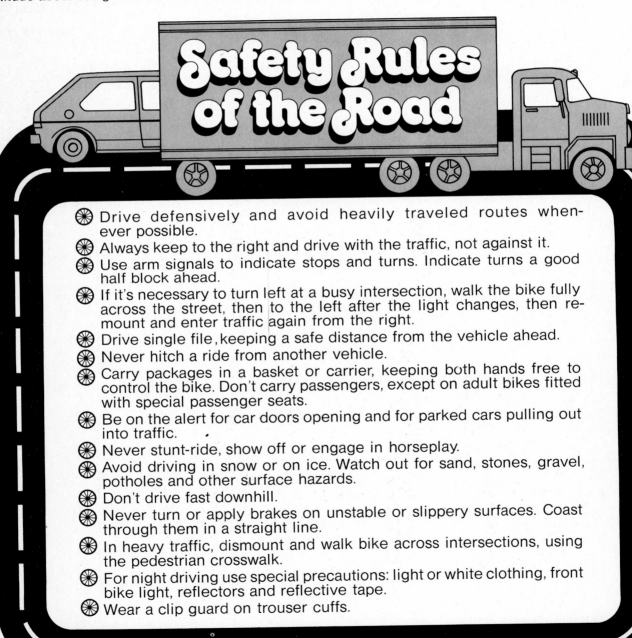

Safety Rules of the Road

- Drive defensively and avoid heavily traveled routes whenever possible.
- Always keep to the right and drive with the traffic, not against it.
- Use arm signals to indicate stops and turns. Indicate turns a good half block ahead.
- If it's necessary to turn left at a busy intersection, walk the bike fully across the street, then to the left after the light changes, then remount and enter traffic again from the right.
- Drive single file, keeping a safe distance from the vehicle ahead.
- Never hitch a ride from another vehicle.
- Carry packages in a basket or carrier, keeping both hands free to control the bike. Don't carry passengers, except on adult bikes fitted with special passenger seats.
- Be on the alert for car doors opening and for parked cars pulling out into traffic.
- Never stunt-ride, show off or engage in horseplay.
- Avoid driving in snow or on ice. Watch out for sand, stones, gravel, potholes and other surface hazards.
- Don't drive fast downhill.
- Never turn or apply brakes on unstable or slippery surfaces. Coast through them in a straight line.
- In heavy traffic, dismount and walk bike across intersections, using the pedestrian crosswalk.
- For night driving use special precautions: light or white clothing, front bike light, reflectors and reflective tape.
- Wear a clip guard on trouser cuffs.

Closely check your youngster's awareness of traffic safety before allowing him to venture out into the street or travel long distances in traffic. Here is another game to help you determine his preparedness:

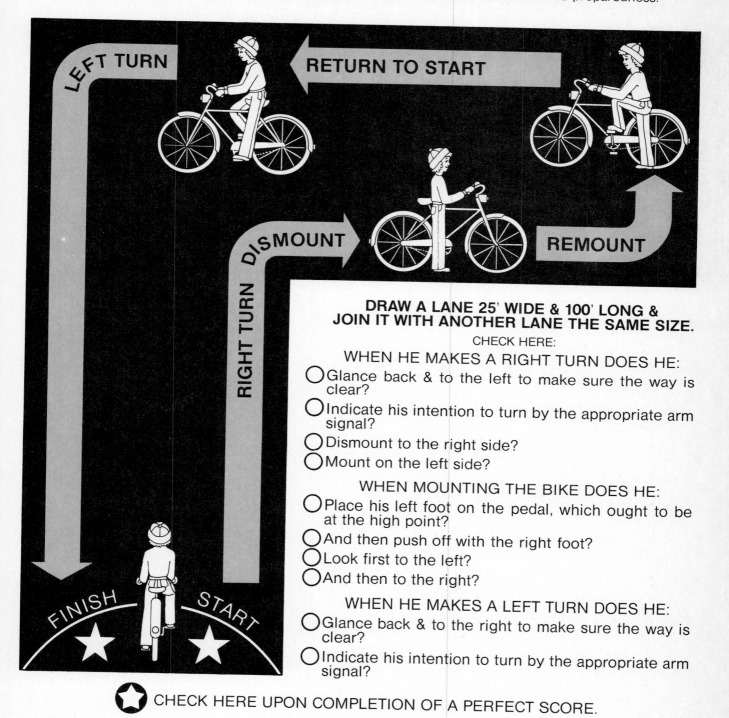

LEFT TURN

RETURN TO START

RIGHT TURN DISMOUNT

REMOUNT

FINISH ★ START ★

**DRAW A LANE 25' WIDE & 100' LONG &
JOIN IT WITH ANOTHER LANE THE SAME SIZE.**

CHECK HERE:

WHEN HE MAKES A RIGHT TURN DOES HE:

○ Glance back & to the left to make sure the way is clear?

○ Indicate his intention to turn by the appropriate arm signal?

○ Dismount to the right side?

○ Mount on the left side?

WHEN MOUNTING THE BIKE DOES HE:

○ Place his left foot on the pedal, which ought to be at the high point?

○ And then push off with the right foot?

○ Look first to the left?

○ And then to the right?

WHEN HE MAKES A LEFT TURN DOES HE:

○ Glance back & to the right to make sure the way is clear?

○ Indicate his intention to turn by the appropriate arm signal?

★ CHECK HERE UPON COMPLETION OF A PERFECT SCORE.

When you are satisfied with your child's driving skill and his knowledge of traffic regulations, it's time to test how well he performs in normal traffic.

Pick out a route about 20 blocks long that requires your youngster to turn, stop, cross intersections and, if possible, ride up and down a hill. Follow him at a safe distance in your car or, preferably, on your bike. Look for how well he demonstrates his understanding of traffic safety and how well he performs under actual driving conditions. At the completion of the drive, talk over his performance with him, calling his attention to any errors you noted.

Playground & Sports Safety

Particularly in the city, playgrounds are among the few spaces set aside for the vigorous play of childhood. Although not without their hazards, they are far less dangerous than open streets, abandoned buildings and other improvised play areas. Most playground accidents are of the minor cut, scrape and bump variety, yet more serious injuries can also occur. Not all playgrounds have the right physical environment, nor are they always safely equipped and supervised. And even in the best of them, whenever a group of children is actively climbing, swinging and jumping, there is always the possibility that someone will get seriously hurt.

This chapter sums up the most common playground dangers and the ways they can be kept to a minimum. The recommended preventions apply equally to public playgrounds and the play equipment you may have set up in your own backyard. We end with some further recommendations about sports safety, since when the child outgrows the playground he usually moves on to the athletic field and court.

THE PHYSICAL ENVIRONMENT

Before letting your child spend time in a playground, check it out yourself to make sure the play area is safe. Here's what to look for:

● The playground should be surrounded by fences to prevent younger children from wandering in and out and to allow the area to be closed off when no supervisor is present. Fences also insure that the equipment will only be approached from the proper direction.

● The equipment should be arranged according to the age group for which it is intended. Facilities for younger children should be separated from facilities for older children. This will keep the younger child away from equipment that requires a strength and skill he doesn't yet have and will protect him from being caught up in the more vigorous, potentially dangerous, activities of older kids.

● Adequate space should be marked off for each activity to protect both the participants and the passersby. Boundaries must be clearly indicated by physical barriers or painted lines. Make sure your child understands the importance of staying outside them when he's not actively playing.

● Particularly around equipment, the surface of the playground should consist of relatively soft materials such as grass, earth, sand or tanbark. Concrete, asphalt and other hard, unyielding surfaces greatly increase the chances of serious injury. Check that the surface is given the necessary maintenance to keep it safe.

● Make sure the playground is kept clear of broken glass, bottles, metal tabs from cans and other debris, especially around slides, sandboxes and swings.

PLAYGROUND EQUIPMENT

Broken-down, dilapidated structures are obviously dangerous and should never be used. However, every piece of equipment used in the playground must be examined to make sure it is in good repair and safe for your child's play.

● The equipment must be firmly anchored into the ground. In most public playgrounds, the apparatus is safely embedded in concrete. Backyard equipment anchored with pegs must be checked regularly to make sure they haven't worked their way loose. All

anchoring devices should be buried well below ground where they won't be tripped over.

● Check that the equipment hasn't shifted with use. Structural components designed to be horizontal or vertical must be maintained that way. Shifts in position can impose a strain on the structure which may eventually lead to its breaking or collapsing.

● Screws and bolts holding the equipment together must not be loose or missing. Exposed screws and bolts should fit flush or be capped and any protruding parts covered with tape. Fittings must be examined frequently to make sure they remain securely in place.

● Split-link chains, S-hooks and similar fittings separate easily and are extremely dangerous.

● Hanging rings should either be much smaller than a child's head or much larger, under 5 inches (12.7 cm.) or over 10 inches (25.4 cm.).

● Metal structures should be kept free from rust.

● Wooden equipment should be protected against deterioration and restored or replaced as required. Check for splinters.

For a more detailed look at individual pieces of equipment, turn the page and take a tour of our Ideal Playground.

The Ideal Playground

SEESAWS

● To be used only by youngsters under 12. Older children often attempt unsafe stunts.
● The fulcrum is enclosed or otherwise protected against catching fingers.

SLIDES

● No higher than 6 feet for children under 8; no higher than 8 feet for older children.
● Should be shaded from the sun, particularly if made of metal.
● Clean sand, sawdust or tanbark is placed under the bottom of the slide.
● Steps, braces and handrails are secure. Both the bed and the sides are free of slivers, screws, nails and rough spots.
● Wooden slides are frequently waxed or oiled with raw linseed oil, not washed with soap and water.

DRINKING FOUNTAINS

● Free of paper, stones and rubbish.

SANDBOX

● Should be shaded from the sun.
● No glass or other debris.
● The frame is free of splinters.
● The sand is raked often to keep it clean and expose it to the sun and air.
● The box is covered at night to protect it from moisture, dogs and cats.

WADING POOLS

● Kept clean by frequent emptying.

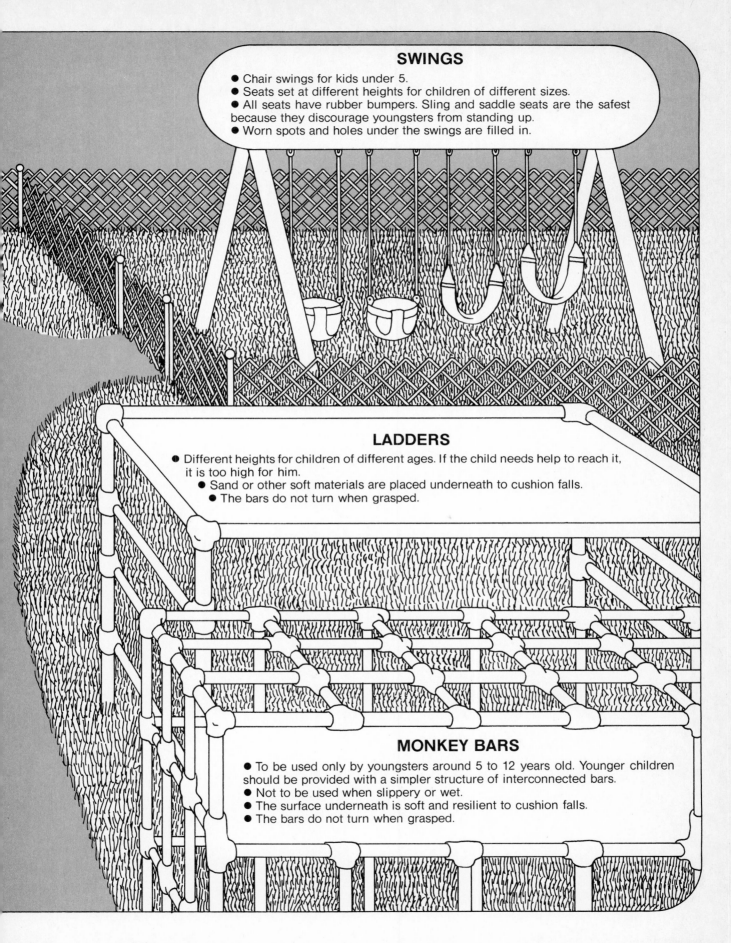

SWINGS

- Chair swings for kids under 5.
- Seats set at different heights for children of different sizes.
- All seats have rubber bumpers. Sling and saddle seats are the safest because they discourage youngsters from standing up.
- Worn spots and holes under the swings are filled in.

LADDERS

- Different heights for children of different ages. If the child needs help to reach it, it is too high for him.
- Sand or other soft materials are placed underneath to cushion falls.
- The bars do not turn when grasped.

MONKEY BARS

- To be used only by youngsters around 5 to 12 years old. Younger children should be provided with a simpler structure of interconnected bars.
- Not to be used when slippery or wet.
- The surface underneath is soft and resilient to cushion falls.
- The bars do not turn when grasped.

Playground Safety Rules

Even in our Ideal Playground, a child can be seriously injured if he doesn't use the equipment safely. Talk over these playground safety rules with your youngster and be sure he understands them.

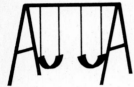

SWINGS

- No kneeling or standing on the swings.
- Hold on tightly with both hands.
- Wait for the swing to come to a full stop before getting off. Never jump off.
- Don't hold anyone on your lap or ride double.
- Never climb the supports.

DRINKING FOUNTAIN

- Fooling around at the fountain can cause broken teeth.

WADING POOL

- Never go wading if you're overheated, sick or have a skin infection.

SEESAWS

- Hold on tightly with both hands and sit facing each other.
- Keep your hands and feet out from under the board as it nears the ground.
- Don't stand or run on the board.
- Never bump the board on the ground.
- Warn the other person before getting off.
- To get off, hold the board tightly and let it rise gradually until the other child has his feet on the ground.

SLIDES

- Climb one step at a time, keeping a safe distance from the child in front of you.
- Only one person should slide down at a time. Slide sitting up with your feet in front of you. Don't hold on to the sides.
- Quickly move away from the bottom of the slide.
- Don't try to crawl or run up the slide or slide down backwards.
- Never go sliding in a wet bathing suit.

SANDBOX

- For younger children only.
- Don't take food into the sandbox.
- No sharp or pointed playthings should be brought into the sand.

LADDERS

- Don't use a ladder if you can't reach it by yourself.
- Climb in one direction only, either up or down.
- Don't put your head or feet through the rungs.

- No Pushing.
- No Fighting.
- No Dogs.
- No Bikes.
- Never play with the equipment when it's wet or icy.

Buying Backyard Equipment

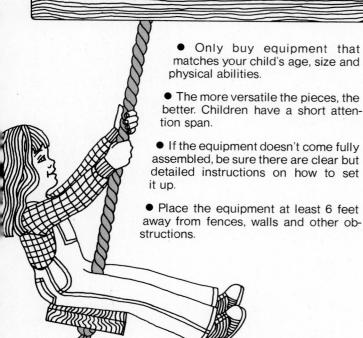

- Only buy equipment that matches your child's age, size and physical abilities.

- The more versatile the pieces, the better. Children have a short attention span.

- If the equipment doesn't come fully assembled, be sure there are clear but detailed instructions on how to set it up.

- Place the equipment at least 6 feet away from fences, walls and other obstructions.

- Install it over grass, sand, soft earth, etc., never over concrete or other hard surfaces.

- Make sure the equipment is stable. It should come with anchoring devices to hold it firmly to the ground.

- Don't buy structures with sharp edges, rough surfaces or open-ended hooks.

- Check that all nuts, bolts and clamps are tight.

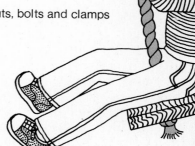

SPORTS

When a youngster outgrows the playground, he usually turns to sports to satisfy his need for excitement and challenging physical activity. Every sport has its own special hazards and benefits, but the principles of accident prevention are essentially the same for all of them:

- The playing area should be large enough to keep children from running into walls and other obstacles, with sufficient space around it to let other people pass by safely. Goal supports and other obstructions that can't be removed must be well padded to reduce injuries from accidental collisions. Playing surfaces should be smooth and even.

- The child should be provided with the equipment the game requires: body padding, cleated shoes and a helmet for tackle football, basketball sneakers for basketball, etc. If your youngster wears eyeglasses, make sure he has unbreakable lenses or eyeglass guards.

- The child should be in the proper physical condition and have practiced the basic skills the sport requires. When he is prepared for the demands of the game, he is less likely to suffer accidental injury and will also enjoy himself more. The greater the inherent risk of injury in a sport, the more time should be given to preparation. Remember that youngsters often attempt things beyond their strength and skill and that every athletic activity makes its own unique demands on co-ordination, stamina and judgment.

- Don't let your child play when he has a sore arm or leg, and encourage him to play different positions over the course of an afternoon, particularly if he likes to catch or pitch. Children's bones are soft and vulnerable and can be damaged by constant strain. For the same reason, never push a child beyond his capabilities or endurance.

- Competitive sports should always involve children of about the same age, size and physical skill. This will minimize the risk of injury and allow everyone to develop a sound attitude about competition by enjoying at least some success.

- The child should have a good general awareness of sports safety as well as an understanding of the hazards of a particular activity. Before allowing him out on the playing field, make sure he appreciates the importance of placing the safety of self and playmates above everything else. Ask him to identify the potential dangers in a given sport and call his attention to any he may have overlooked.

Hiking & Camping Safety

HIKING

Hiking is a simple, enjoyable recreation that provides excellent exercise and gets your youngster outdoors into the world of nature. The following precautions will keep his hiking experiences safe as well as pleasurable:

● The length and difficulty of the hike should always match the child's age and skill. Young or new hikers should start off with short walks along a road or clearly marked trail. Long hikes over unmarked, rough terrain are best left to older, more experienced children.

● Make sure your youngster has the necessary supervision or companionship. Solo hikes should be reserved for older children who have demonstrated their mastery of hiking skills. Until then, it's best to have at least three people along on an outing. The companionship adds to the fun, and in case of an accident, someone can stay with the injured child while a third person goes for help.

● All hikes should be planned and prepared for in advance. The longer the hike and the rougher the terrain, the more planning and preparation that are required. For even short outings, you should know where your child is going and when to expect him back. Be sure he understands never to set out on a hike without your knowledge and approval.

● See to it that your child is properly dressed to protect himself from sun and insects and unexpected changes in weather. He should always carry a water-repellent jacket or poncho in case of rain.

● Footwear should be appropriate to the length of the hike and the terrain to be traveled. Rubber and other flexible soles provide good footing in the woods, but leather soles are too slippery. Boots are essential for rough ground. Sneakers and other low laced shoes are satisfactory for roads or improved trails.

● Shoes and boots should fit comfortably and already be broken in. Treat new boots with one of the various waterproofing products specifically designed to make them water repellent. To prevent blisters, check that the child's heels don't slip when he walks. Two pairs of socks are preferable. The inner layer should be orlon or cotton and the second pair thick wool.

● A peaked cap will help keep the rain and sun out of your child's eyes. Sunglasses also add comfort and protection.

● Your youngster should carry along with him all the food and drink he'll need. For a short outing, a canteen (not a glass jug) of water, a sandwich and an apple or orange should suffice. Unless he is extremely knowledgeable about wood lore, he should never eat fruit, nuts, berries or other vegetation found along the way. They might well be poisonous.

● Even on a short hike, your child should always take along a first-aid kit to deal with cuts, scrapes and blisters as well as more serious emergencies. Check that it contains such basic items as adhesive bandages and sterile dressings.

● He should also carry a compass and a map of the area and know how to use them. Emphasize that until he learns these skills, he is never to hike alone or leave the marked path or road. A flashlight is also helpful for reading road signs and avoiding bad footing when it gets dark.

● Teach your youngster not to panic or wander about aimlessly if he gets lost, but to stay where he is until help arrives. Explain to him that when he doesn't get back home when expected, a search party will look for him along the route he originally projected. He should always carry a whistle among his emergency supplies and know the universal distress signal—three short blasts repeated frequently. The signal will help rescuers find him even in darkness.

● Make sure he understands the dangers of lightning and never to seek shelter under a tall tree, especially if it stands alone in a clearing or is higher than the trees around it. If he's caught in the woods during a storm and can't find any other protection, the safest spot is under a group of young trees of about the same height. In open countryside, he should look for a protected spot away from anything tall.

● Your youngster should never approach a strange dog or other animal he might encounter in the woods or along a country road. If a dog comes up to him, he should stand still with his hands at his sides, let the dog sniff him to get his scent and speak to it in a calm, low voice. Sudden movements, yelling or running away will only increase the chance of attack.

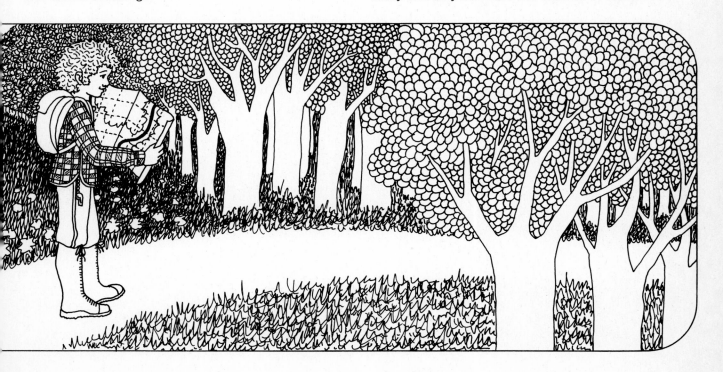

CAMPING

After gaining some experience in hiking, many youngsters want to begin camping out in the woods for several days at a time. Camping requires greater preparation, more elaborate equipment and specialized knowledge and skills. Initial trips should be made with parents or other adults or as part of organized youth activities. Before letting your child camp out, make sure he is in good physical condition and doesn't have a cold or other ailment which might be aggravated by sleeping outdoors. If he has any special medical problems, consult his doctor to see what safeguards are required. Here are some other basic precautions that will insure his comfort and safety:

● Find out as much as you can in advance about the camping area. Talk with people who have already camped there for their suggestions and warnings. Obtain a detailed map of the area so your youngster can familiarize himself with such major features of the countryside as mountains, valleys, swamps, rivers and streams. The map will also help him choose the best routes and campsites and steer him away from natural or man-made hazards. Superior inexpensive maps of the United States are available from the United States Geological Survey, G.S.A. Building, U.S. Department of the Interior, Washington, D.C. 20242. (Road maps are made for drivers and don't usually show the details a camper needs.)

● Work out a timetable with your child so you'll know where he'll be at various times and when he'll return home. Stress the importance of sticking to this schedule. He should also have an alternate plan in case the weather turns out unsuitable for camping.

● While your youngster shouldn't be overloaded with equipment, he should certainly take along everything he will need for his enjoyment and safety. This will vary according to the length of the outing, the character of the countryside and the weather likely to be encountered, but the basics include:

  ● Food and water. Depending on his size, a child requires between one and two pounds of food a day. Cans are bulky and heavy and glass jars break, so dehydrated foods are the best alternative. Have your child sample them at home first to be sure he finds them palatable.

  ● A change of clothes, a warm sweater, extra socks, a cap and a waterproof jacket or poncho. It's always safest to assume it will be cold and damp at night and rainy during the day.

  ● Sleeping and cooking equipment: a tent or tarp, a warm, lightweight sleeping bag, a ground pad and nylon ground cloth, a canteen, eating utensils, a collapsible cup, a cooking pot, aluminum foil, a good folding saw and several waterproof containers of matches to be carried in different pockets. Meals should be simple to prepare but nourishing and tasty.

  ● A first-aid kit, insect repellent, soap, a toothbrush and other toilet equipment, a pocketknife, whistle and a compass and map.

● A campsite should always be selected well before nightfall. Tell your child to look for a level spot out in the open, preferably near good water and firewood. It should be somewhat higher than its surroundings so water will drain away if it rains.

● See to it that he knows how to build a campfire safely. The area 10 feet around the fire should be cleared of grass, brush and anything else that might accidentally ignite, and the fire should be no larger than necessary for cooking and warmth. If he builds it in a shallow pit he has dug in the ground, the wind won't scatter the embers. Tents should be set up a safe distance from the fire and one or two buckets of water kept nearby as a safety measure.

● Check that your youngster's tent is light in weight, easily assembled and fire retardant. No tent is truly fireproof, so he should never light a campfire or camp stove inside it. Nor should he use paraffin or kerosene to make it water repellent since this will make it more flammable. Show him how to use it properly and keep it in good repair. The fine netting provided to keep out mosquitoes and other insects will work well if it is kept tightly closed and free of holes.

● A camper shouldn't attempt to feed or play with any animals he may come across. In the woods, all animals are wild, and no matter how cute or friendly they seem, they can inflict nasty bites and scratches. Large animals usually avoid humans, but raccoons, skunks, porcupines and the like may visit the camp, particularly if food or garbage is left in the open. If the camp is kept clean at all times, they'll have little reason to come around.

● Make sure your youngster can recognize poisonous snakes and knows to stay away from them. Photocopy the emergency treatment for **SNAKEBITE** on pages 96-99 and put it in his first-aid kit.

COPPERHEAD

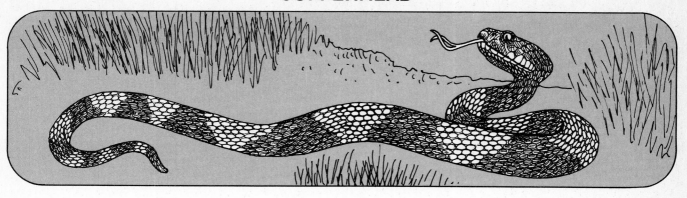

CORAL SNAKE

RATTLESNAKE

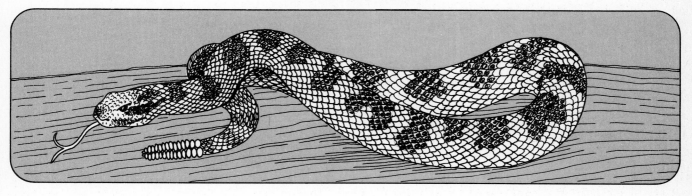

WATER MOCCASIN

Water Safety

The principal danger from water is, of course, drowning, a tragic mishap that claims thousands of young lives each year. Many, perhaps all, these children might have been saved if their parents had been better informed and taught them how to stay out of harm's way. This chapter details the most common causes of childhood drowning accidents and the recommended preventions. After reading it yourself, we suggest you review it with your youngster, your baby-sitter and anyone else who shares responsibility for your sons' and daughters' safety.

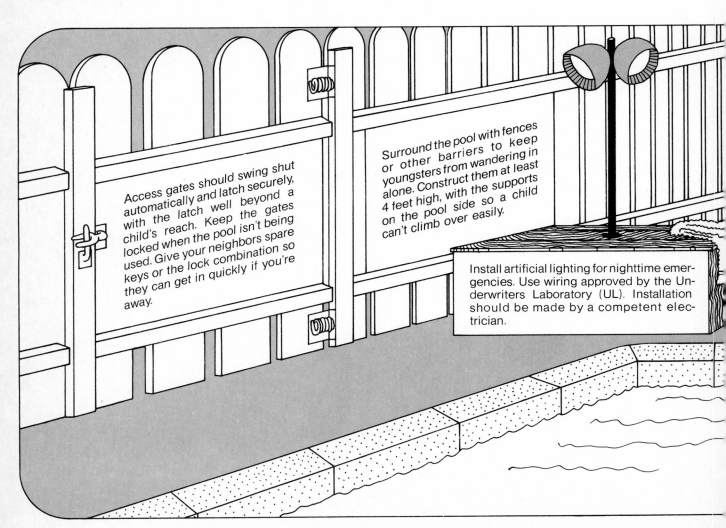

Access gates should swing shut automatically and latch securely, with the latch well beyond a child's reach. Keep the gates locked when the pool isn't being used. Give your neighbors spare keys or the lock combination so they can get in quickly if you're away.

Surround the pool with fences or other barriers to keep youngsters from wandering in alone. Construct them at least 4 feet high, with the supports on the pool side so a child can't climb over easily.

Install artificial lighting for nighttime emergencies. Use wiring approved by the Underwriters Laboratory (UL). Installation should be made by a competent electrician.

AROUND THE HOME

For infants, toddlers and younger children, the best protection against drowning accidents around the home is close adult supervision. Never leave a baby alone near water for even the briefest moment. A drowning accident can take only a few seconds. If you're bathing your child and the telephone or doorbell rings, wrap him in a towel and bring him with you while you tend to it. When he becomes old enough not to need constant watching, continue to stay nearby, keeping an ear tuned to the sounds of his talk and play.

Full bathtubs and wading pools are obvious hazards, but even an open toilet, diaper pail or vaporizer can be dangerous. If there's enough water to cover an infant's or toddler's nose and mouth, there's enough to drown him. Your child may be attracted to the light shimmering on the surface, the sound of water running or by something floating on top. His curiosity aroused, he may tumble in headlong and not have the strength or coordination to pull himself out. To prevent this sort of accident, never draw water until you are ready to use it, never leave it within your child's reach, and discard it as soon as you're done with it. Always keep the lids on diaper pails, drain scrub buckets and store them away promptly, and empty bathtubs when they're not being used.

Outdoors, don't let your child play around cesspools, puddles and ditches. Empty small wading pools after each use and turn them over or deflate them to keep rain from collecting.

Many drowning accidents around the home take place in larger backyard swimming pools, so the following precautions are particularly important:

● Keep the pool covered during the months it isn't in use. Rigid covers are preferable to flexible models because they won't collect rain.

● Teach your child never to play in any pool away from home without your knowledge and approval. Fully 1/3 of all childhood drownings occur in the pools of neighbors.

● If there's a pond near your home, make sure the safe swimming areas are marked off and the danger points indicated with warning signs. The pond should be supplied with the same rescue devices shown below for pools:

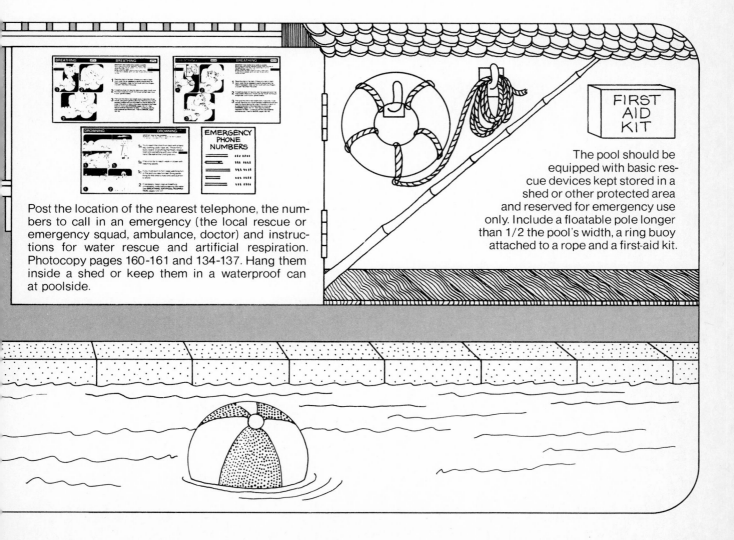

Post the location of the nearest telephone, the numbers to call in an emergency (the local rescue or emergency squad, ambulance, doctor) and instructions for water rescue and artificial respiration. Photocopy pages 160-161 and 134-137. Hang them inside a shed or keep them in a waterproof can at poolside.

The pool should be equipped with basic rescue devices kept stored in a shed or other protected area and reserved for emergency use only. Include a floatable pole longer than 1/2 the pool's width, a ring buoy attached to a rope and a first-aid kit.

SWIMMING

The single best protection against drowning is knowing how to swim. With professional instruction, most children can begin learning at a very early age, and the younger they start the better. Good programs are offered by the Red Cross, the Boy and Girl Scouts, the "Y" and other community organizations. If your child isn't ready to swim, he can still learn to float.

Even good swimmers under the age of 12 or so still need adult supervision. Infants, toddlers and young non-swimmers require it constantly. Don't let a lifeguard do your watching for you, particularly in a crowded pool. Make sure you're not responsible for so many small children that you can't keep track of all of them all the time. Never let a toddler run loose near a pool. Pool decks are often slippery, and he could easily fall in. It's best not to let a non-swimmer enter the water without you, and you should certainly always keep him within immediate reach.

Know the water you're letting your child play in.

Check out an unfamiliar pool before letting your youngster use it. Enter the shallow end and walk toward the deep end to determine the depths, traction and slope of the bottom. Make sure pool slides and diving boards are well-constructed and in good shape. Pool ladders and stairs should be equipped with handrails on both sides. Before allowing a non-swimmer to enter the water, make certain it really is shallow enough for him to stand in comfortably, without unexpected sharp drop-offs or an irregular or slippery bottom. He should never go out over his head, and should only use inflated tubes, rafts and water wings with adult supervision. They build false confidence and may drift him into deep water.

Your child should know the rules for playing safely in the water by the time he is old enough to go off to a pool or beach without you. Make sure he learns and understands the following precautions:

Never go swimming alone. Always use the "buddy system."

When swimming with a group, choose someone as lookout to oversee everyone's safety, even if a lifeguard is present.

Swim only in protected areas. Obey the posted rules and the lifeguard's instructions. Never swim at a public beach if there isn't a lifeguard present. Don't swim where people are actively engaged in water sports.

Before wading, swimming or diving in an unfamiliar place, find out the depth of the water and whether there are any strong currents, sudden drop-offs or hidden rocks, branches or roots. Stay out of very cold or fast-moving water and watch out for undertows.

Don't engage in horseplay, roughhousing or showing off.

Check that diving boards and pool slides are sturdy and not slippery. Make sure the water underneath them isn't too shallow. Never run on diving boards or dive off the sides. Learn how to dive properly.

Always pay attention to the weather. Stay out of the water if it's going to storm.

Know your limitations and never push yourself beyond them.

Never swim when you are tired, overheated or chilled.

Wait at least an hour after eating before you enter the water.

Before swimming in the ocean, find out about the changes in the tides and whether there's any danger of sharks or poisonous marine life. Remember that ocean swimming is much more difficult and exhausting than fresh-water swimming.

Be careful about hyperventilating before swimming underwater. Excessive deep breathing can inactivate the body's warning signals—that you need a fresh breath, and you may black out before you can surface.

Never dive from rocks or under buoys or boats.

If you find yourself in trouble in deep water, stay calm and think out the best plan of action.

BOATING

Particularly for younger children, the boating environment is filled with hazards—poisons, gas cans, sharp objects, low doorways and ceilings, stairways, ropes, holes, protrusions, etc. Always check it out carefully and watch your child closely to keep him out of trouble.

Know where poisonous substances are kept and make sure they are securely closed and placed where your child can't get to them. Sharp objects should be stored out of a youngster's reach and ropes kept where he can't get tangled up in them. Keep him away from stairways and places where he might trip or fall or bump into protruding objects. Stairways should always be closed off when not in use.

When you take your child out on a boat, continue to supervise him carefully and be sure you're prepared for any emergency. There should be personal flotation devices (PFD) for everyone on board, and non-swimmers should wear them constantly. Your youngster's PFD should fit him snugly enough to keep him from slipping out. Make sure that for every child who doesn't swim there's an expert swimmer who will keep an eye on him. Take a first-aid kit with you as well as rescue lines or life preservers. Check that you have bailing cans and that a motorboat is equipped with a fire extinguisher.

Before a child takes out a boat himself, he should be a skilled swimmer and understand all the above precautions. It's equally important that he knows the following basics of safe boating:

⊙ Know how to handle the boat. Learn from a qualified person. Before taking it out in deep water, put in the necessary hours practicing near shore. Know how to right a capsized canoe and climb back into it and how to handle a boat in a sudden squall or storm.

⊙ Be sure the boat is in good repair and properly equipped.

⊙ Know the water you are boating in.

⊙ Never overload a boat. Distribute the weight evenly and keep it low. Keep the passengers down to a safe number.

⊙ Never smoke around fuel. Closed in fueling areas must be ventilated before a motorboat is started, and all fuel spills wiped up promptly.

⊙ Know how to conduct yourself safely on board. Never engage in horseplay or showing off. Be careful around slippery decks. Don't stand upright in a canoe or rowboat. A youngster should always sit toward the middle of a rowboat or motorboat, never in the bow, where any sudden movement could knock him into the water.

⊙ Know about right-of-way rules, channel markings, anchorages, the correct use of lights and the relevant boating laws.

⊙ Never go out if there's a chance of storm. Check the weather forecasts in advance.

⊙ Have a plan of travel and leave this information with someone on shore.

WATER-SKIING, SURFING, SNORKELING AND SCUBA DIVING

These water sports involve many of the same dangers as swimming and boating as well as their own special hazards. Before letting your child take part in them, make sure he understands these fundamentals:

- Know how to swim expertly and be in good physical condition. Don't scuba dive if you have a respiratory ailment.

- Learn the basics of the sport from a qualified teacher. Build up your skills gradually without trying to do too much at once. As with swimming, know your limitations and don't push yourself beyond them.

- Never use restricted areas. Keep away from swimmers and stay conscious of other water skiiers, surfers and divers.

- Make sure your equipment is in good shape, particularly for scuba diving.

- When water skiing, wear a PFD and have a third person along to keep watch and pass your signals to the driver.

- Don't go out in bad weather or rough water.

FISHING

Fishing is much more reposeful than surfing or water skiing, but it is not without its dangers. Your child should pay attention to the following precautions:

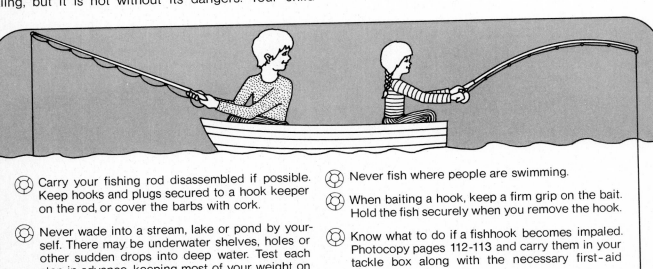

- Carry your fishing rod disassembled if possible. Keep hooks and plugs secured to a hook keeper on the rod, or cover the barbs with cork.

- Never wade into a stream, lake or pond by yourself. There may be underwater shelves, holes or other sudden drops into deep water. Test each step in advance, keeping most of your weight on the foot that's already grounded. Be on the alert for stumps, roots and other tripping hazards.

- Maintain plenty of distance between yourself and other fishermen.

- Never fish where people are swimming.

- When baiting a hook, keep a firm grip on the bait. Hold the fish securely when you remove the hook.

- Know what to do if a fishhook becomes impaled. Photocopy pages 112-113 and carry them in your tackle box along with the necessary first-aid supplies.

SURVIVAL TECHNIQUES

Even an experienced swimmer may sometimes find himself in danger and should know how to cope with it beforehand. The following survival techniques will help your child through most emergencies. Talk them over with him and, where possible, practice them together in a pool until he has them mastered. Knowing what to do in advance will build up his confidence and decrease the chance of panic. His survival could depend on his ability to remain calm and bring himself to safety quickly.

● **Cramps:** Every swimmer occasionally experiences a cramp, a painful muscle contraction which greatly impedes the body's movement. Make sure your child understands a cramp need not be serious if he keeps calm and takes proper action. When he feels his muscle tighten, he should take a deep breath, roll to a face-down position in the water and grasp the cramped area firmly with one or both hands **(Figure 1).** Continued firm pressure will release the cramp and permit him to move to land. He can also ease a leg cramp by straightening his leg and forcing his toes upward toward the knee **(Figure 2).** Cramps are most likely to occur when muscles are tired and the water is particularly cold, good reasons for taking relatively short swims at the start of the summer.

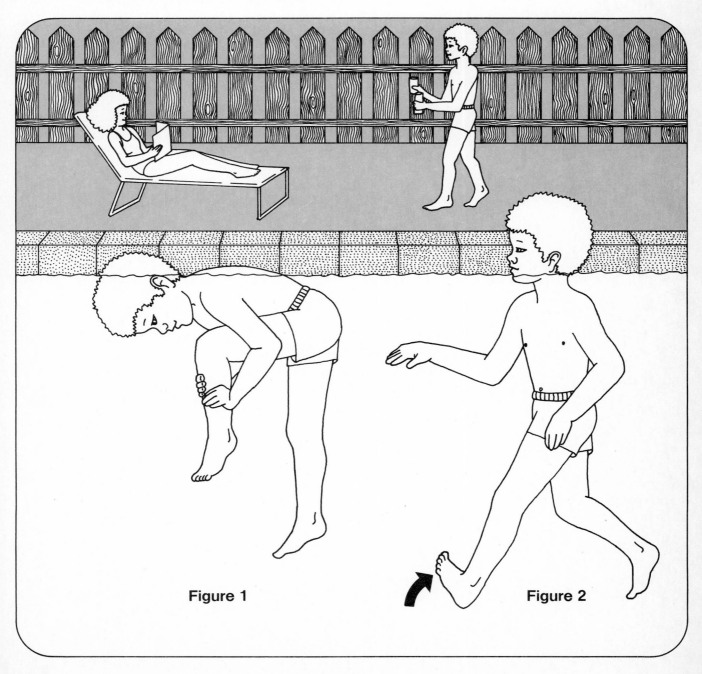

Figure 1

Figure 2

● **Drownproofing:** Should your child ever find himself caught out in deep water, the following technique will keep him afloat and conserve his energy between active efforts to reach safety or until help arrives:

❶ Take a breath through your mouth and allow yourself to sink below the surface. Hang there loosely with your arms, legs and head relaxed. The air in your lungs will bring you effortlessly back to the surface.

❷ When your head is partly out of water, stretch out your arms and at the same time move one leg forward and the other back, as in a scissors kick.

❸ To take a fresh breath, gently pull your arms downward toward your hips and bring your legs together, pressing against the water with your soles and heels. As soon as your arms start downward (not before),

begin to exhale through your nose and continue exhaling until your nose rises above the surface. Be sure to keep your eyes open. Then inhale through your mouth. Your chin should be right on the water, not above it.

❹ Just as your head goes under again, give a slight downward push with your arms or legs or with both of them together. This will keep you from sinking too deeply.

❺ Rest underwater completely relaxed. Stay under until you would **like** a fresh breath, not until you absolutely **must have** one.

If the child becomes chilled, he can conserve his body warmth by drawing his arms and legs up to his chest and keeping his head above water.

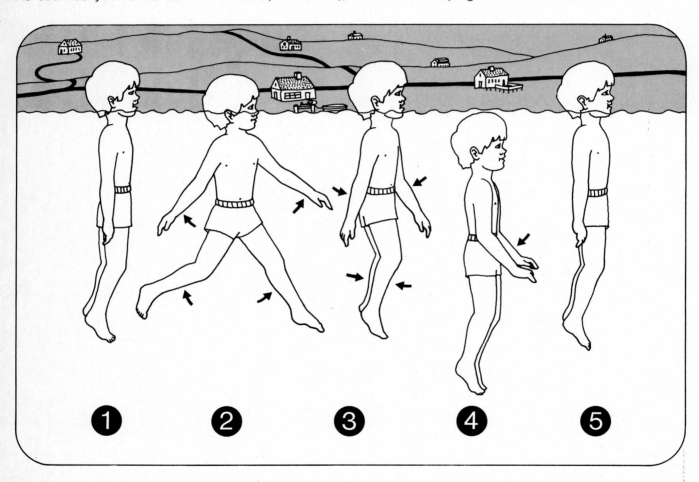

● **Improvising A Float:** Show your youngster how he can use such clothing as his trousers or shirt to help stay afloat in an emergency. Air forced into wet clothing will form a buoyant air pocket that will last as long as it is kept submerged.

To inflate a shirt or jacket, button it to the neck, hold the lower front out and away from your body with one hand, then cup your other hand and drive it down into the water, letting the air trapped in your palm escape out of the water and into the garment. Repeat the process until an air pocket forms, and replenish

the air as it gradually leaks out.

Trousers work even better because they can hold more air. To inflate a pair of pants, **❶** take them off, close the zipper, and knot each leg at the cuff. **❷** As you tread water, hold the pants at the waist, swing the legs behind your head, then quickly whip the waist down into the water, trapping the air in the legs. Take a relaxed floating position and use small underwater strokes. **❸** Or lie on your back, holding the float to your chest while kicking with your feet.

● **Capsized Boats:** Teach your child to stay near a boat that has capsized or flooded. Even when submerged a few inches under the surface, it will probably continue to float because of its natural buoyancy or the air trapped inside. A youngster can conserve his strength until rescue arrives by clinging to the bottom of an overturned boat, and by kicking with his feet as he holds on he may be able to propel himself back to land. It is also possible to sit within a boat that has become completely flooded and paddle back to safety with your hands. Floating objects from a capsized boat —a thermos jug, oar, life preserver, etc.—can also help you back to shore. You can gain additional flotation as you hold on by keeping only your nose above water.

● **Strong Currents:** A river current can be exceedingly strong and may easily carry a young swimmer away from land. Make sure your child knows that if he is caught in a strong current he will probably exhaust himself if he tries to fight it. Instead, he should swim diagonally across the current with its flow, even though he may come to land some distance away. Most river currents make their way closer to shore eventually.

● **Broken Ice:** Should your youngster ever break through the ice while skating or playing on the frozen surface, he shouldn't try to climb out immediately. If the ice is thin or weakened, his efforts will only break more of the ice and subject him to repeated dunkings. Rather, he should kick his feet to the surface and to the rear to avoid going under the ice, extend his hands and arms in front of him onto the unbroken ice and slide forward onto the solid surface. If the ice breaks again, then continue to slide forward until the ice is firm enough to give the needed support. To distribute his weight over the widest possible area, he should remain prone as long as the ice is still thin and inch himself along in that position, rather than stand upright and put his full weight on one small area.

● **Helping Someone In Trouble:** Besides knowing how to save himself from drowning, your child should also know how to rescue someone else without jeopardizing his own safety. Unless he is fully trained in lifesaving techniques, he should never try to swim to the aid of a drowning person. Instead, he should use the following methods of assistance, which are also treated on pages 160-161:

• Near shore, use a reaching assist. Drop to the ground, extend your head and chest over the water and reach out a hand to the person in trouble. If you can't reach him without losing your own balance, reverse the position and extend your legs while holding onto a branch or other firm handhold.

• If the person is just out of body reach, look around for something else to reach him with—a stick, fishing pole, rope, etc. A shirt or coat held by the sleeve may be long enough to pull him to safety. Even if the person is underwater, as long as he is still conscious, he will instinctively grasp anything thrust into his hands or pushed against his chest.

• Find a float. Anything buoyant—a thermos, board, log, buoy, oar, boat, etc.—that can be gotten within reach of a drowning person can provide at least momentary relief while you seek further help.

Emergency Medical Information

This page provides an immediate overview of your youngster's medical history and can save valuable time in an emergency. If you have more than one child, make as many extra photocopies as you need and tape them into the book. You should also give copies to your children's teachers, camp counselors and the other adults with whom they spend significant time. Be sure to keep the information current.

CHILD'S NAME _____ DATE OF BIRTH _____
ADDRESS _____ HOME PHONE _____
FATHER'S PHONE AT WORK _____ MOTHER'S PHONE AT WORK _____

PEDIATRICIAN: NAME _____ OFFICE PHONE _____ HOME PHONE _____
FAMILY DOCTOR: NAME _____ OFFICE PHONE _____ HOME PHONE _____
ALTERNATE DOCTOR: NAME _____ OFFICE PHONE _____ HOME PHONE _____
DENTIST: NAME _____ OFFICE PHONE _____ HOME PHONE _____
MEDICAL INSURANCE: COMPANY NAME _____
ADDRESS _____ POLICY NUMBER _____

DATES OF MOST RECENT IMMUNIZATIONS

TETANUS _____ DIPHTHERIA _____ POLIO _____
MEASLES _____ OTHER _____

BLOOD TYPE _____
RH FACTOR   RH NEGATIVE _____
(CHECK ONE) RH POSITIVE _____

PRESENT MEDICAL PROBLEMS & CHRONIC CONDITIONS (EPILEPSY, ASTHMA, ETC.)

_____ _____ _____
_____ _____ _____

ALLERGIES (DRUGS, INSECT BITES, ETC.)

_____ _____ _____
_____ _____ _____

MEDICINES TAKEN REGULARLY

NAME _____ REASON TAKEN _____ DOSE & FREQUENCY _____
NAME _____ REASON TAKEN _____ DOSE & FREQUENCY _____
NAME _____ REASON TAKEN _____ DOSE & FREQUENCY _____

SPECIAL PRECAUTIONS & OTHER INFORMATION _____
_____
_____

	NATURE	DATE	DOCTOR	PHONE
HOSPITALIZATIONS	____			
	____			
SURGERY	____			
	____			
MAJOR INJURIES	____			
	____			
PSYCHIATRIC CARE OR COUNSELING	____			

Stocking Up: First-Aid Supplies

Every household should have a first-aid kit stocked with the basic supplies necessary for treating childhood emergencies. You can put your own kit together by purchasing the individual items listed on this page. Check off each item as you place it in the kit. If you prefer to buy a commercial kit that is already assembled, use this list to make sure its contents are complete. Always keep the kit stored in the same place, well out of a youngster's reach, and be sure your family and babysitter know where to find it. Keep it fully stocked and replace supplies as they are used.

You should also have first-aid kits for your car or boat and for hiking and camping expeditions. For hiking and camping, you might also buy a special snakebite kit containing a constricting band, sterile blades and a suction device. If your child has severe allergic reactions to insect bites and stings, have his doctor prescribe an insect sting kit and keep it with your other emergency supplies.

- ☐ Absorbent Cotton
- ☐ Adhesive Strip Bandages, assorted sizes
- ☐ Adhesive Tape, 1/2 to 1 inch wide
- ☐ Butterfly Bandages
- ☐ Cotton-Tipped Swabs
- ☐ Large Triangular Bandages
- ☐ Sterile Eye Pads
- ☐ Sterile Gauze Bandages, assorted sizes 1/2 to 2 inches wide
- ☐ Sterile Gauze Pads, 2 x 4 inches
- ☐ Tourniquet: A short, sturdy stick and a clean cloth 2 inches wide and 20 inches long. See **BLEEDING: TOURNIQUET,** pages 104-107, before using.

- ☐ Ammonia Inhalant (for fainting)
- ☐ Calamine Lotion
- ☐ Children's Aspirin Substitute (use only as directed by your doctor)
- ☐ Hydrogen Peroxide
- ☐ Oil of Cloves (for minor toothache)
- ☐ Petroleum Jelly
- ☐ Rubbing Alcohol
- ☐ Salt or Salt Tablets (for heat exhaustion)

- ☐ Drinking Cups (paper or plastic)
- ☐ Measuring Cup
- ☐ Measuring Spoons
- ☐ Safety Pins
- ☐ Sharp Needles (to remove splinters; sterilize first)
- ☐ Sharp scissors with rounded ends
- ☐ Thermometer (rectal for infants)
- ☐ Tongue Depressors
- ☐ Tweezers

FOR ACCIDENTAL POISONING
- ☐ Syrup of Ipecac (to induce vomiting)
- ☐ Activated Charcoal (to absorb poison)
- ☐ Epsom Salts (a strong laxative; **use only as directed by your Poison Control Center**)

See **SWALLOWED POISONS,** page 226.

SPECIAL KITS AVAILABLE
Insect Sting Kit: For persons with severe allergic reactions. Available by prescription only.

Snakebite Kit: Contains a constricting band, sterile blades and a suction device.

Poison First-Aid Kit: Contains syrup of ipecac, activated charcoal and Epsom salts.

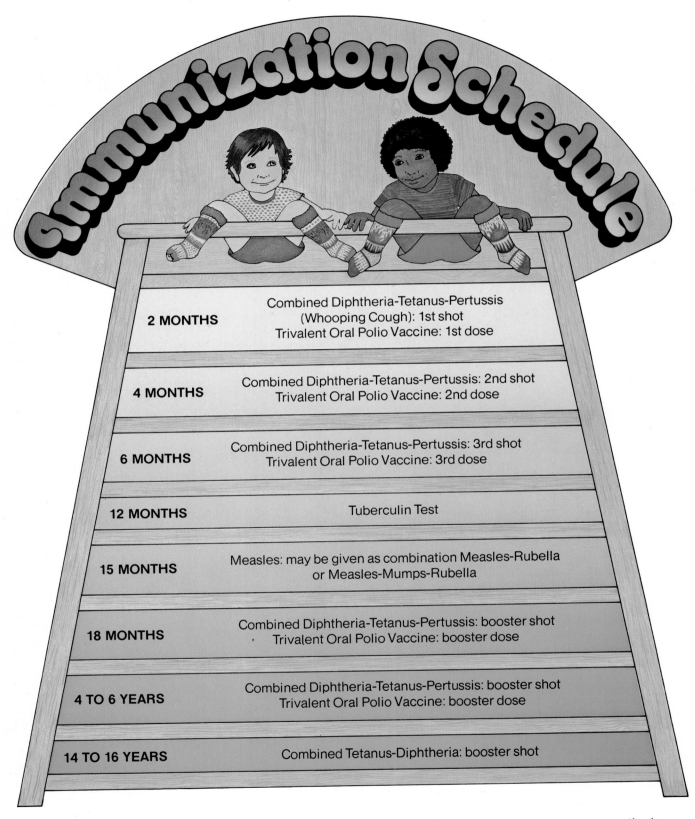

Immunization Schedule

2 MONTHS	Combined Diphtheria-Tetanus-Pertussis (Whooping Cough): 1st shot Trivalent Oral Polio Vaccine: 1st dose
4 MONTHS	Combined Diphtheria-Tetanus-Pertussis: 2nd shot Trivalent Oral Polio Vaccine: 2nd dose
6 MONTHS	Combined Diphtheria-Tetanus-Pertussis: 3rd shot Trivalent Oral Polio Vaccine: 3rd dose
12 MONTHS	Tuberculin Test
15 MONTHS	Measles: may be given as combination Measles-Rubella or Measles-Mumps-Rubella
18 MONTHS	Combined Diphtheria-Tetanus-Pertussis: booster shot Trivalent Oral Polio Vaccine: booster dose
4 TO 6 YEARS	Combined Diphtheria-Tetanus-Pertussis: booster shot Trivalent Oral Polio Vaccine: booster dose
14 TO 16 YEARS	Combined Tetanus-Diphtheria: booster shot

• If there is a measles epidemic, the child should be given a measles shot even if he is not yet 15 months old.
• For deep punctures or severe wounds, a tetanus shot should be given immediately.

• Smallpox immunization is no longer routinely recommended.
• For foreign travel, follow your doctor's recommendations.

Immunization Record

NAME _____ DATE OF BIRTH _____

DIPHTHERIA-TETANUS-PERTUSSIS

1st DATE _____ PHYSICIAN _____
2nd DATE _____ PHYSICIAN _____
3rd DATE _____ PHYSICIAN _____
Booster DATE _____ PHYSICIAN _____
Booster DATE _____ PHYSICIAN _____

TRIVALENT ORAL POLIO VACCINE

1st DATE _____ PHYSICIAN _____
2nd DATE _____ PHYSICIAN _____
3rd DATE _____ PHYSICIAN _____
Booster DATE _____ PHYSICIAN _____
Booster DATE _____ PHYSICIAN _____

TUBERCULIN TEST
DATE _____ PHYSICIAN _____

MEASLES-MUMPS-RUBELLA
DATE _____ PHYSICIAN _____

TETANUS-DIPHTHERIA BOOSTER
DATE _____ PHYSICIAN _____

OTHER VACCINES (INFLUENZA, ETC.)

TYPE _____ DATE _____ PHYSICIAN _____
TYPE _____ DATE _____ PHYSICIAN _____
TYPE _____ DATE _____ PHYSICIAN _____
TYPE _____ DATE _____ PHYSICIAN _____
TYPE _____ DATE _____ PHYSICIAN _____

NAME _____ DATE OF BIRTH _____

DIPHTHERIA-TETANUS-PERTUSSIS

1st DATE _____ PHYSICIAN _____
2nd DATE _____ PHYSICIAN _____
3rd DATE _____ PHYSICIAN _____
Booster DATE _____ PHYSICIAN _____
Booster DATE _____ PHYSICIAN _____

TRIVALENT ORAL POLIO VACCINE

1st DATE _____ PHYSICIAN _____
2nd DATE _____ PHYSICIAN _____
3rd DATE _____ PHYSICIAN _____
Booster DATE _____ PHYSICIAN _____
Booster DATE _____ PHYSICIAN _____

TUBERCULIN TEST
DATE _____ PHYSICIAN _____

MEASLES-MUMPS-RUBELLA
DATE _____ PHYSICIAN _____

TETANUS-DIPHTHERIA BOOSTER
DATE _____ PHYSICIAN _____

OTHER VACCINES (INFLUENZA, ETC.)

TYPE _____ DATE _____ PHYSICIAN _____
TYPE _____ DATE _____ PHYSICIAN _____
TYPE _____ DATE _____ PHYSICIAN _____
TYPE _____ DATE _____ PHYSICIAN _____
TYPE _____ DATE _____ PHYSICIAN _____

NAME _____ DATE OF BIRTH _____

DIPHTHERIA-TETANUS-PERTUSSIS

1st DATE _____ PHYSICIAN _____
2nd DATE _____ PHYSICIAN _____
3rd DATE _____ PHYSICIAN _____
Booster DATE _____ PHYSICIAN _____
Booster DATE _____ PHYSICIAN _____

TRIVALENT ORAL POLIO VACCINE

1st DATE _____ PHYSICIAN _____
2nd DATE _____ PHYSICIAN _____
3rd DATE _____ PHYSICIAN _____
Booster DATE _____ PHYSICIAN _____
Booster DATE _____ PHYSICIAN _____

TUBERCULIN TEST
DATE _____ PHYSICIAN _____

MEASLES-MUMPS-RUBELLA
DATE _____ PHYSICIAN _____

TETANUS-DIPHTHERIA BOOSTER
DATE _____ PHYSICIAN _____

OTHER VACCINES (INFLUENZA, ETC.)

TYPE _____ DATE _____ PHYSICIAN _____
TYPE _____ DATE _____ PHYSICIAN _____
TYPE _____ DATE _____ PHYSICIAN _____
TYPE _____ DATE _____ PHYSICIAN _____
TYPE _____ DATE _____ PHYSICIAN _____

Childhood Illnesses

	SYMPTOMS	INCUBATION	DURATION
BRONCHITIS	Frequent coughing. Labored breathing. Possible fever.	1 to 7 days	2 to 4 days
CHICKEN POX	Fever. Discomfort. Itching. Pink or red spots on the chest, stomach and back, which may spread to the scalp and face. Spots change to blisters, which eventually crust.	10 to 21 days	7 to 10 days
COMMON COLD	Sneezing. Stuffed or runny nose. Sore throat. Watery eyes. Possible cough, chills, low fever.	1 to 7 days	2 to 14 days
CROUP	Labored breathing. Hoarseness. Loud hacking cough. Often comes on at night.	2 to 6 days	4 to 5 days
GERMAN MEASLES (RUBELLA)	Chills. Low fever (sometimes high). Runny nose. Painful swelling of glands behind the ears. Usually there is a slightly raised fine red rash, which begins on the face, then spreads over the entire body.	14 to 21 days	3 to 6 days
INFLUENZA (VIRUS, FLU)	Chills. Drowsiness. Weakness. Sudden high fever. Headache. Aches and pains. Sore throat. No appetite. Possible nausea and dizziness.	1 to 3 days	3 to 7 days
MEASLES	Early symptoms include low fever, slight hacking cough, fatigue, discomfort, eye irritation. Around the 4th day, fever and cough worsen and a rash of faint pink spots appears on the neck and cheeks, then spreads to the rest of the body.	10 to 15 days	8 to 12 days
MUMPS	Swollen glands on one or both sides of the jaw. Mild headache. Fever.	12 to 24 days	6 to 10 days
PNEUMONIA	Coughing. Fever. Rapid breathing. Discomfort. Chills. Weakness. Possible nausea and vomiting. Sudden fever lasting several days.	2 to 14 days	About 7 days
ROSEOLA	Sudden fever lasting several days. After fever is gone, a rash of flat or raised spots appears on the chest, stomach or back, then spreads to the rest of the body.	10 to 14 days	5 to 6 days
SCARLET FEVER	Painful sore throat. Fever. Nausea and vomiting. Within 3 days a fine rash appears on the neck, armpit and groin, then spreads over the body.	1 to 5 days	6 to 8 days
STREP THROAT	Painful sore throat. Fever. Nausea and vomiting.	2 to 5 days	About 6 days

VOMITING AND DIARRHEA

Consult your doctor if vomiting or diarrhea persists for more than 6 hours, contains blood or is accompanied by high fever. Have the child rest and keep him off solid foods. When he starts to feel better, give him low fat foods and frequent small amounts of liquid.

COMMUNICABILITY	TREATMENT*	SPECIAL PRECAUTIONS
2 days before symptoms appear to 2 days after	**Consult your doctor.** If the child has fever, make sure he rests, give him plenty of juice and use a vaporizer.	
1 day before spots appear to about 6 days after. The child should be isolated until blisters crust and dry.	**Consult your doctor.** Rest is essential. Relieve itching with calamine lotion. Trim the child's nails so he doesn't scratch himself.	Keep his utensils and dishes separate.
2 days before symptoms appear to 2 days after	If the child has fever, make sure he rests, give him plenty of juice and use a vaporizer. Keep him warm and avoid chilling.	Consult your doctor if the symptoms persist or worsen.
2 days before symptoms appear to 5 days after	**Consult your doctor.** Use a vaporizer. Keep the child on a light, low-fat diet.	
7 days before symptoms appear to 5 days after. **Pregnant women should never be exposed to this illness.**	If the child has fever, make sure he rests, give him plenty of juice and use a vaporizer.	Keep the child's hands clean. Launder his linen and clothes separately.
1 day before symptoms appear to 7 days after	**Consult your doctor.** If the child has fever, make sure he rests, give him plenty of juice and use a vaporizer.	Keep his utensils and dishes separate.
4 days before rash appears to 5 days after	**Consult your doctor.** If the child's eyes are sensitive to light, keep the room dim. If he has fever, make sure he rests, give him plenty of juice and use a vaporizer.	Keep his utensils and dishes separate.
7 days before symptoms appear to 9 days after	**Consult your doctor.** Rest is essential. Apply cool compresses to the cheeks. **Do not** give the child citrus juices.	Keep his utensils and dishes separate.
Varies	**Consult your doctor.** Make sure the child rests. Give him plenty of juice. Use a vaporizer. Keep him on a light, low-fat diet.	
Varies	**Consult your doctor.**	
1 day before symptoms appear to 6 days after	**Consult your doctor.** Make sure the child rests. Give him plenty of fluids.	Check other family members for symptoms.
1 day before symptoms appear to 6 days after	**Consult your doctor.** If the child has fever, make sure he rests and give him plenty of juice.	Check other family members for symptoms.

*If a fever reaches 103°F. (39.46°C.), see **FEVER,** pages 178-179

Drug Identification

IMPORTANT: Watch breathing closely. If it stops, see **BREATHING: ARTIFICIAL RESPIRATION,** pages 134-137.

For any drug overdose, call your local Poison Control Center immediately. Also seek medical aid.

For ingested drugs, induce vomiting if the child is conscious. See **SWALLOWED POISONS,** page 228, and follow treatment **B**.

Do not panic or threaten a child intoxicated by a drug. Be supportive, tolerant and gentle.

Keep the environment quiet and peaceful if the drug is being well-tolerated. The effects will gradually wear off.

SEDATIVES

EFFECTS OF HABITUAL USE MAY INCLUDE: Sleepiness. Slurred speech. Irritability. Lack of coordination. Confused thinking. Dulled reactions. Impaired memory. Coma.
When taken with alcohol, may be fatal.

BARBITURATES
(Amytal, Nembutal, Phenobarbital, Seconal, Tuinal, Etc.)

Amytal   Nembutal   Seconal   Tuinal

IMPORTANT: Barbiturates are highly addictive.
Duration: 4 to 8 hours

HYPNOTICS
(Doriden, Quaalude, Sopor, Etc.)

Doriden   Quaalude   Sopor

Duration: 4 to 8 hours

TRANQUILIZERS
(Equanil, Librium, Miltown, Placidyl, Valium, Etc.)

Equanil   Librium   Miltown   Placidyl   Valium

Duration: 2 to 8 hours

TREATMENT FOR AN OVERDOSE
- **Seek medical aid immediately.**
- If the child has trouble breathing, see **BREATHING: ARTIFICIAL RESPIRATION,** pages 134-137.
- Treat for **SHOCK,** pages 242-245.
- A heavily addicted user should not try to withdraw abruptly.

STIMULANTS

EFFECTS MAY INCLUDE: Elation. Loss of appetite. Increased energy and alertness. **Frequent large doses can produce** trembling, muscle spasms, deep depression, hallucinations, convulsions and coma.

AMPHETAMINES
(Benzedrine, Biphetamine, Desoxyn, Dexamyl, Dexedrine, Methamphetamine, Preludin, Ritalin, Etc.)

Benzedrine   Biphetamine

Desoxyn   Dexamyl

Dexedrine   Methamphetamine

Crystal

Preludin   Ritalin

Further effects can include incessant talking, insomnia, irritability and restlessness, impaired judgment, malnutrition and extreme weight loss, and paranoia.
Duration: 3 to 4 hours.

COCAINE

Further effects can include impaired nasal membranes.
Duration: 15 to 30 minutes

TREATMENT FOR AN OVERDOSE
Seek medical aid and give supportive care.

OPIATES (NARCOTICS)

IMPORTANT: All opiates are highly addictive.
EFFECTS MAY INCLUDE: Tranquil, euphoric feeling. Dizziness, nausea and vomiting. Itchiness. Sweating. Constipation. Loss of appetite and physical energy. Very small pupils. Disassociation. Sluggishness. Drowsiness. Slurred speech. Slow pulse and respiration. Lowered temperature. Weight loss and overall breakdown in health.

HEROIN

Duration: 4 to 6 hours

MORPHINE

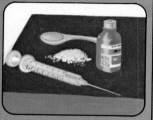

Duration: May last 12 hours or more

METHADONE

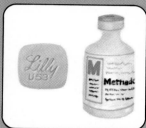

Duration: 4 to 6 hours

OPIUM

Duration: 2 to 6 hours

OTHER OPIUM DERIVATIVES
(Codeine, Demerol, Dilaudid, Paregoric, Etc.)

Codeine	Demerol	Dilaudid	Paregoric

Duration: 2 to 8 hours

TREATMENT FOR AN OVERDOSE
- **Seek medical aid immediately.**
- If the child has trouble breathing, see **BREATHING: ARTIFICIAL RESPIRATION,** pages 134-137.
- If he has trouble staying conscious, arouse him. Keep him awake and moving constantly.
- Treat for **SHOCK,** pages 242-245.
- Keep calm. Stay with the child, giving him emotional support and gentle reassurance.

HALLUCINOGENS

EFFECTS: Vary greatly according to the individual, the dose, the potency and the circumstances. Experiences can be highly pleasurable or frightening and bizarre. Psychotic reactions can be provoked in susceptible persons. Effects may include: Intense visual imagery. Intensification of the senses. Feelings of deep, spiritual transcendence. Distortion of time and space. Hallucinations. Dizziness and nausea. Numbness. Poor coordination. Panic, fear and depression.

LSD (Lysergic Acid Diethylamide)

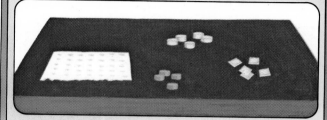

Duration: Varies with dose, potency and user. Usually 6 to 18 hours

MESCALINE

Duration: 6 to 12 hours

PEYOTE BUTTONS

Duration: 6 to 12 hours

PSILOCYBIN

Duration: 5 to 8 hours

TREATMENT FOR AN ADVERSE REACTION
- **Seek medical aid** if the child becomes panicky, violent or severely depressed.
- Protect him from hurting himself.
- Give him emotional support and gentle reassurance. **Do not** frighten or berate him.

CANNABIS (Marijuana, Hashish)

EFFECTS MAY INCLUDE: Reddened eyes. Intensification of mood, feelings and senses. Lessening of anxieties and inhibitions. Increased appetite, particularly for sweets. Distortion of time and space. Euphoria. Lightheadedness. Irritability and nervousness. Fear and paranoia.

Hashish	Marijuana
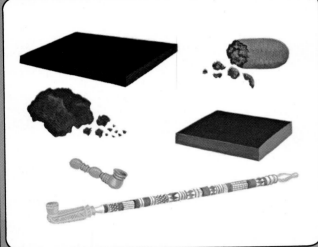	

Duration: 30 minutes to several hours

TREATMENT FOR AN ADVERSE REACTION

- Give the child emotional support and gentle reassurance. **Do not** frighten or berate him.
- **Seek medical aid** if the child becomes panicky, violent or severely depressed.

ALCOHOL

IMPORTANT: Alcohol is highly addictive.

EFFECTS MAY INCLUDE: Drowsiness. Slurred speech. Dizziness, nausea and vomiting. Lack of coordination. Uninhibited behavior. Impaired reactions and judgment. Aggressiveness. Loss of consciousness. Habitual use can damage the liver, brain, nervous system and heart.

INHALANTS (Aerosols, Airplane Glue, Etc.)

Duration: Varies with dosage.

EFFECTS MAY INCLUDE: Slurred speech. Impaired reactions and judgment. Mild euphoria. Lack of coordination. Hallucinations. Rapid pulse. Habitual use can damage the liver, kidneys and brain.

TREATMENT FOR AN OVERDOSE

- **Seek medical aid immediately.**
- If the child has trouble breathing, see **BREATHING: ARTIFICIAL RESPIRATION,** pages 134-137.
- Treat for **SHOCK,** pages 242-245.

ASPIRIN

TREATMENT FOR AN OVERDOSE

Call your local Poison Control Center and seek immediate medical aid. See **SWALLOWED POISONS,** page 226, and follow treatment **B**.

Part Two

Emergencies & Mishaps
First-Aid Procedures

CONTINUED ON NEXT PAGE

Introduction to Part Two

Remember that first aid is not a substitute for professional care. If your child becomes seriously injured or ill, you should always try to obtain the immediate assistance of a physician. Unfortunately, this isn't always possible. Emergencies have a way of happening when help isn't available right away, and if they aren't dealt with promptly the child's life may be jeopardized. Under such circumstances, your ability to provide quick, effective first aid may mean the difference between life and death.

This section presents the most up-to-date first-aid procedures for all the most common emergencies and mishaps. To help you act quickly and correctly, each procedure combines clear, simple instructions printed in large type with easy to follow step-by-step illustrations. As a further help, the back cover of this book is thumb-indexed to give you immediate access to the procedures for the most serious emergencies. Each procedure is also listed in the Contents in the front of the book.

There are several crucial points to keep in mind whenever you have to come to someone's aid:

• It is, of course, terribly distressing to see a loved one suffering from an illness or injury, but if you are to alleviate the emergency, you must do your best to remain calm and clearheaded so you can follow the appropriate procedures correctly.

• If you are unsure about the nature or extent of an emergency, see **ASSESSING THE EMERGENCY**, pages 76-79, before attempting any first aid. There are times when doing the incorrect thing can be more injurious than not doing anything at all.

To reiterate Dr. Solomon's advice in the Introduction, we suggest you read through this section as soon as possible to familiarize yourself with the recommended procedures before you ever need to use them. Don't forget that the basic purpose of first aid is to preserve the victim's life and prevent further physical and psychological harm until help arrives. We also suggest that you keep this book in an accessible place known to your baby-sitters and the other members of your family.

To obtain the best possible preparation for medical emergencies, sign up for the first-aid courses offered by your local chapter of the American National Red Cross. The basic and advanced programs provide training and supervised practice in virtually every aspect of emergency care. **Special training for cardiopulmonary resuscitation (CPR), the first-aid technique for heart failure, is especially important**; the procedure can cause serious harm if used unnecessarily or incorrectly.

With the proper foresight, many medical emergencies can be prevented altogether. We strongly urge you to study Part One of this book, **Preventions: Reducing the Odds**.

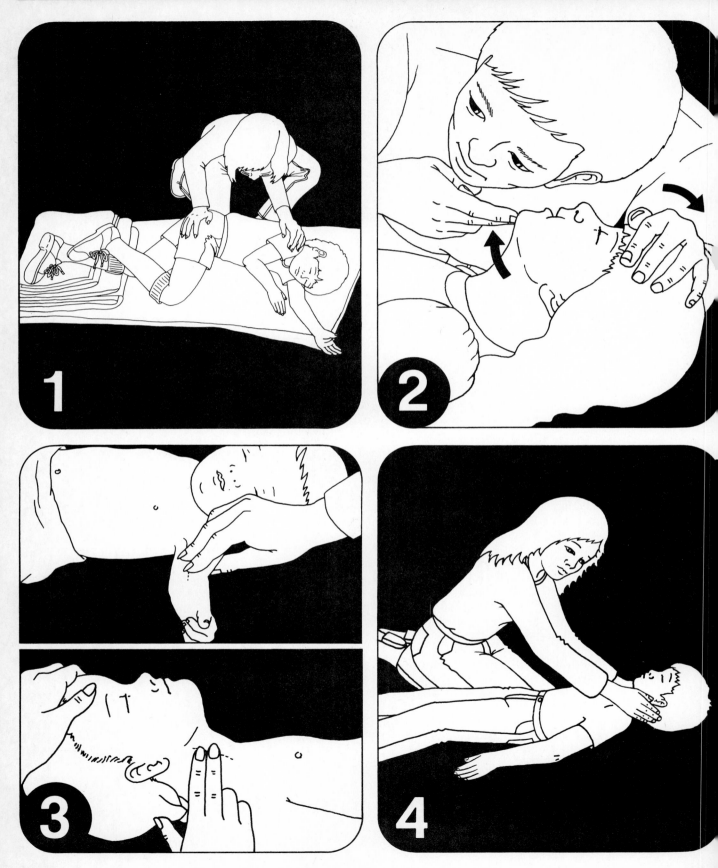

IMPORTANT

- **If the injury seems at all serious, send for medical aid immediately.**

- **Do not** move the child unless you absolutely must. You may cause further harm. If it does become necessary, see **TRANSPORTING THE INJURED**, pages 258-261.

- Remain calm and offer reassurance and comfort.

- Treat the most serious injuries first.

- Check the child for emergency medical information tags or cards.

- Try to get an account of what happened. Ask the child or bystanders who have witnessed the event.

1 **If the child is unconscious**, see **UNCONSCIOUSNESS**, pages 262-263.

2 **Check the child's breathing.** If necessary, see **BREATHING: ARTIFICIAL RESPIRATION**, pages 134-137.

3 **Check the pulse**; see **TAKING THE PULSE**, pages 256-257. If no pulse is felt, see **HEART FAILURE**, pages 192-207.

4 **Check for bleeding**. Quickly and gently examine the child's head and body for injuries. Make sure not to overlook any concealed wounds. Control the most serious bleeding first. See **BLEEDING: CUTS & WOUNDS**, pages 100-115.

CONTINUED ON NEXT PAGE

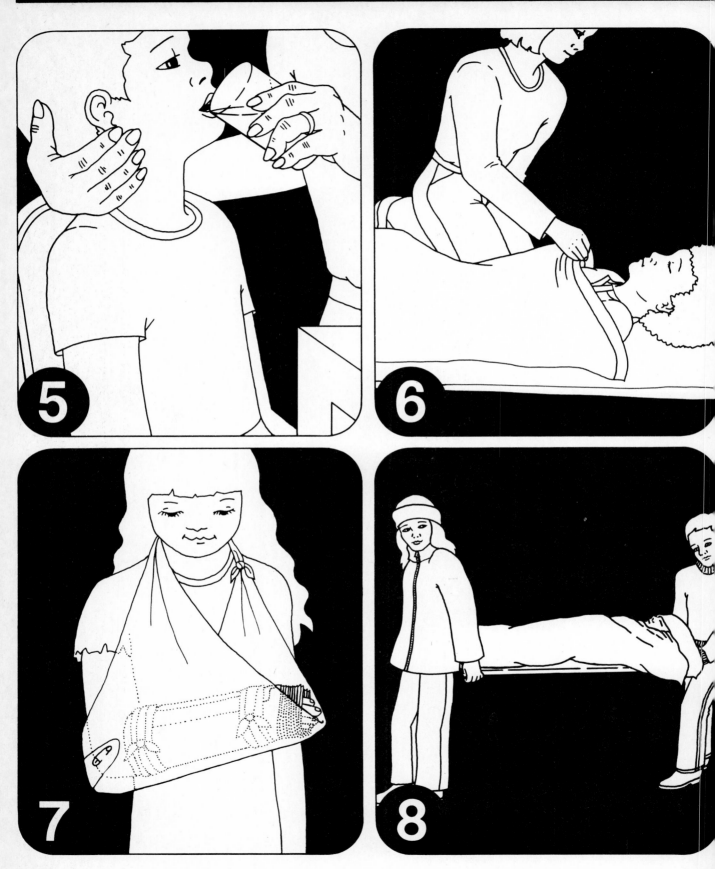

5

6

7

8

5 If there are burns or stains on the child's mouth or other signs of poisoning (pills, chemicals, poisonous plants, etc.), see **POISONING**, pages 226-241.

6 If the child is seriously injured, treat for **SHOCK**, pages 242-245.

7 For broken bones, see **BREAKS: FRAC-TURES & DISLOCATIONS**, pages 122-133.

8 In cool or cold weather, particularly if it is windy and the child is wet, see **HYPOTHERMIA (COLD EXPOSURE)**, pages 216-219.

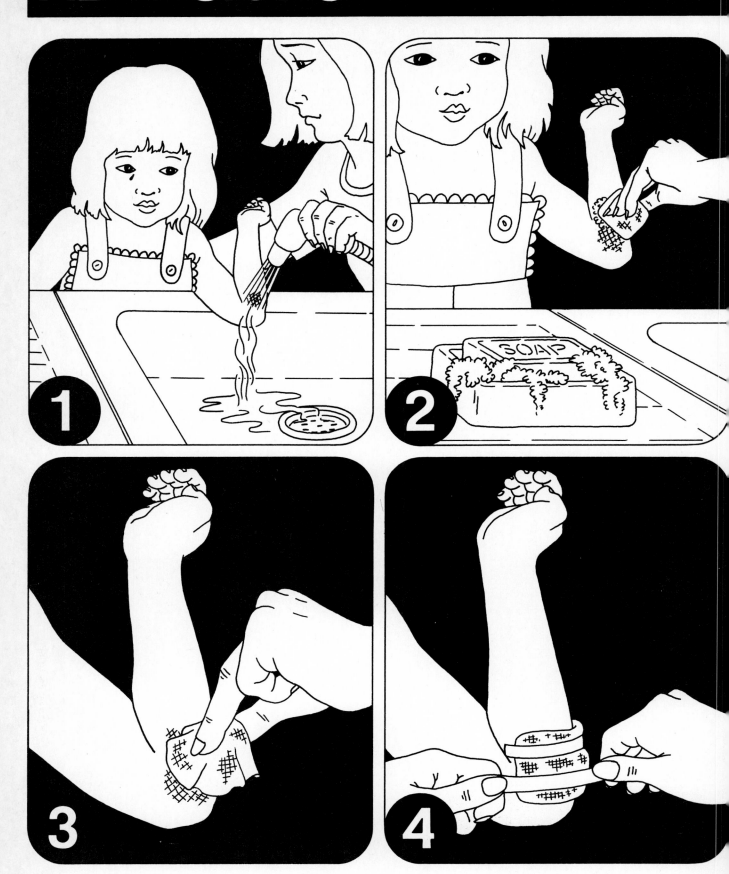

IMPORTANT

- **Seek medical aid immediately if an eye or a large area of the body is affected, if dirt or foreign substances have been ground into the wound or if there is evidence of infection. Do not** treat these abrasions yourself.

SYMPTOMS

Surface of the skin is scraped, scratched or rubbed away. Reddening of the affected area. May or may not bleed, depending on severity.

1 Place the affected area under running water to loosen and wash away dirt. If necessary, gently remove foreign matter with a sterile gauze pad or clean cloth.

2 Wash the affected area with soap and water.

3 Gently blot dry with sterile gauze or a clean cloth.

4 Cover with a clean, nonadhering dressing or cloth. Hold it in place with adhesive tape.

ASTHMA ATTACK

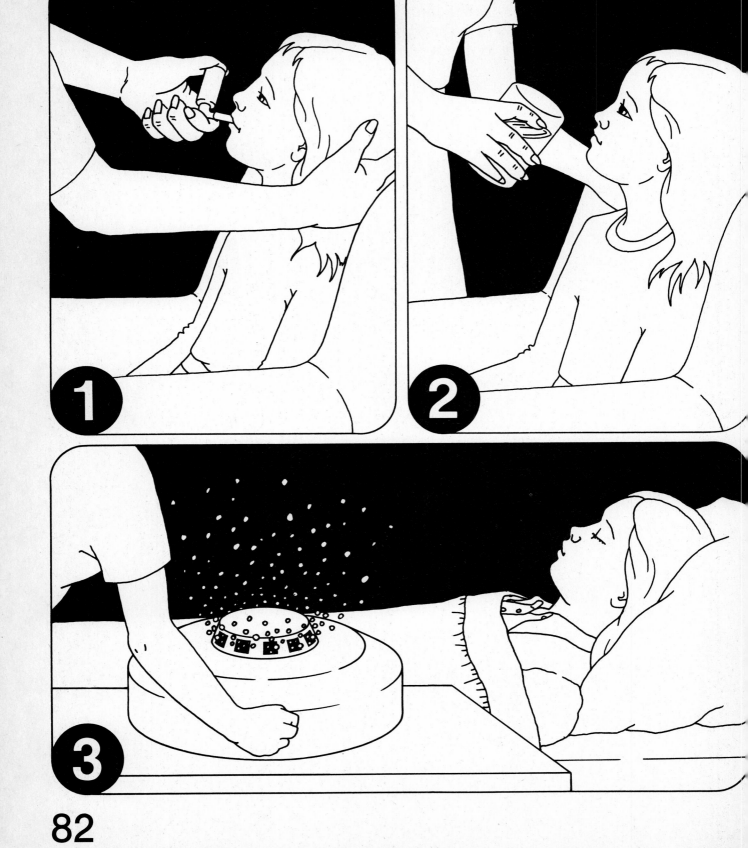

IMPORTANT

- **Seek medical aid if the attack is severe or occurring for the first time**.
- Watch breathing closely. If necessary, see **BREATHING: ARTIFICIAL RESPIRATION**, pages 134-137.
- Someone with a history of asthma should avoid known or suspected causes of attacks.

SYMPTOMS

In early stages: Respiratory discomfort resembling a cold. Coughing. Nasal congestion. **May progress to:** Labored breathing with whistling or wheezing sounds. Anxiety. **In advanced cases:** Feeling of suffocation. Pale or bluish lips, gums, skin and fingernails. **May progress to:** Respiratory failure.

1 As soon as symptoms are noticed, take the child to a quiet area and place her in the most comfortable position possible, preferably seated with her shoulders relaxed. Provide good ventilation. If medicine has been prescribed, help her take it.

2 Have the child rest. Comfort and reassure her; anxiety may worsen the attack. Encourage her to drink plenty of liquids — water, fruit juices, etc., but **not** milk.

3 A cool-mist vaporizer may help ease distressed breathing.

BACK & NECK INJURIES

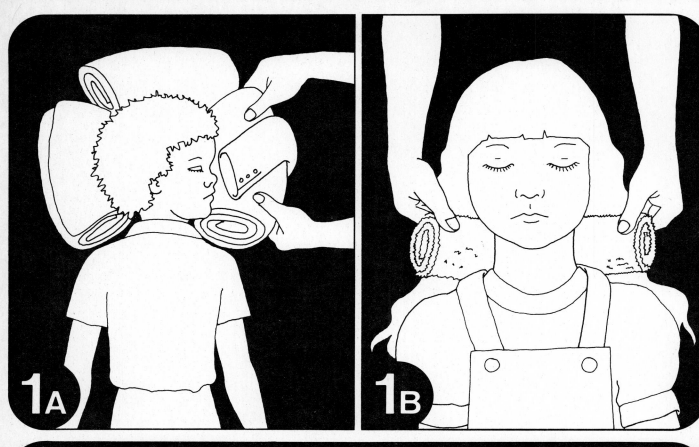

1A

1B

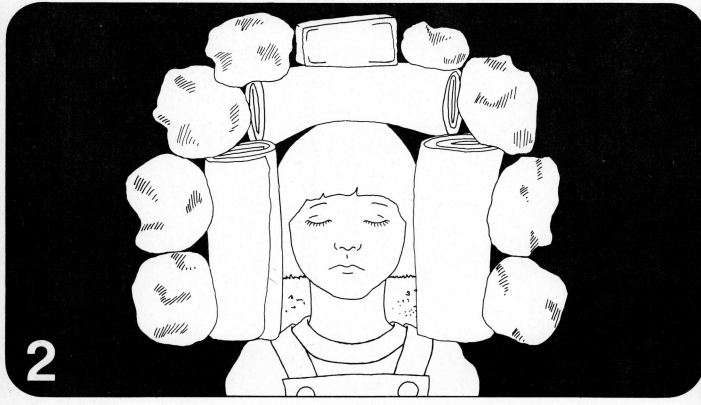

2

BACK & NECK INJURIES

IMPORTANT

- **Seek medical aid immediately.**
- **Do not** bend or twist the neck or body.
- **Do not** move the child unless you absolutely must. If it does become necessary, see **TRANSPORTING THE INJURED**, pages 258-259.
- If the child has trouble breathing, see **BREATHING: ARTIFICIAL RESPIRATION**, pages 134-137.

1A Immobilize the head in the position found by placing rolled-up clothing, blankets, etc. around the head and the sides of the neck and shoulders. For back injuries, also immobilize the torso.

1B If the child is on her back, slide a small towel or pad under her neck without moving her head. (**Do not** place anything bulky under the head.)

2 Hold restraining materials in place with bricks, stones, etc.

BITES & STINGS: ANIMAL & HUMAN BITES

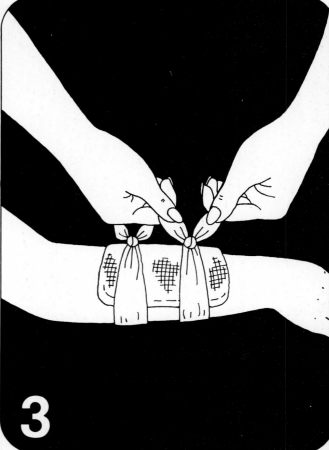

IMPORTANT

- **If the skin is penetrated, seek medical aid immediately.** Human bites can be particularly dangerous.

- Try to capture or confine the animal for examination. Be careful not to get bitten yourself.

- Observe for **SHOCK**, pages 242-245.

1 Control the bleeding. See **BLEEDING: CUTS & WOUNDS**, pages 100-103.

2 Wash the wound with soap and water. **Do not** use antiseptics, ointments or other medications.

3 Apply a sterile dressing or clean cloth, and hold it in place with a bandage.

IMPORTANT

- **Seek medical aid immediately for bites and stings from BLACK WIDOW and BROWN RECLUSE SPIDERS, SCORPIONS and TARANTULAS, particularly if the child is subject to hay fever, asthma or an allergic reaction.** Also observe for **SHOCK**, pages 242-245.

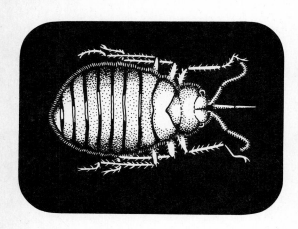

BEDBUG

SYMPTOMS

Welts. Swelling. Irritation.

WHAT TO DO

Wash thoroughly with soap and water.

BEE (WASP, HORNET & YELLOW JACKET)

IMPORTANT

Seek medical aid immediately if the child is subject to allergic reactions or if there is severe swelling anywhere on his body. Also observe for **SHOCK**, pages 242-245. Watch breathing closely. If necessary, see **BREATHING: ARTIFICIAL RESPIRATION**, pages 134-137.

SYMPTOMS

Pain. Local swelling. Burning and itching. Allergic reaction may also cause nausea, shock, unconsciousness and severe swelling.

WHAT TO DO

For a bee sting, remove the venom sac by scraping gently, not by squeezing. (Wasps, hornets and yellow jackets do not leave venom sacs.) Wash with soap and water. For severe reactions, see first aid for **BLACK WIDOW**, page 89.

BLACK WIDOW SPIDER

SYMPTOMS

Severe pain. Profuse sweating. Muscle cramps. Difficulty breathing. Nausea.

WHAT TO DO

Watch breathing closely. If it stops, see **BREATHING: ARTIFICIAL RESPIRATION**, pages 134-137. Keep the child quiet and avoid unnecessary movement. Keep the affected part below heart level. Place a constricting band 2 to 4 inches above the wound. **Do not** bind too tightly. You should be able to slide your finger under it. Apply ice wrapped in a cloth. Remove the band after 30 minutes.

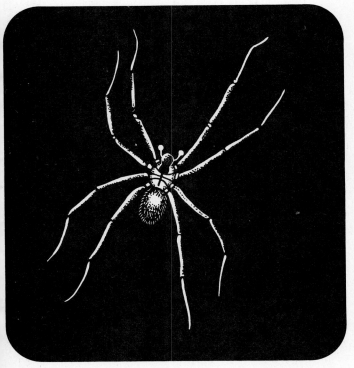

BROWN RECLUSE SPIDER

SYMPTOMS

The bite may be hardly noticed, but hours later severe pain, swelling and blisters occur.

WHAT TO DO

Follow first aid for **BLACK WIDOW**, above.

CONTINUED ON NEXT PAGE

89

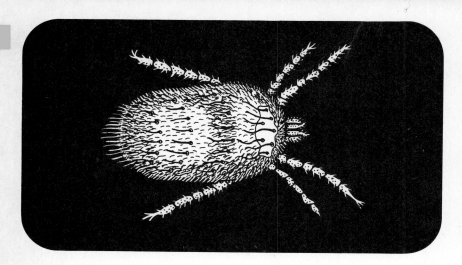

CHIGGER

SYMPTOMS

Itching. Irritation. Local pain. Small red welts.

WHAT TO DO

Wash with soap and water. Soothe irritation with cold compresses or calamine lotion.

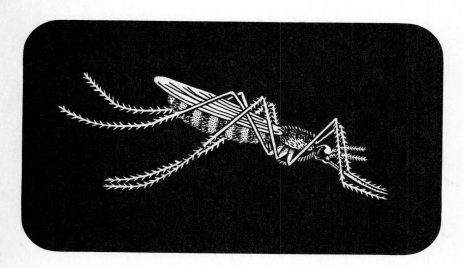

MOSQUITO

SYMPTOMS

Itching. Irritation. Local pain. Small red welts.

WHAT TO DO

Wash with soap and water. Soothe irritation with cold compresses or calamine lotion.

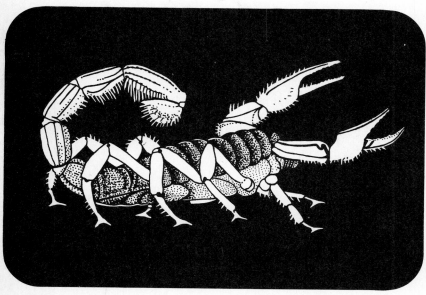

SCORPION

SYMPTOMS

Excruciating pain at the sting. Swelling. Fever. Nausea. Stomach pains. Difficulty speaking. Worsening convulsions. Coma.

WHAT TO DO

Follow first aid for **BLACK WIDOW**, page 89.

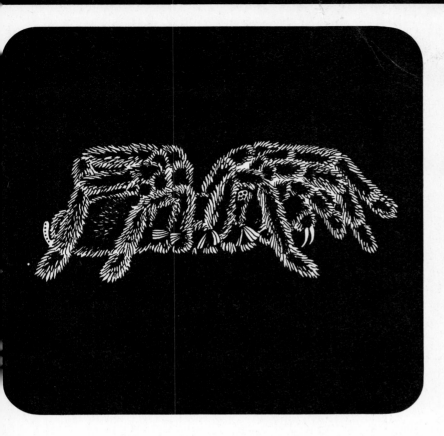

TARANTULA

SYMPTOMS

May vary from pinprick to severe wound.

WHAT TO DO

Wash with soap and water. Cover lightly with a sterile dressing or clean cloth. For severe reactions, see first aid for **BLACK WIDOW**, page 89.

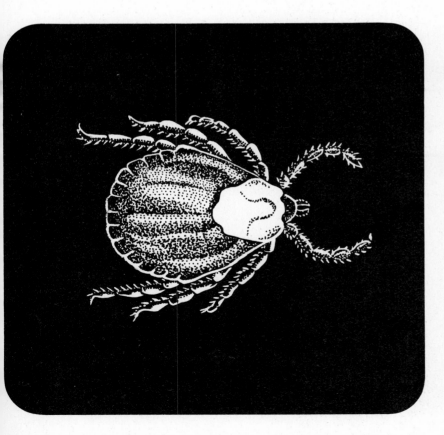

TICK

SYMPTOMS

The tick may be visible on the skin as a dark spot.

WHAT TO DO

Do not pull the tick from the child's skin. Apply heavy oil to the area, then after 30 minutes remove the parts carefully with tweezers. Wash with soap and water.

BITES & STINGS:

IMPORTANT

- **Seek medical aid immediately.**
- Watch breathing closely. If necessary, see **BREATHING: ARTIFICIAL RESPIRATION**, pages 134-137.
- Observe for **SHOCK**, pages 242-245.

CONE SHELL

SYMPTOMS

Vary from a slight sting to severe pain, numbness, tingling, difficulty swallowing, tightness in the chest, partial paralysis, impaired vision, collapse.

WHAT TO DO

Place a constricting band 2 to 4 inches above the wound. **Do not** bind too tightly. You should be able to slide your finger under it. Soak in hot water or apply hot compresses for 30 minutes, then remove the band.

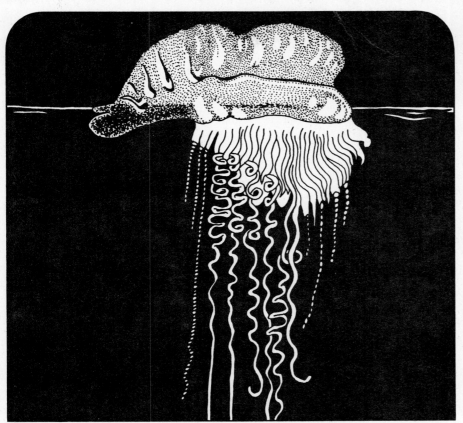

MAN OF WAR & JELLYFISH

SYMPTOMS

Burning pain. Rash. Swelling. Difficulty breathing. Cramps. Nausea. Vomiting. Collapse.

WHAT TO DO

Gently remove the tentacles with a cloth. Clean affected area with alcohol or diluted ammonia.

CONTINUED ON NEXT PAGE

SEA ANEMONE & HYDROID

SYMPTOMS

Burning or stinging pain. Stomach cramps. Chills. Diarrhea.

WHAT TO DO

Soak in hot water or apply hot compresses.

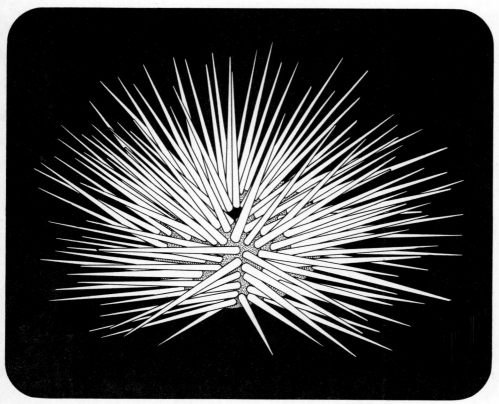

SEA URCHIN

SYMPTOMS

Pain. Dizziness. Muscle tremors. Paralysis.

WHAT TO DO

Follow first aid for **CONE SHELL**, page 92.

94

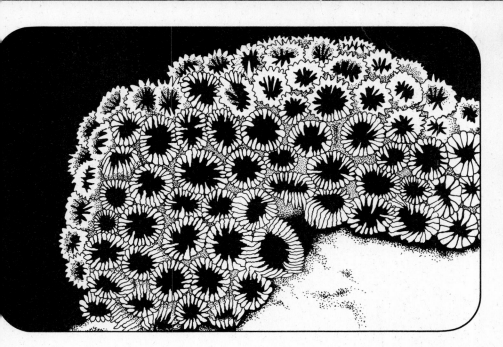

STINGING CORAL

SYMPTOMS

Burning or stinging pain.

WHAT TO DO

Wash thoroughly with soap and water.

STINGRAY

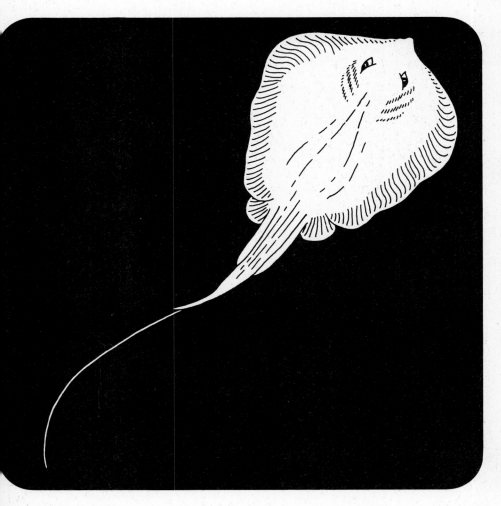

SYMPTOMS

Painful cut or puncture. Swelling. Discoloration. Nausea. Vomiting. Muscle spasms. Convulsions. Difficulty breathing.

WHAT TO DO

Carefully remove the stinger if possible. Wash thoroughly with soap and water. Control the bleeding; see **BLEEDING: CUTS & WOUNDS (DIRECT PRESSURE)**, pages 100-101. Apply a constricting band; see first aid for **CONE SHELL**, page 92.

BITES & STINGS: SNAKEBITE

POISONOUS SNAKE

NONPOISONOUS SNAKE

1

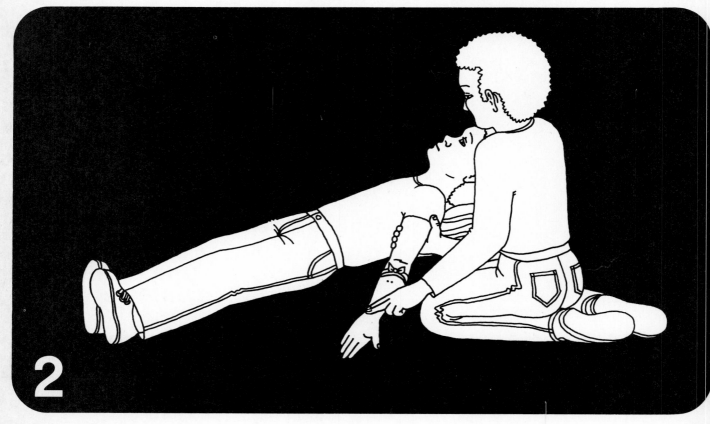

2

IMPORTANT

- **Seek medical aid immediately for any suspected snakebite.**

- **Do not cut through a snakebite (Step 3) if you are within several hours of medical aid.**

- **Do not** let the child walk or move the affected part unless absolutely necessary. Whenever possible, carry him carefully.

- **Do not** use cold compresses or pack in ice.

- Watch breathing closely. If necessary, see **BREATHING: ARTIFICIAL RESPIRATION**, pages 134–137.

- Treat for **SHOCK**, pages 242–245.

SYMPTOMS

Mild to moderate: Pain. Swelling. Nausea. Weakness. **Severe:** Slurred speech. Severe nausea. Vomiting. Shock. Paralysis. Convulsions. **May progress to:** Unconsciousness. No breathing and circulation.

1 Determine if the bite is from a poisonous snake by looking for 1 or more fang marks at the wound. If nonpoisonous, see Step 5 only.

2 **If any symptoms occur:** Apply a constricting band between the bite and the heart 2 to 4 inches above the puncture. **Do not** bind too tightly. Check the pulse below the wound. If you can't feel it, loosen the band until it returns. The wound should ooze. Keep the affected part below heart level.

CONTINUED ON NEXT PAGE

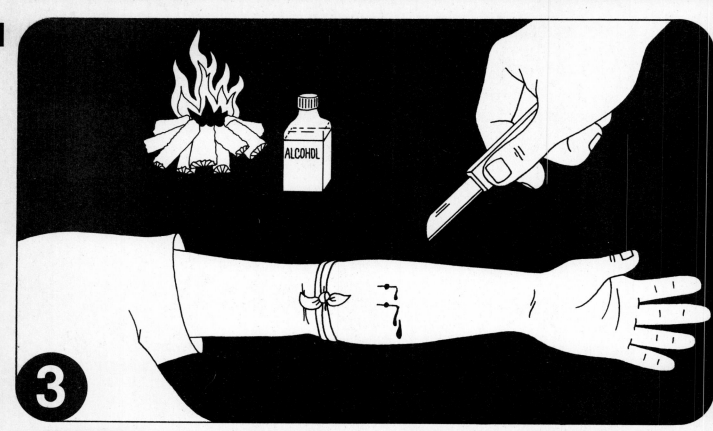

3

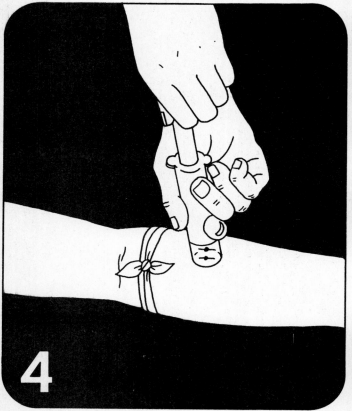

4

5

3 **If severe symptoms occur and you cannot get to medical aid within several hours, then:** Clean the wound with alcohol or soap and water. Sterilize a knife or razor blade over an open flame, and make a **shallow vertical incision about ⅛ inch deep and ¼ inch long through each fang mark (as shown).** **Do not** cut deeply or crisscross. **Do not** make incisions on the head, neck or torso.

4 Draw the venom from the wound with a suction cup or your mouth, if it is free of open sores. **Do not** swallow the venom. Maintain suction for 30 minutes.

5 Wash thoroughly with soap and water.

DIRECT PRESSURE

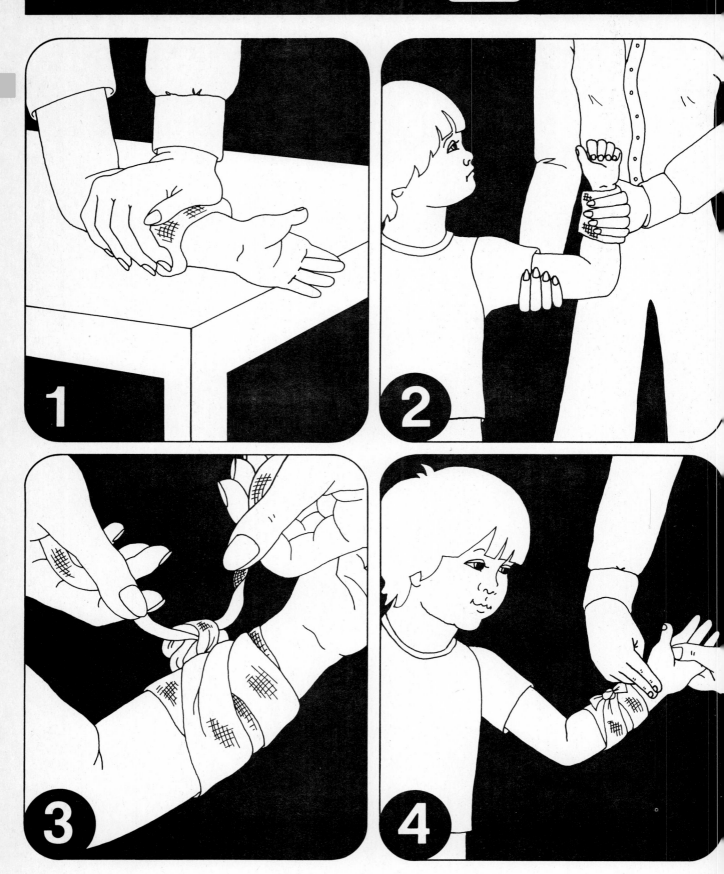

IMPORTANT

- **Seek medical aid for any serious bleeding.**
- **Do not** apply direct pressure on breaks.
- Observe for **SHOCK**, pages 242-245.

- **First try to control the bleeding by direct pressure; see below.**
- **If you cannot control the bleeding, use pressure points while continuing direct pressure; see BLEEDING: CUTS & WOUNDS (PRESSURE POINTS), pages 102-103.**
- **If serious blood loss continues and becomes critical, apply a tourniquet as a last resort; see BLEEDING: CUTS & WOUNDS (TOURNIQUET), pages 104-107.**

1 Press gauze or a clean cloth directly over the wound.

2 Elevate injured limbs higher than the heart unless there is evidence of fracture or it causes pain.

3 After bleeding is controlled, bandage firmly but not too tightly.

4 Check the pulse below the wound; see **TAKING THE PULSE**, pages 256-257, for normal pulse rates. If you can't feel it, loosen the bandage until it returns, then observe for **SHOCK**, pages 242-245.

ARM

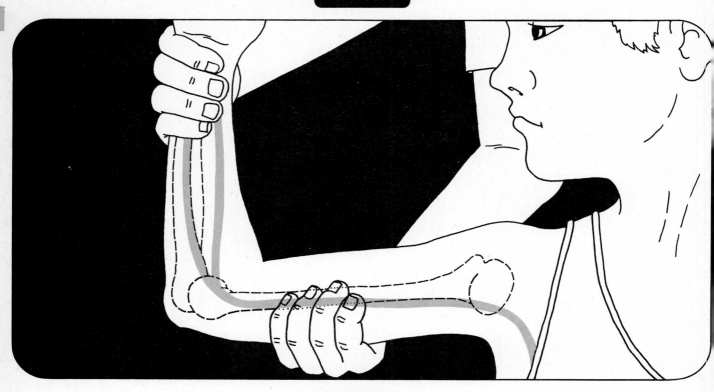

LEG

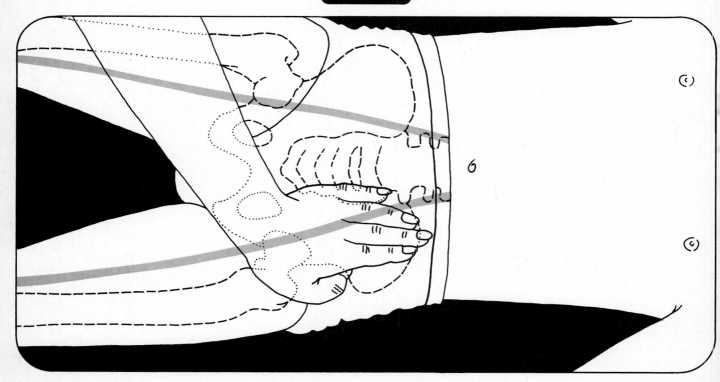

IMPORTANT

- **Seek medical aid for any serious bleeding.**
- Continue **DIRECT PRESSURE**, pages 100-101.
- Observe for **SHOCK**, pages 242-245.

ARM

Elevate the injured arm higher than the heart unless there is evidence of fracture or it causes pain. Place your fingers on the inner side of the arm, pressing in the groove between the muscles. Keeping your thumb on the outside of the arm, press toward the bone.

LEG

Elevate the injured leg higher than the heart unless there is evidence of fracture or it causes pain. Place the heel of your hand on the inner thigh at the midpoint of the crease of the groin. With your arm straight and your elbow locked, press against the bone.

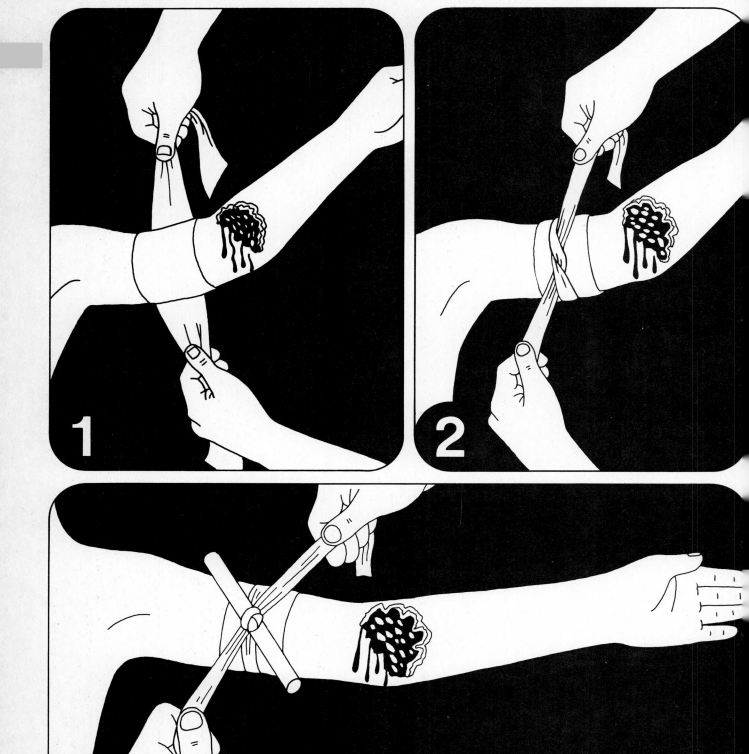

IMPORTANT

- Seek medical aid immediately.
- Use of a tourniquet may lead to later amputation of the limb. Do not use except in a critical emergency where all other methods fail to control serious bleeding and it is a matter of life and death. First try direct pressure and pressure points; see BLEEDING: CUTS & WOUNDS (DIRECT PRESSURE), pages 100–101, and BLEEDING: CUTS & WOUNDS (PRESSURE POINTS), pages 102–103.
- The tourniquet band must be at least 2 inches wide.

1 Place the tourniquet band around the limb **about ½ inch above** the wound. If a joint intervenes, position the band above the joint.

2 Wrap the band tightly around the limb twice and tie a half-knot.

3 Place a short, strong stick on the band and complete the knot on the top of the stick.

CONTINUED ON NEXT PAGE

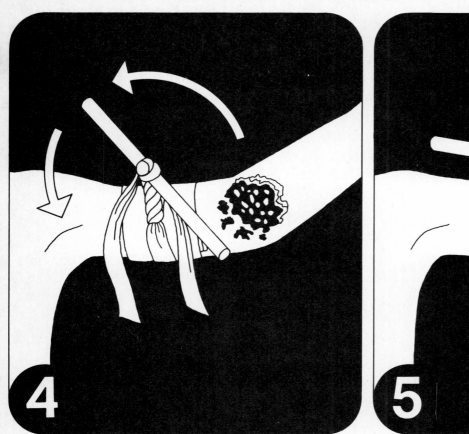

4

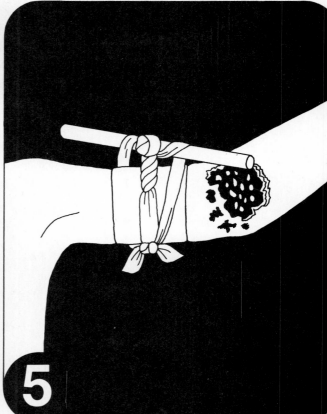

5

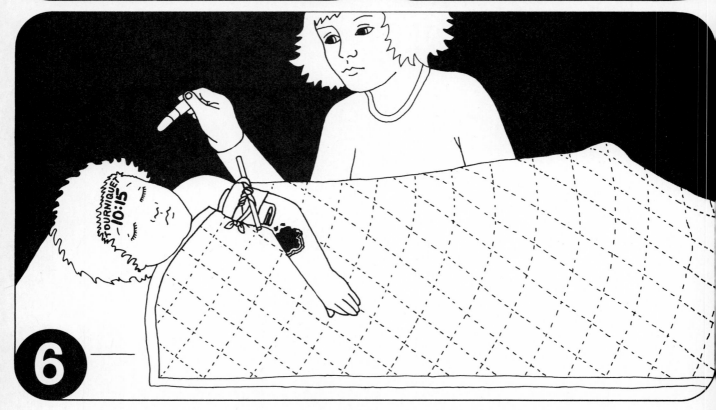

6

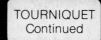

CONTINUED

4 Twist the stick until the bleeding stops.

5 Secure the stick in place. **Do not** loosen unless a doctor so advises.

6 Write down the exact time the tourniquet was applied. Attach it as a note to the child's clothing or write it on his forehead with lipstick, etc. Treat for **SHOCK**, pages 242-245, and **get to the hospital immediately**. **Do not** cover the tourniquet.

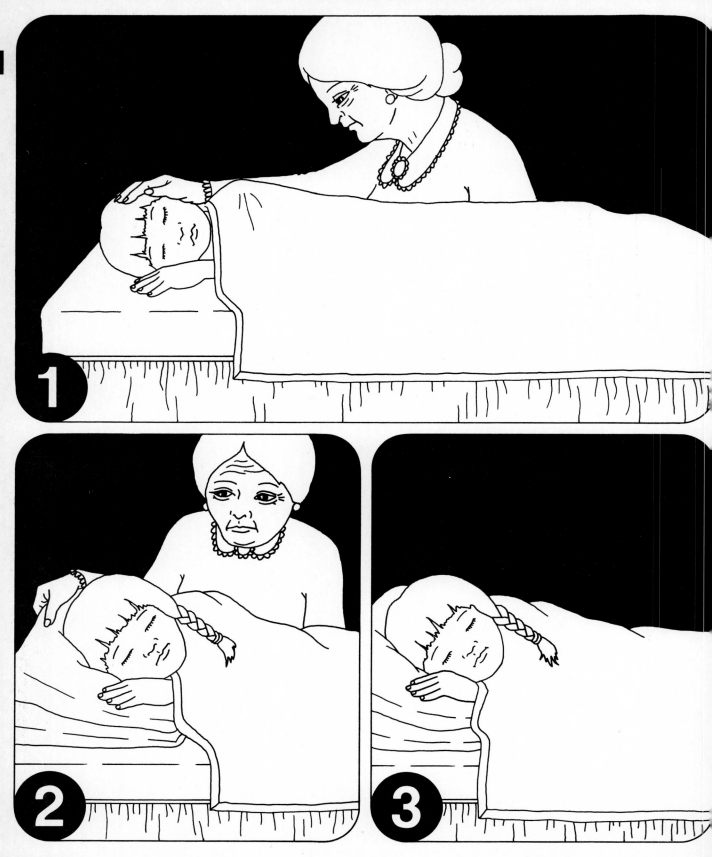

IMPORTANT

- To be suspected if the child has had a sharp blow or crushing injury to the abdomen, chest or torso.
- **Seek medical aid immediately.**
- **Do not** give the child anything to drink.

SYMPTOMS

Stomach: Vomit is bright red, dark red or the color and size of large coffee grounds.

Intestines: Excrement contains dark tar-like material or bright red blood.

Chest and Lungs: Bright red foamy blood is coughed up.

1 Keep the child lying down and covered lightly. Turn her to one side to keep the air passage clear.

2 Raise her head and shoulders if she has difficulty breathing. If necessary, see **BREATHING: ARTIFICIAL RESPIRATION**, pages 134-137.

3 Treat for **SHOCK**, pages 242-245.

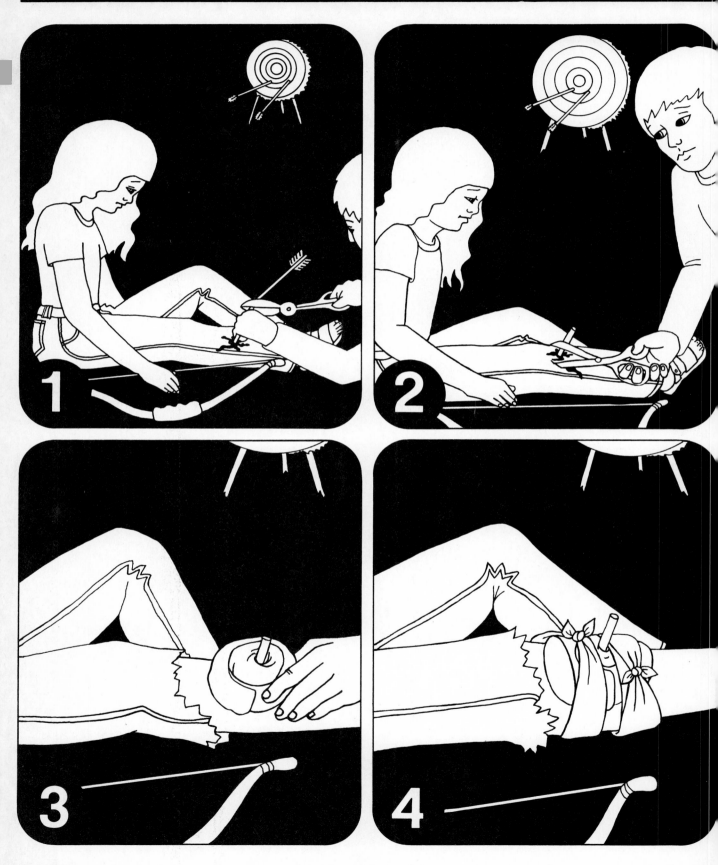

IMPORTANT

- **Call for an ambulance or get to the hospital immediately.** If necessary, see **TRANSPORTING THE INJURED: STRETCHERS & CARRIES**, pages 260-261.

- **Do not** move the child off an impaling object unless her life is in imminent danger. If you must, remove her as gently as possible, then tend to her wounds immediately and treat for **SHOCK**, pages 242-245.

1 If possible, cut off the impaling object several inches from the wound **without moving or removing it.**

2 Carefully cut away the clothing from around the wound.

3 Immobilize the object by placing a bulky dressing around it.

4 Secure the dressing in place with bandages. Treat for **SHOCK**, pages 242-245.

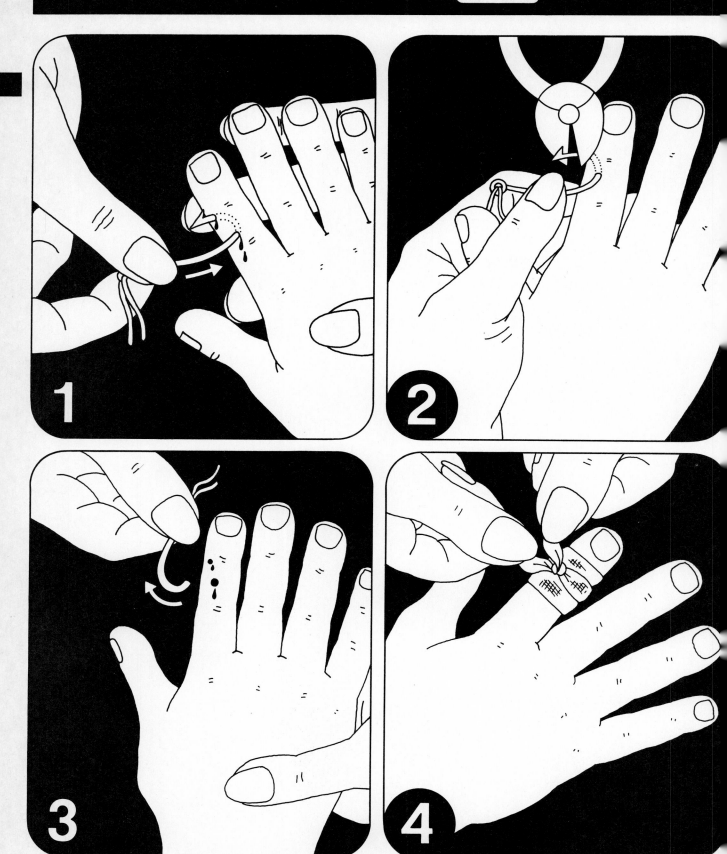

IMPORTANT

- **Do not** attempt to remove a fishhook from the face. **Seek medical aid immediately.**

1 Push the shank through the skin until the point appears.

2 Holding the shank steady, cut off the barbed end with clippers or pliers.

3 Remove the shank from the wound.

4 Wash the wound with soap and water. Cover with gauze or a clean cloth. **Consult your doctor.**

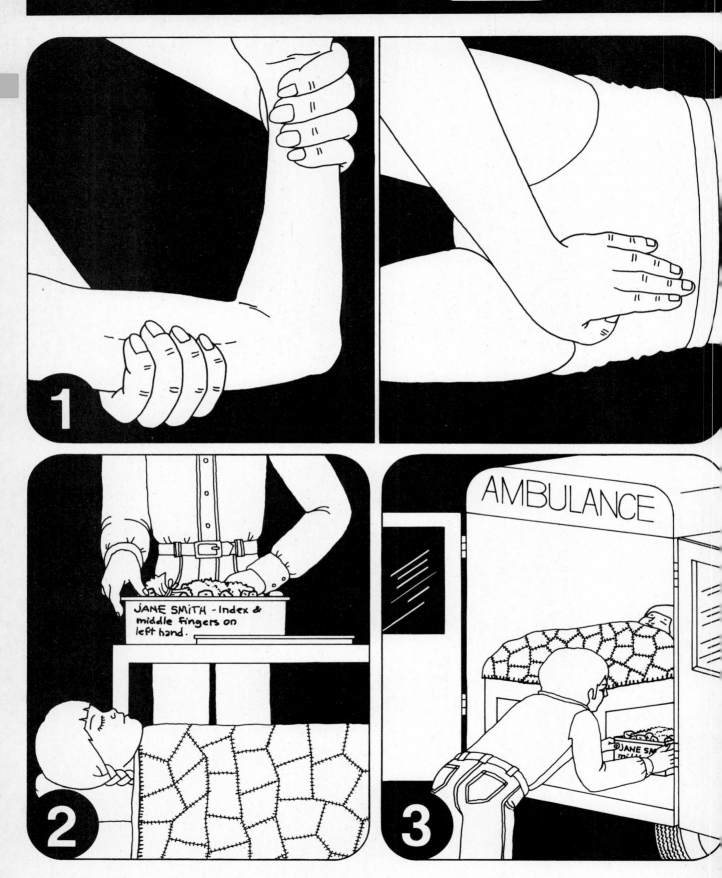

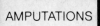
IMPORTANT

- **Stay calm and act quickly. Bleeding must be stopped as soon as possible.**
- **Seek medical aid immediately.**
- **Do not** put severed parts in water, alcohol or any other liquid. Keep them dry. Avoid freezing.

1 Control the bleeding through direct pressure and pressure points; see **BLEEDING: CUTS & WOUNDS (DIRECT PRESSURE)**, pages 100-101, and **BLEEDING: CUTS & WOUNDS (PRESSURE POINTS)**, pages 102-103. As a last resort, a tourniquet may be necessary; see **BLEEDING: CUTS & WOUNDS (TOURNIQUET)**, pages 104-107.

2 Treat for **SHOCK**, pages 242-245.

3 Wrap severed parts in a dry, clean dressing and put in a plastic bag. Wrap the plastic bag in towels and place it in a container with ice. Write the name of the child and the severed parts on the outside of the container. **Take the container and the child to a hospital immediately.**

BLISTERS

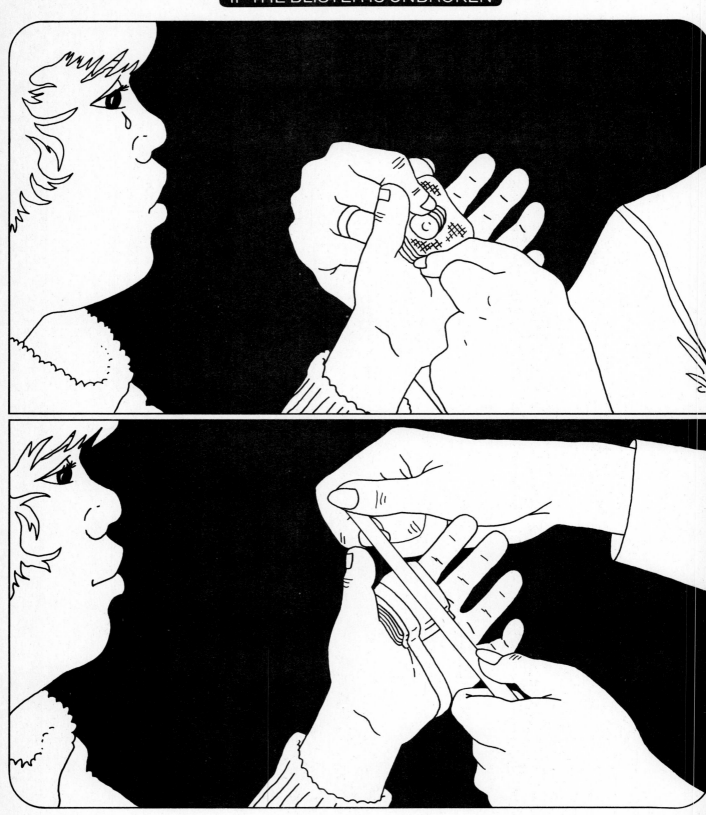

IMPORTANT

- **Seek medical aid if blisters are large, affect deep tissues of the hands or soles of the feet, cover a large portion of the body or become infected.**

- **Do not** break or open blisters caused by burns, frostbite or irritation from insect bites, poison ivy or heat rash.

SYMPTOMS

A well-defined cushion-like raised area filled with clear fluid. May be uncomfortable or painful, particularly if broken.

IF THE BLISTER IS UNBROKEN

Try to keep the blister from breaking by improvising a protective shield: Cut a hole in the center of several gauze pads slightly larger than the affected area. Place the hole in each pad over the blister, taking care not to touch the blister. Add sufficient layers to protect the blister from contact, then cover the opening with a pad fastened loosely in place with adhesive tape. If possible, try to keep the child from using the affected area.

CONTINUED ON NEXT PAGE

BLISTERS Continued

IF YOU CANNOT PREVENT THE BLISTER FROM BREAKING

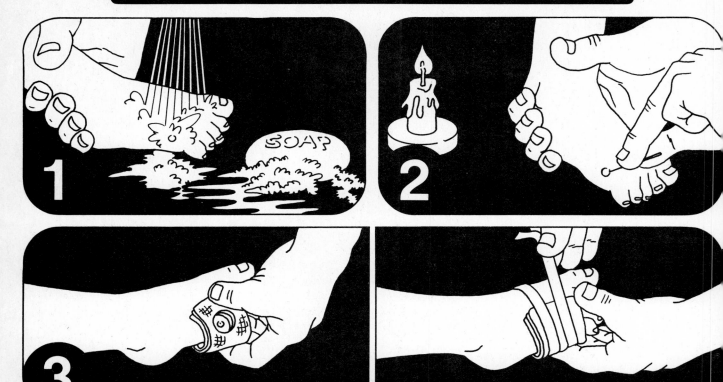

IF THE BLISTER HAS BROKEN

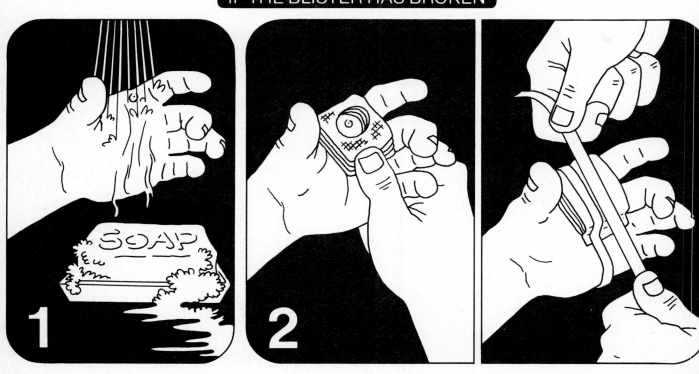

118

1 Gently wash the affected area thoroughly with soap and water.

2 Sterilize a needle by holding it over an open flame or soaking it for 10 minutes in rubbing alcohol or boiling water, then carefully puncture the edge of the blister to allow fluids to drain out.

3 Improvise a protective shield with gauze pads; see procedure for unbroken blister, pages 116-117.

IF THE BLISTER HAS BROKEN

1 Gently wash the affected area thoroughly with soap and water.

2 Improvise a protective shield with gauze pads; see procedure for unbroken blister, pages 116-117.

BOILS & CARBUNCLES

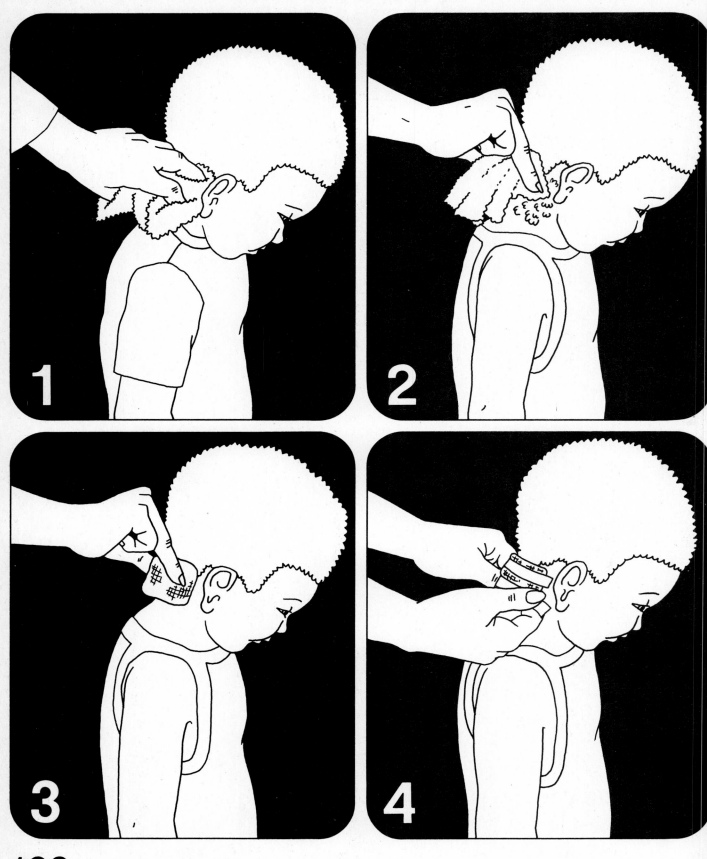

1

2

3

4

120

BOILS & CARBUNCLES

IMPORTANT

- **Seek medical aid, particularly if the central area of the face, underarm or groin is affected or if the boils spread, form clusters (carbuncles) or become chronic.**

- **Do not** puncture or squeeze boils.

SYMPTOMS

Caused by inflamed and infected hair follicles. Usually take 3 to 5 days to develop. Often affect the skin of the face, neck, chest or buttocks. Itching. Redness. Tenderness or acute pain. Possible throbbing. May come to a head, open and drain a mixture of pus and blood. **In severe cases:** May spread and form clusters. Chills. Fever.

1 Apply hot wet compresses to affected area for 10 minutes, 3 to 4 times a day. Between compresses, prevent pressure or friction by covering the affected area with a gauze pad or clean cloth loosely fastened in place with adhesive tape. Continue until the boil comes to a head, opens by itself and begins to drain.

2 After the boil opens, use soap and water to help keep the area clean and free of debris. Wipe from edge of boil toward center to prevent further contamination.

3 Gently blot dry with sterile gauze or clean cloth.

4 Cover with a clean, nonadhering dressing or cloth. Hold the dressing in place with adhesive tape.

COLLARBONE & SHOULDER

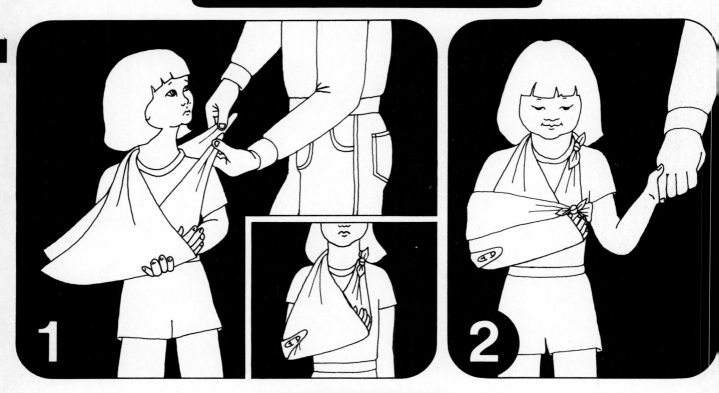

BENT ELBOW

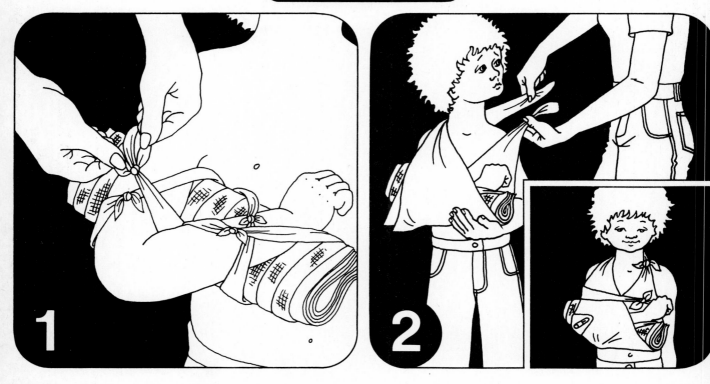

IMPORTANT

- **Seek medical aid.**
- **Do not** try to reset dislocations yourself. Treat the same as fractures.
- If any bones protrude, control the bleeding, then cover the bone and the wound with a large clean dressing or cloth. **Do not** clean the wound. See **BLEEDING: CUTS & WOUNDS (PRESSURE POINTS)**, pages 102-103.
- Observe for **SHOCK**, pages 242-245.

COLLARBONE & SHOULDER

1 Make a sling to support the weight of the arm. Be sure the hand rests 4 to 5 inches above the elbow.

2 Stabilize the arm by tying a band over the sling and around the body.

BENT ELBOW

1 Immobilize in the position found with a padded splint. Use boards, magazines, etc. for rigidity; cloth for padding.

2 Make a sling to support the weight of the arm and bind it to the body. Be sure the fingers are above elbow level. Check the fingertips for circulation. If they become blue or swollen, loosen the binding.

STRAIGHT ELBOW

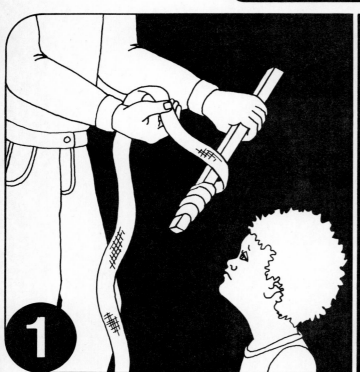

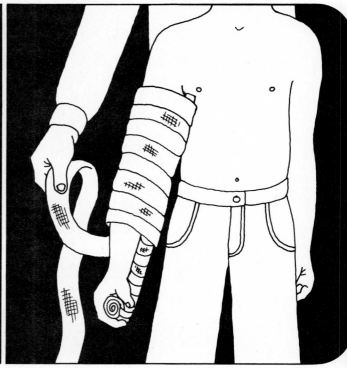

FINGER

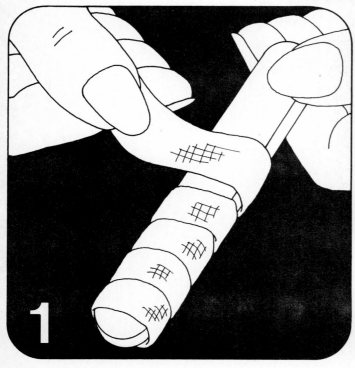

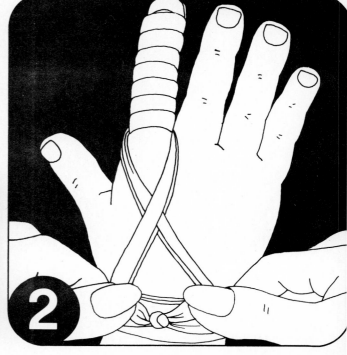

124

IMPORTANT

- **Seek medical aid.**
- **Do not** try to reset dislocations yourself. Treat the same as fractures.
- If any bones protrude, control the bleeding, then cover the bone and the wound with a large clean dressing or cloth. **Do not** clean the wound. See **BLEEDING: CUTS & WOUNDS (PRESSURE POINTS)**, pages 102-103.
- Observe for **SHOCK**, pages 242-245.

STRAIGHT ELBOW

1 Immobilize the elbow in position found with a padded splint extending from the armpit to the hand. Use boards, magazines, etc. for rigidity; cloth for padding. Bind in place.

FINGER

1 **Do not** try to straighten the finger. Immobilize it in position found with a padded splint made from a tongue depressor or the like.

2 Bind the splint to the finger with cloth or tape.

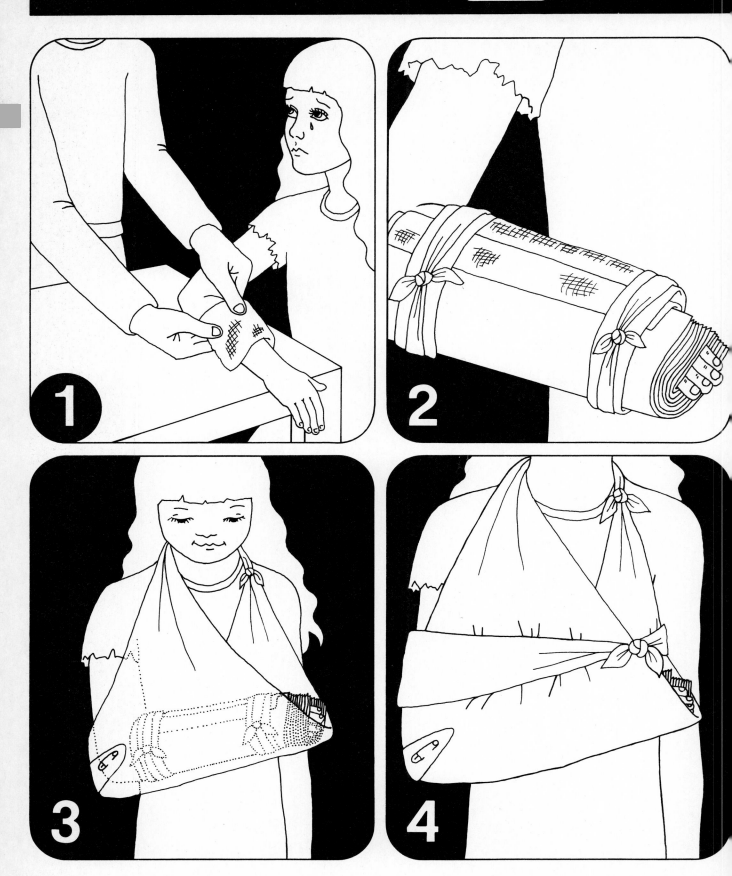

IMPORTANT

- **Seek medical aid.**
- **Do not** try to reset dislocations yourself. Treat the same as fractures.
- Observe for **SHOCK**, pages 242-245.

1 If any bones protrude, control the bleeding, then cover the bone and the wound with a large clean dressing or cloth. **Do not** clean the wound. See **BLEEDING: CUTS & WOUNDS (PRESSURE POINTS)**, pages 102-103.

2 Immobilize with a padded splint. Use boards, magazines, etc. for rigidity; cloth for padding. **Do not** tie too tightly. Check fingertips for circulation. If they become blue or swollen, loosen the binding.

3 Make a sling to support the weight of the arm. Be sure the fingers are above elbow level.

4 For a broken arm, immobilize the shoulder and elbow by binding the arm to the body.

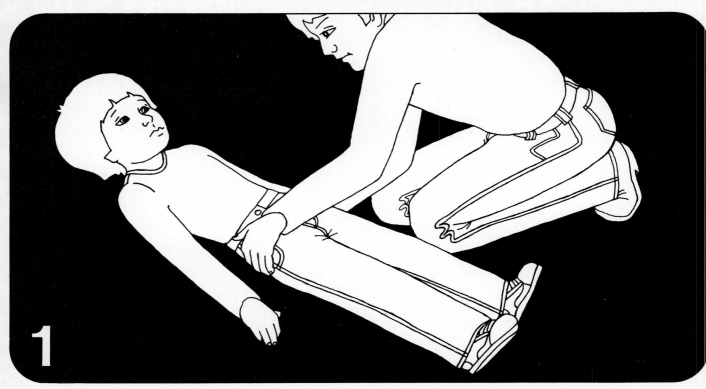

1

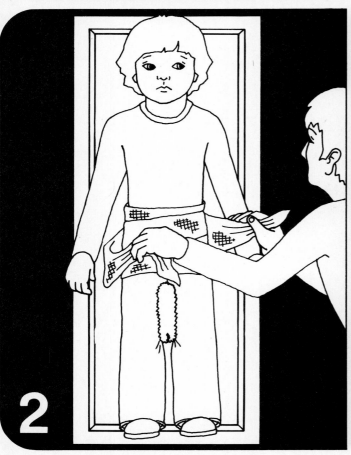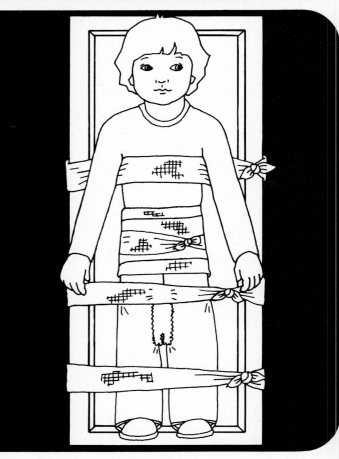

2

IMPORTANT

- **Seek medical aid.**
- **Do not** try to reset dislocations yourself. Treat the same as fractures.
- Observe for **SHOCK**, pages 242-245.

1 Check for fracture by gently feeling the bones in the pelvic and hip areas. Note where it hurts the child when you touch him.

2 To immobilize the child, place thick padding between his thighs, then tie him down on a board, door, etc. with bandages, belts or the like.

KNEE

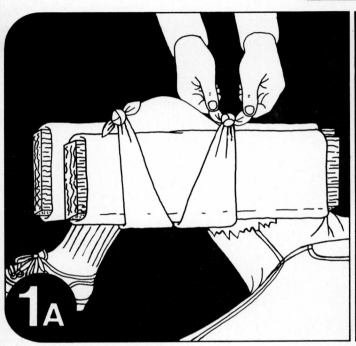

1A

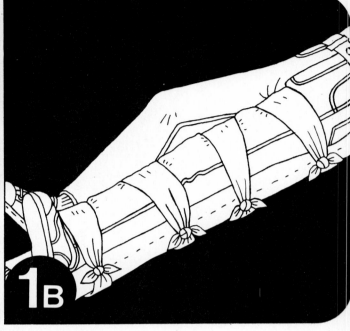

1B

LEG & ANKLE

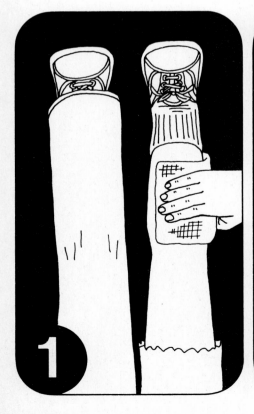

1

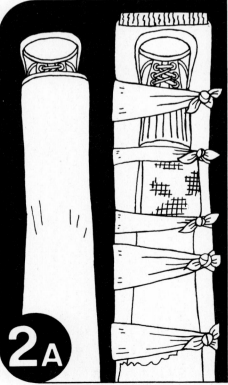

2A

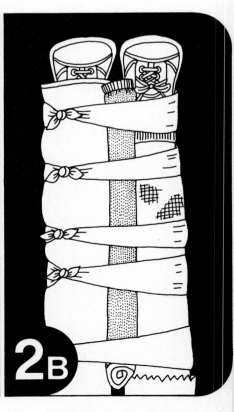

2B

IMPORTANT

- **Seek medical aid.**
- **Do not** try to reset dislocations yourself. Treat the same as fractures.
- Observe for **SHOCK**, pages 242-245.

KNEE

1A Immobilize in the position found with a padded splint. Use boards, magazines, etc. for rigidity; cloth for padding.

1B For a straight knee, extend the splint from the buttock to the heel.

LEG & ANKLE

1 If any bones protrude, control the bleeding, then cover the bone and the wound with a large clean dressing or cloth. **Do not** clean the wound. See **BLEEDING: CUTS & WOUNDS (PRESSURE POINTS)**, pages 102-103.

2A Immobilize with a padded splint. Use boards, magazines, etc. for rigidity; cloth or a pillow for padding.

2B If unable to improvise a splint, place padding between the legs and tie them together.

131

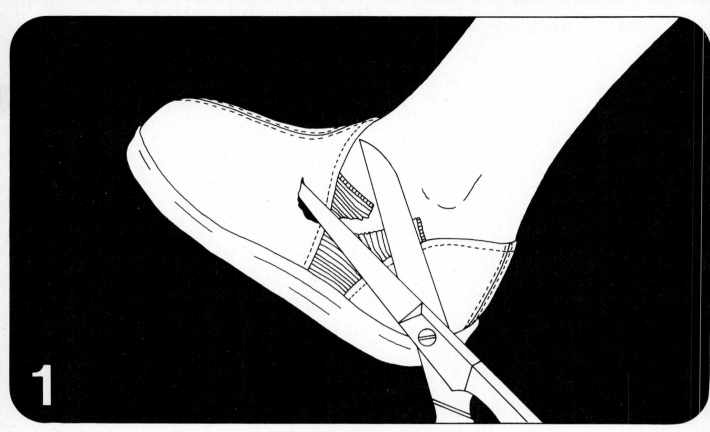

1

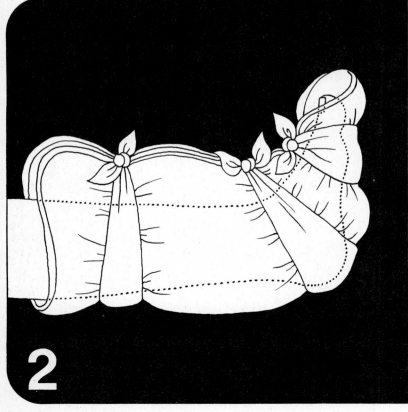

2

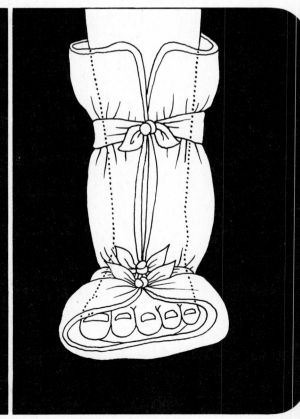

IMPORTANT

- **Seek medical aid.**
- **Do not** try to reset dislocations yourself. Treat the same as fractures.
- If any bones protrude, control the bleeding, then cover the bone and the wound with a large clean dressing or cloth. **Do not** clean the wound. See **BLEEDING: CUTS & WOUNDS (PRESSURE POINTS)**, pages 102-103.
- Observe for **SHOCK**, pages 242-245.

1 Remove or cut away the shoe or boot if possible.

2 Immobilize with a padded splint made from a blanket, pillow, etc. Tie it snugly but not too tightly.

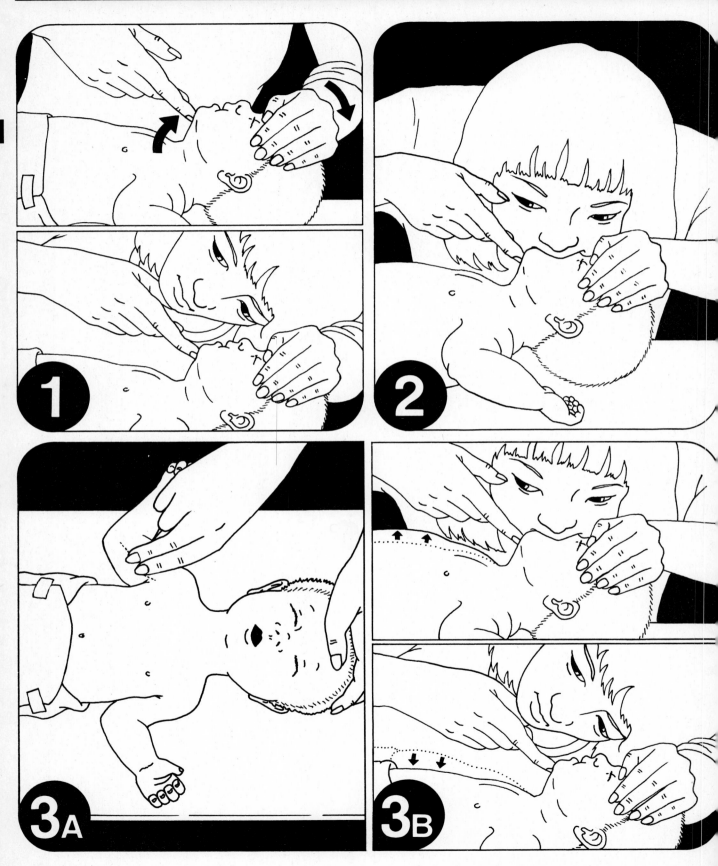

1

2

3A

3B

IMPORTANT

- **Seek medical aid as quickly as possible.**

- **Do not** tip back the head if there is a neck or back injury. To open the air passage, gently pull open the jaw without moving the head.

1 Place the infant on his back on a firm surface. If there is no neck or back injury, open the air passage by using the **head-tilt/chin-lift:** Place your hand—the one closest to his head—on his forehead. Place 1 or 2 fingers (**not** the thumb) of your other hand under the bony part of his jaw at the chin. Gently tilt his head back to a neutral position by applying gentle backward pressure on his forehead and lifting his chin. **Do not** close the infant's mouth completely. If necessary, clear out his mouth with your fingers. **Check for breathing by looking and listening for air leaving his lungs.**

2 **If breathing does not resume,** place your open mouth over the infant's nose and mouth, forming an airtight seal. Give 2 slow, gentle breaths (1 to 1½ seconds each). **Remove your mouth between breaths and look and listen for air leaving his lungs.**

3A **If breathing still has not resumed,** check the pulse by placing the tips of your fingers (**not** your thumb) on the inside of the upper arm. **If you cannot feel the pulse,** see **HEART FAILURE**, pages 192–195.

3B **If there is a pulse,** then give the infant a new breath every 3 seconds (20 per minute), using slow gentle breaths lasting 1 to 1½ seconds each. **Remove your mouth between breaths and look and listen for air leaving his lungs.** If the entry or return of air seems blocked or the chest does not move, re-tip the infant's head (as in Step 1) and repeat Step 2. If air still seems blocked, see **CHOKING**, pages 150–153, then resume artificial respiration at Step 1. Recheck the pulse and breathing after the first minute of artificial respiration, then recheck every few minutes thereafter. Continue rescue breathing until the infant breathes on his own or professional help arrives. Treat for **SHOCK**, pages 242–245.

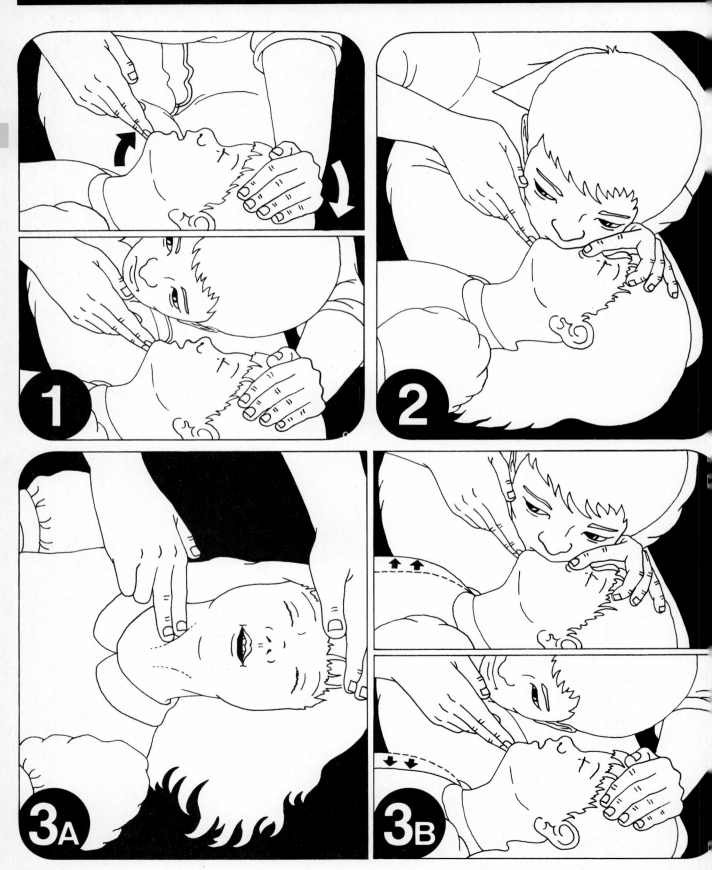

IMPORTANT

- **Seek medical aid as quickly as possible.**

- **Do not** tip back the head if there is a neck or back injury. To open the air passage, gently pull open the jaw without moving the head.

1 Place the child on her back on a firm surface. If there is no neck or back injury, open the air passage by using the **head-tilt/chin-lift:** Place your hand—the one closest to her head—on her forehead. Place 2 or 3 fingers (but **not** the thumb) of your other hand under the bony part of her jaw at the chin. Gently tilt her head back to a neutral-plus position by applying gentle backward pressure on her forehead and lifting her chin. **Do not** close the child's mouth completely. If necessary, clear out her mouth with your fingers. **Check for breathing by looking and listening for air leaving her lungs.**

2 **If breathing does not resume**, use the thumb and index finger of the hand that is on the child's forehead to pinch her nose closed. Place your open mouth over her open mouth, forming an airtight seal. Give 2 slow, full breaths (1 to 1½ seconds each). **Remove your mouth between breaths and look and listen for air leaving her lungs.**

3A **If breathing still has not resumed**, check the pulse at the large artery in the neck; see **TAKING THE PULSE**, pages 256–257. If you cannot feel the pulse, see **HEART FAILURE**, pages 196–201 for **small child** or pages 202–207 for **older child**.

3B **If there is a pulse**, then give the child a new breath every 4 seconds, 15 per minute. (Each breath should last 1 to 1½ seconds.) **Remove your mouth between breaths and look and listen for air leaving her lungs.** If the entry or return of air seems blocked or the chest does not move, re-tip the child's head (as in Step 1) and repeat Step 2. If air still seems blocked, see **CHOKING**, pages 154–157, then resume artificial respiration at Step 1. Recheck the pulse and breathing after the first minute of artificial respiration, then recheck every few minutes thereafter. Continue rescue breathing until the child breathes on her own or professional help arrives. Treat for **SHOCK**, pages 242-245.

BURNS: CHEMICAL

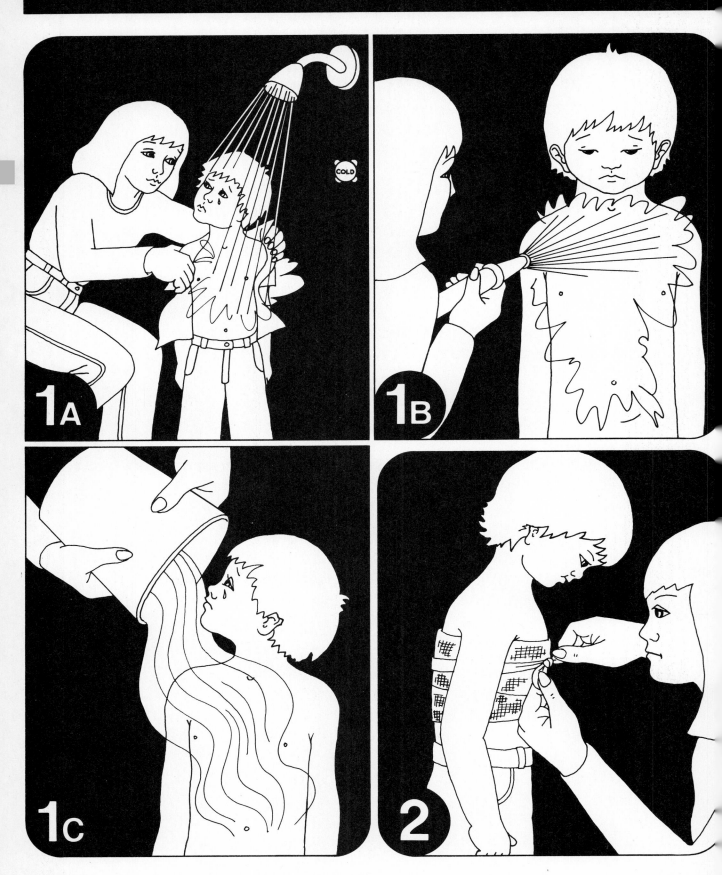

IMPORTANT

- **Seek medical aid as soon as possible.**

1A Place the child under a heavy, cool shower immediately. Remove all contaminated clothing. Keep him there at least 5 minutes, until all traces of the chemical have washed away.

1B If a shower is not available, use a hose.

1C If a hose isn't available, keep pouring cool water over the burn.

2 Cover with a dry, clean dressing or cloth. Treat for **SHOCK**, pages 242-245.

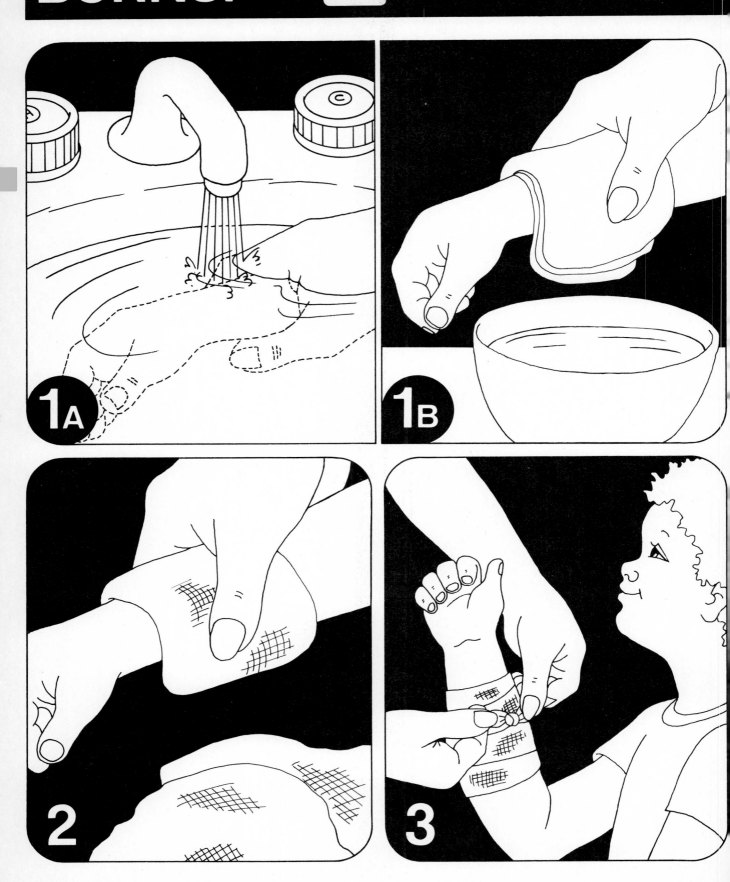

IMPORTANT

- **Do not** remove shreds of tissue or break blisters.
- **Do not** use antiseptic sprays, ointments or home remedies.
- **Do not** put pressure on burned areas.
- Treat for **SHOCK**, pages 242-245.
- **Seek medical aid.**

Determine the degree of the burn and treat accordingly. If the skin is broken or there is any question as to the severity of the burn, treat for Third Degree.
- **First Degree:** Red or discolored skin. **See below.**
- **Second Degree:** Blisters and red or mottled skin. **See below.**
- **Third Degree:** White or charred skin. **See next page.**

1A **If the skin isn't broken**, immerse in cold **(not ice)** water for 5 to 10 minutes or until pain subsides.

1B Or lightly apply cold clean compresses that have been wrung out in cold water, until pain subsides.

2 Gently blot dry with sterile gauze or a clean cloth.

3 Cover loosely with a dry clean dressing. Elevate burned arms or legs higher than the heart.

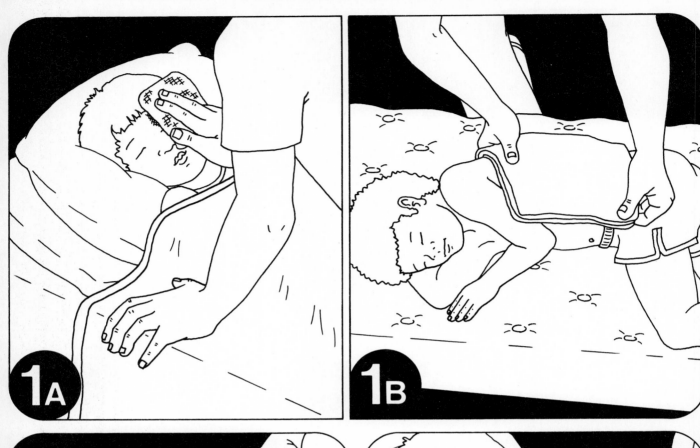

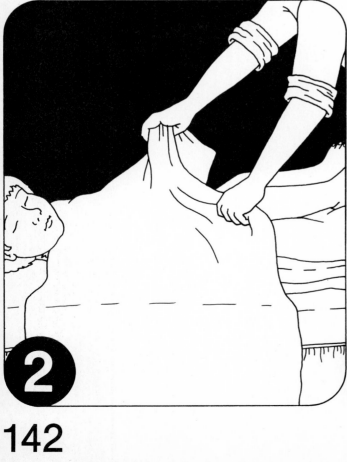

IMPORTANT

- **Call for an ambulance or doctor immediately.**
- **Do not** apply water, antiseptic sprays, ointments or home remedies.
- **Do not** apply ice or immerse in water.
- **Do not** remove adhered particles of clothing.
- **Do not** remove shreds of tissue or break blisters.
- **Do not** use absorbent cotton.
- **Do not** give the child anything to drink (unless Step 3 becomes necessary).
- Treat for **SHOCK**, pages 242-245.

1A If the **face** has been burned, sit or prop the child up and apply a dry cool compress (an ice bag wrapped in a towel or ice wrapped in a thick towel). Watch breathing closely. If necessary, see **BREATHING: ARTIFICIAL RESPIRATION**, pages 134-137.

1B Lightly cover **other burned areas** with a dry sterile dressing, clean dry sheet or cloth, or kitchen plastic wrap.

2 Elevate burned arms or legs higher than the heart.

3 **If you cannot obtain professional medical care for an hour or more** and the child is conscious and not vomiting, have him sip a small amount of lukewarm water (1 ounce for an infant, 2 ounces for a small child, 4 ounces for an older child) containing salt and baking soda (1 level teaspoon salt and ½ level teaspoon baking soda **per quart**). Discontinue liquid if the child vomits. **Do not** give an unconscious child anything to drink.

CHEST INJURIES: CRUSHED CHEST

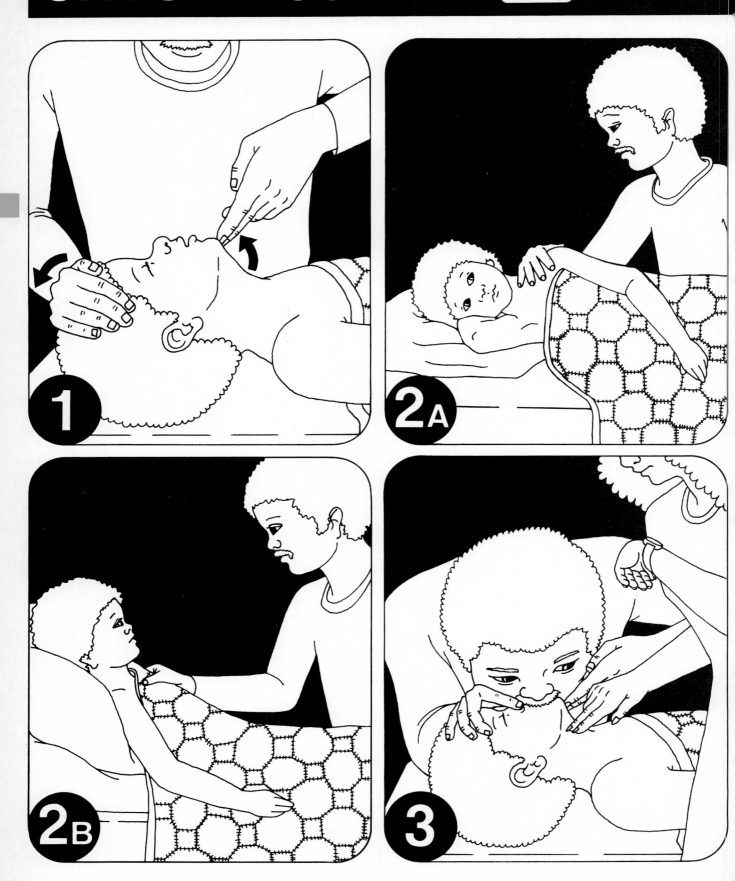

IMPORTANT

- **Seek medical aid immediately.**
- Observe for **SHOCK**, pages 242-245.

SYMPTOMS

Many broken ribs. The chest may collapse rather than expand when the child tries to inhale.

1 If he has difficulty breathing, open the child's air passage by using the **head-tilt/chin-lift: For an infant**, see pages 134–135 and follow Step 1. **For a child over 1 year old**, see pages 136–137 and follow Step 1.

2A If the injury is only on one side, turn the injured side down if possible, and try to make the child comfortable.

2B If the injury is in the center or on both sides of the chest or if he has trouble breathing, prop him up in a comfortable position.

3 If necessary, begin rescue breathing immediately; see **BREATHING: ARTIFICIAL RESPIRATION**, pages 134–137. Watch his pulse closely; see **TAKING THE PULSE**, pages 256–257. If it stops, treat for heart failure immediately; see **HEART FAILURE**, pages 192–207.

CHEST INJURIES: OPEN CHEST WOUNDS

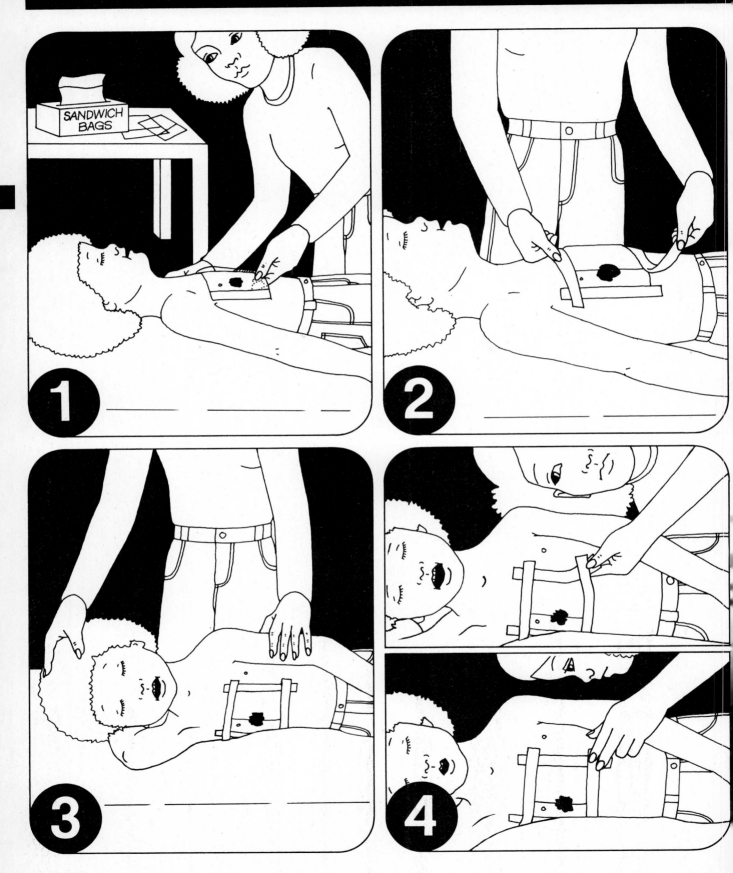

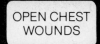

OPEN CHEST WOUNDS

IMPORTANT

• **Seek medical aid immediately.**

1 Seal the wound immediately with a nonporous dressing — plastic wrap, aluminum foil, etc. **Be sure** the seal extends beyond the edges of the wound.

2 Tape the seal in place. If tape is not available, bind the seal with a wide bandage, belt or the like. Be careful not to restrict breathing.

3 Turn the child onto the injured side and keep his air passage open. Treat for **SHOCK**, pages 242-245.

4 If the child worsens shortly after the wound is sealed, his lung may have collapsed, in which case lift one edge of the seal briefly while the child is inhaling and listen for the escape of air. Replace the seal quickly before air is sucked into the wound.

CHEST INJURIES: RIBS

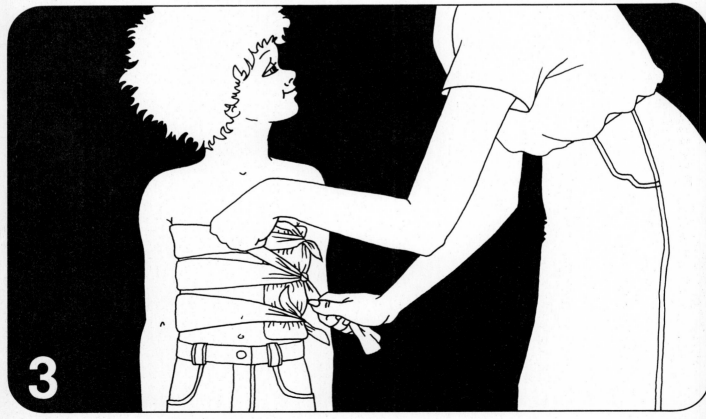

CHEST INJURIES: RIBS

IMPORTANT

- **Seek medical aid.**
- **Do not** interfere with breathing.

SYMPTOMS

The child feels pain when he inhales or when the rib area is touched.

1 Restrict the movement of the chest by binding it with three wide cloth bandages. Place the first bandage around the center of the chest and bring the ends together in a loose half-knot on the uninjured side of the body.

2 Use a handkerchief or other folded cloth to prevent discomfort from the knots. Place a second and third bandage above and below the first one. Then gently tie the half-knots. **Do not** tie too tightly. The binders should apply gentle pressure to the injured area.

3 To complete the knots, ask the child to exhale and hold his breath. Then take out the slack and finish tying the knots before he starts his next breath.

CHOKING:

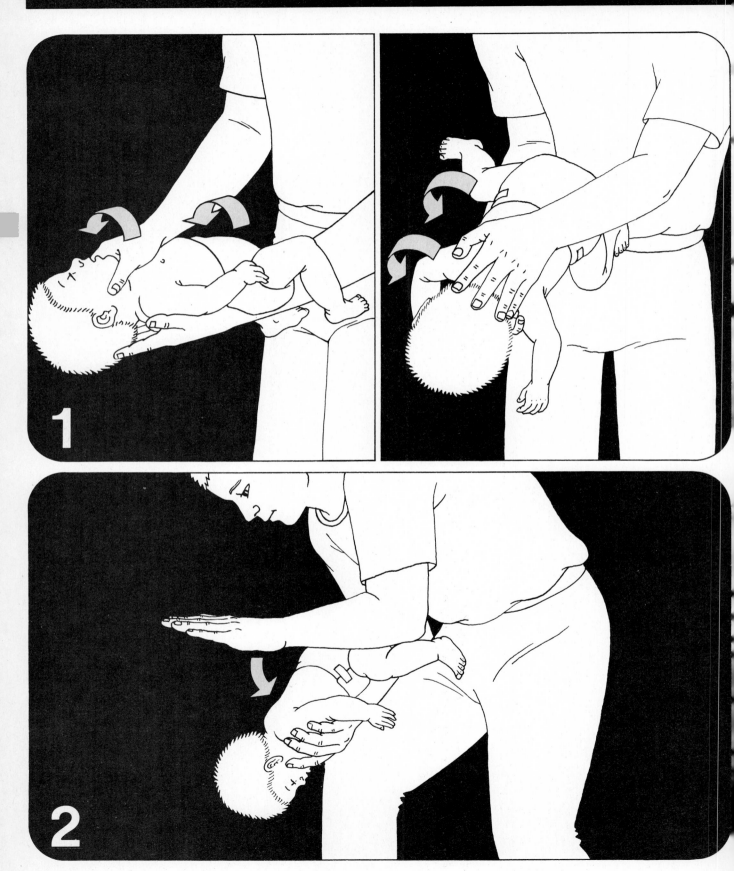

1

2

150

IMPORTANT

- **If the infant is unconscious and not breathing,** see **BREATHING: ARTIFICIAL RESPIRATION**, pages 134–135.

- **Do not** interfere with the infant's own efforts to free the obstruction if he can breathe, speak or cough. If he cannot free the obstruction, do the following:

1 Supporting his head, neck and chest with one hand, place him face down on your forearm.

2 With the heel of the other hand, give him 4 rapid forceful blows between the shoulder blades.

CONTINUED ON NEXT PAGE

151

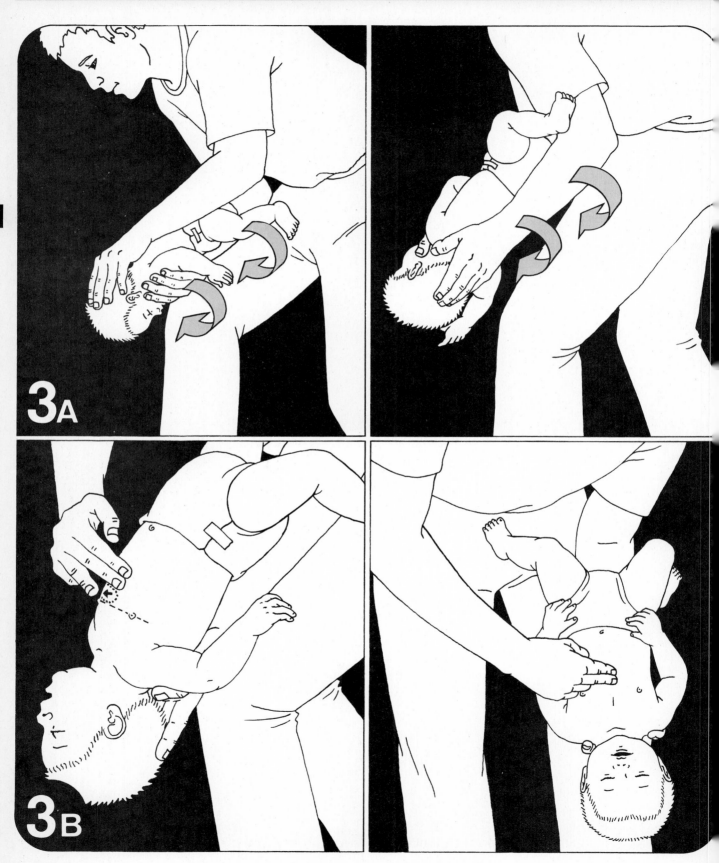

3A

3B

CONTINUED

3A **If the obstruction is not cleared,** place him face up on your forearm with the head lower than the body. Support your arm with your thigh.

3B Place the pad of your ring finger just below the imaginary line between the infant's nipples. Then place the pads of your middle and index fingers next to the ring finger. Now lift your ring finger (see illustration 3B on opposite page) and make 4 quick thrusts downward toward his chest. **Do not** thrust to either side. **Adjust the force of your thrusts to the child's size. Repeat if necessary.** Watch breathing closely. If necessary, see **BREATHING: ARTIFICIAL RESPIRATION**, pages 134–135.

CHOKING:

CHILD (OVER 1 YEAR OLD)

IF HE IS STANDING OR SITTING

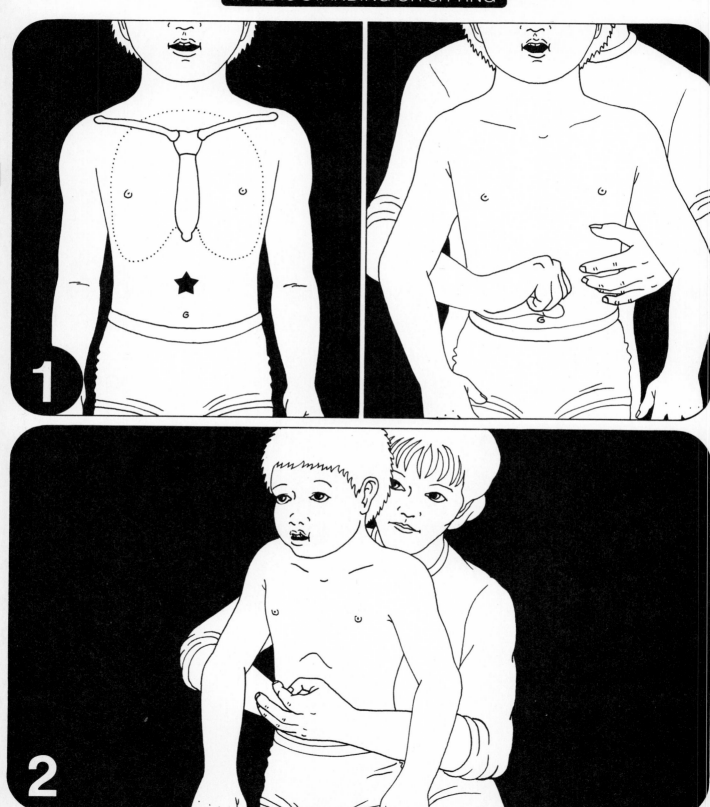

1

2

IMPORTANT

- **If the child is unconscious and not breathing,** see **BREATHING: ARTIFICIAL RESPIRATION**, pages 136–137.

- **Do not** interfere with the child's own efforts to free the obstruction if he can breathe, speak or cough. If he cannot free the obstruction, do the following:

IF HE IS STANDING OR SITTING

1 Place your arms around the child with the thumb side of your fist against his stomach above the navel and well below the sternum.

2 Grasp your fist with your other hand and make a quick upward thrust at the exact spot shown. **Do not** thrust to either side. **Adjust the force of your thrusts to the child's size. Repeat if necessary.** Watch breathing closely. If necessary, see **BREATHING: ARTIFICIAL RESPIRATION**, pages 136-137.

CONTINUED ON NEXT PAGE

IF HE IS LYING DOWN

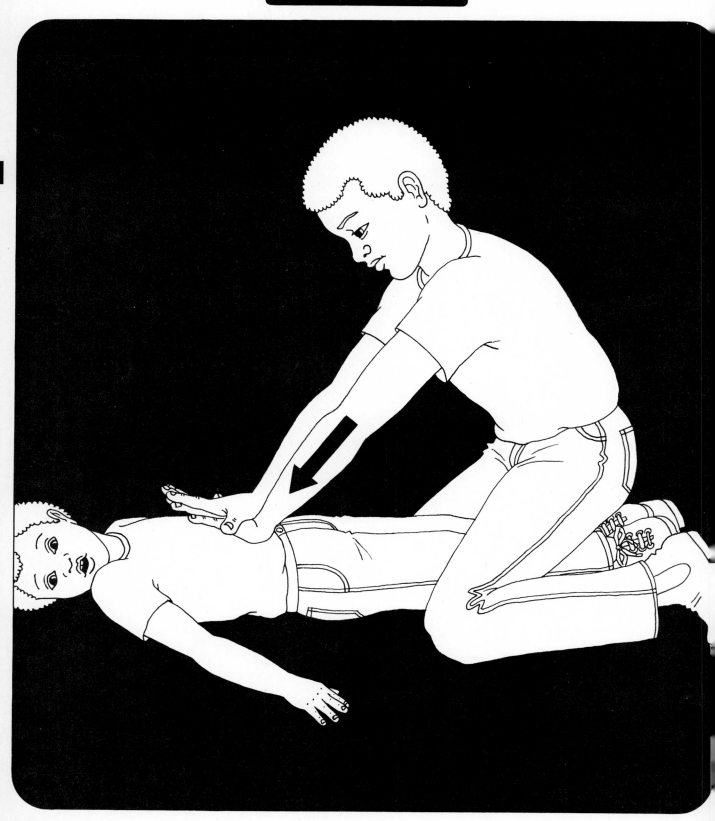

IMPORTANT

- **If the child is unconscious and not breathing**, see **BREATHING: ARTIFICIAL RESPIRATION**, pages 136–137.

- **Do not** interfere with the child's own efforts to free the obstruction if he can breathe, speak or cough. If he cannot free the obstruction, do the following:

IF HE IS LYING DOWN

Roll him on his back and straddle his legs. Place the heel of one hand on his stomach above the navel and well below the sternum. Place your other hand on top of the first. Give 6 upward thrusts, trying to expel the obstruction with each thrust. **Do not** thrust to either side. **Adjust the force of your thrusts to the child's size.** Between each thrust, check if the obstruction has been expelled. **Repeat cycle of thrusts if necessary.** Watch breathing closely. If necessary, see **BREATHING: ARTIFICIAL RESPIRATION**, pages 136–137.

CONVULSIONS & SEIZURES

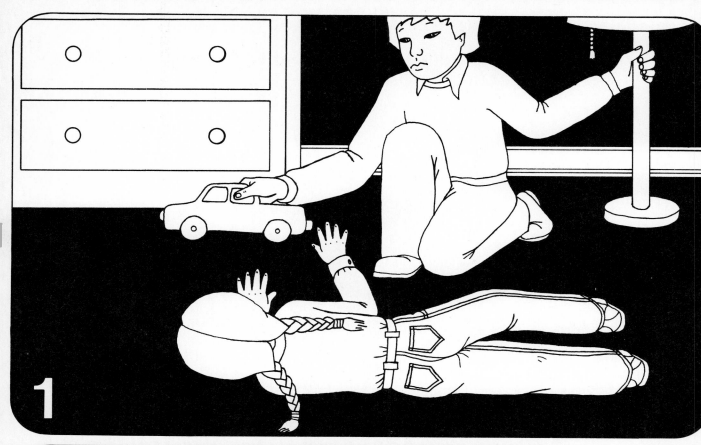

1

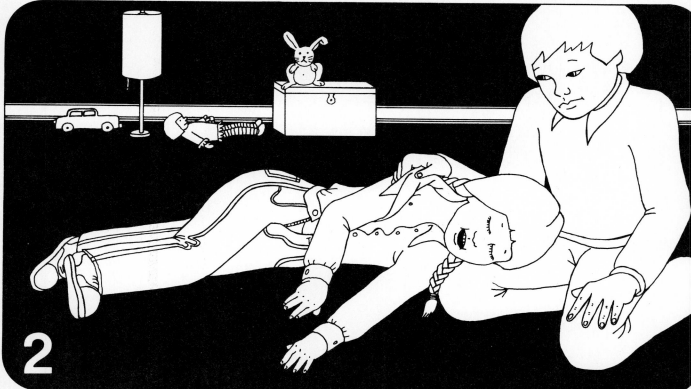

2

IMPORTANT

- **Do not** give the child anything to drink during the convulsion.
- Tell your doctor about all convulsive seizures, no matter how brief.

SYMPTOMS

Falling. Frothing at the mouth. Stiffening of the body. Jerky, uncontrollable movements. Unconsciousness.

1 Clear the area of hard or sharp objects that might cause harm. Try to loosen tight clothing, but **do not** restrain the child.

2 When the convulsion subsides, turn the child onto her side. Watch breathing closely. If necessary, see **BREATHING: ARTIFICIAL RESPIRATION**, pages 134-137.

DROWNING: WATER RESCUE

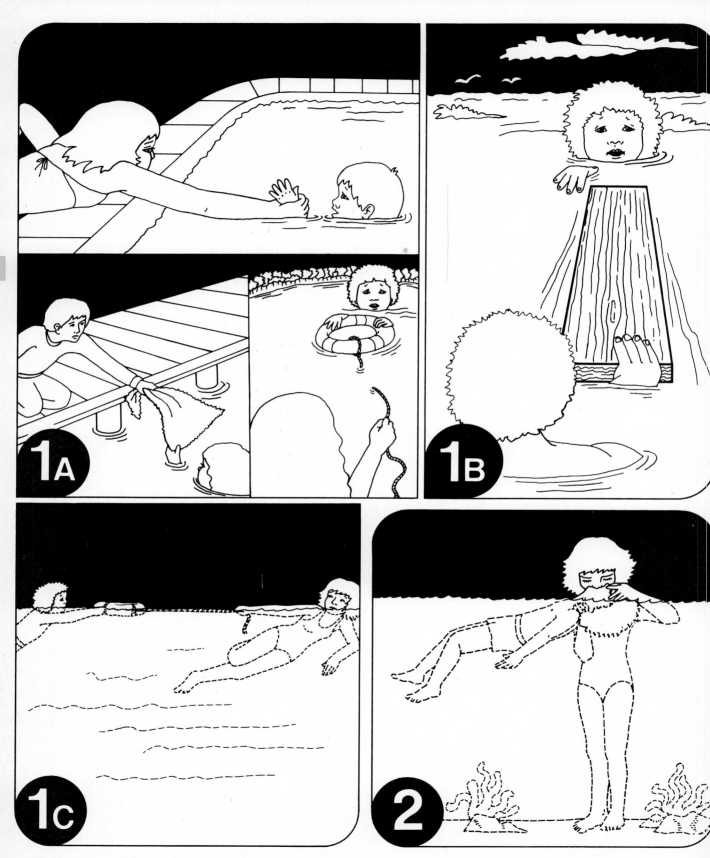

IMPORTANT

- **Send for help immediately.**

- **Do not** swim to the child unless you cannot use reaching assists from land and it is a matter of life or death.

- **Try to touch the child's hand or body with the reaching assist.** He may be too panicked to realize the assist is there if it doesn't touch him directly.

1A Try to reach the child from land with a hand, leg, clothing, pole, rope, etc. Always hold onto something with your other hand. **Do not** let the child grab you. Throw him a buoy, board or anything that floats. Take care not to hit him; you may accidently knock him unconscious. Ropes or objects attached to ropes should be thrown beyond the child, then pulled directly into his grasp.

1B If he is too far to reach, wade in closer with reaching assists.

1C If you must swim to him, keep watching him or the spot you saw him last. Bring something for the child to hold onto and pull him to shore. **Do not** let him grab you.

2 If necessary, begin rescue breathing immediately, even before leaving the water. See **BREATHING: ARTIFICIAL RESPIRATION**, pages 134-137. After he is revived, **do not** let the child walk. Treat for **SHOCK**, pages 242-245, and **seek medical attention immediately.**

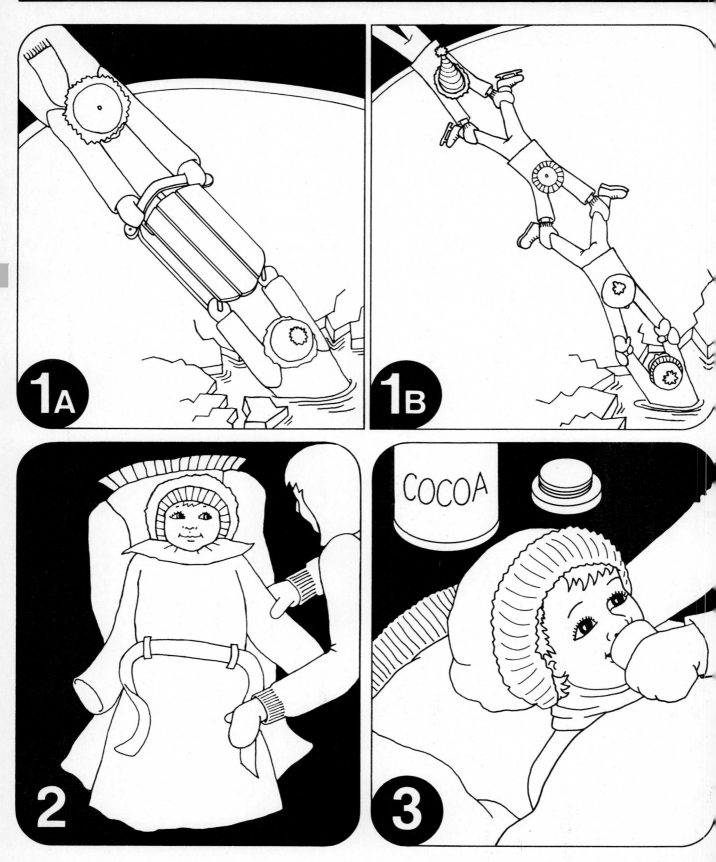

IMPORTANT

- **Send for help immediately.**
- **Do not** walk near the open ice.
- Tell the child not to try to climb out but to slide his arms onto the ice and hold on until you reach him.
- When safely back on firm footing, watch the child's breathing closely. If necessary, begin rescue breathing immediately. See **BREATHING: ARTIFICIAL RESPIRATION**, pages 134-137.
- Treat for **SHOCK**, pages 242-245.
- Observe for hypothermia, even if the child was in the water for only a short time. See **HYPOTHERMIA (COLD EXPOSURE)**, pages 216-219.

1A Try to reach the child from land with a hand, leg, clothing, rope, ladder, sled, board, etc. Tell him to hold onto the reaching assist and slide on his stomach — not walk upright — back to firm footing.

1B If necessary, form a human chain. Each person lies spread-eagled on the ice, holding the ankles of the person in front of him.

2 Quickly but gently remove his wet clothing and warm him with blankets, a sleeping bag, etc. Observe for **HYPOTHERMIA (COLD EXPOSURE)**, pages 216-219.

3 If the child is conscious, can swallow easily and shows no symptoms of hypothermia, give him sips of a warm, sweetened drink. Check for **FROSTBITE**, pages 180-181.

EAR INJURIES:

FOREIGN OBJECTS

CUTS

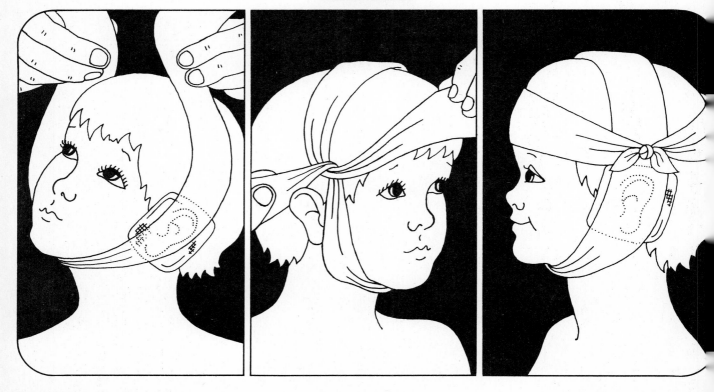

IMPORTANT

- If the ear is severed, see **BLEEDING: CUTS & WOUNDS (AMPUTATIONS)**, pages 114-115.
- Blood or clear fluid coming from the ear suggests a serious injury to the head; see **HEAD INJURIES: CLOSED HEAD INJURIES**, pages 182-183.

FOREIGN OBJECTS

Turn the child's head onto the injured side and **seek medical aid immediately. Do not** try to remove the object yourself.

CUTS

Control the bleeding by pressing gauze or a clean cloth directly over the wound and elevating the child's head. Apply a wide bandage to sustain the pressure.

EAR INJURIES: PERFORATED EARDRUM

IF PERFORATION HAS BEEN CAUSED BY A BLOW TO THE HEAD

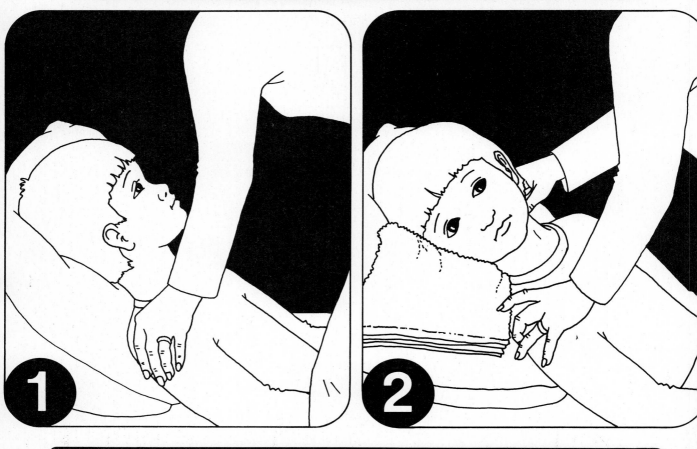

IF PERFORATION HAS NOT BEEN CAUSED BY A BLOW TO THE HEAD

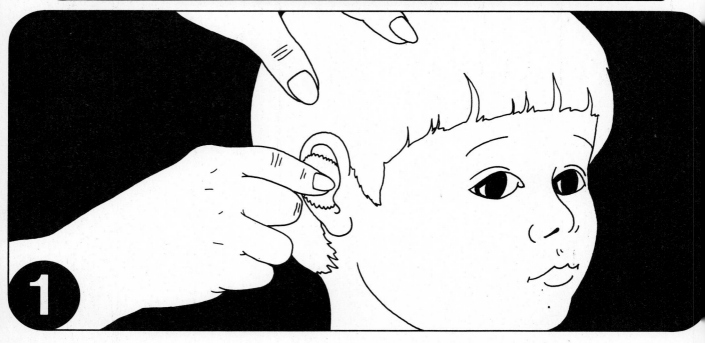

EAR INJURIES:

IMPORTANT

- **Seek medical aid immediately.**
- If the child has received a blow to the head, check for symptoms of serious head injuries before treating the ear; see **HEAD INJURIES: CLOSED HEAD INJURIES**, pages 182-183.
- **Do not** insert drops, fingers or instruments into the ear if you suspect a perforated eardrum.
- **Do not** permit the child to hit the side of his head in an effort to restore lost hearing.

SYMPTOMS

Sudden severe pain. Reduction in hearing. Ringing in the ears. Possible dizziness. Possible blood or fluid draining from the ear.

IF PERFORATION HAS BEEN CAUSED BY A BLOW TO THE HEAD

1 Keep the child lying down. If there is no sign of neck injury, place a pillow, jacket, etc. under both his head and shoulders, **not** his head alone.

2 Turn the head toward the affected side so fluids may drain from the ear. **Do not** stop the flow of fluid or clean the ear canal.

IF PERFORATION HAS NOT BEEN CAUSED BY A BLOW TO THE HEAD

1 Place a piece of gauze loosely in the outer ear canal.

ELECTRIC SHOCK

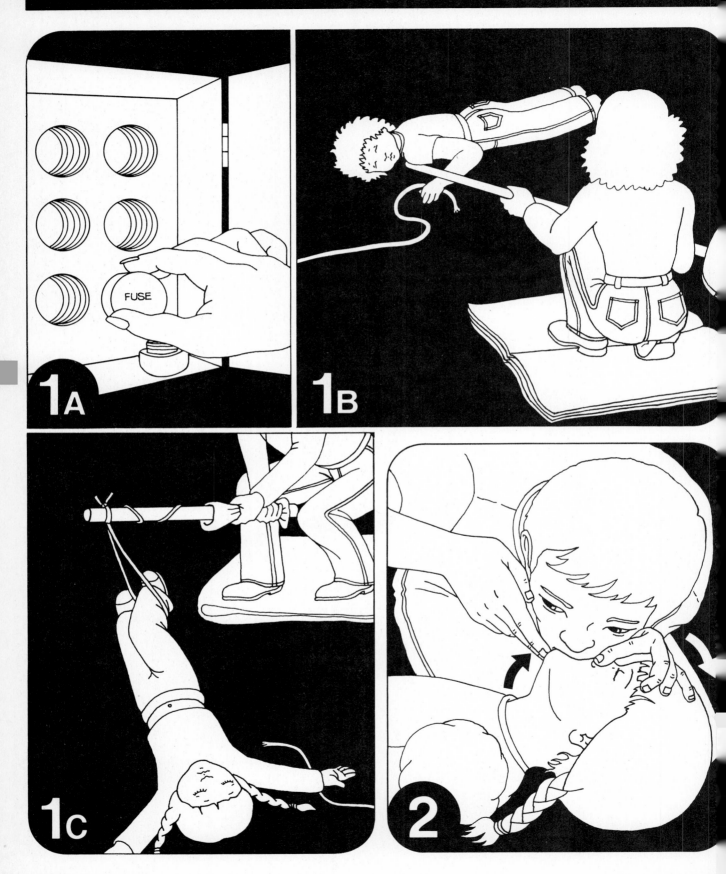

IMPORTANT

- **Do not** touch the child directly while he remains in contact with the current.

1A Try to break the contact by turning off the current, removing the fuse or unplugging the electrical cord from the outlet.

B If that isn't possible, stand on something dry — a blanket, rubber mat, newspapers, etc. — and push away the child or the source of the shock with a dry board or pole.

1C Or pull the child away with a dry rope looped over the foot or arm.

2 If necessary, begin rescue breathing immediately; see **BREATHING: ARTIFICIAL RESPIRATION**, pages 134-137. Treat for **SHOCK**, pages 242-245. Also treat for **BURNS**, pages 140-143.

EYE INJURIES: FOREIGN OBJECTS & CHEMICALS

FOREIGN OBJECTS: UPPER EYELID

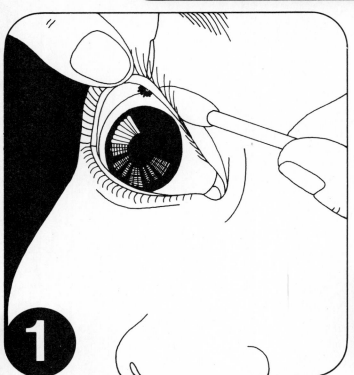

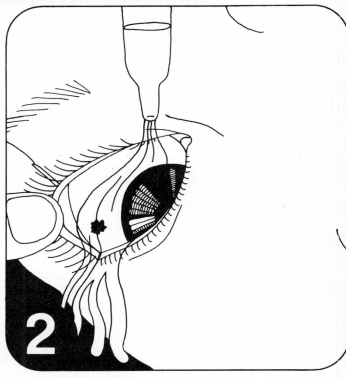

CHEMICALS IN THE EYE

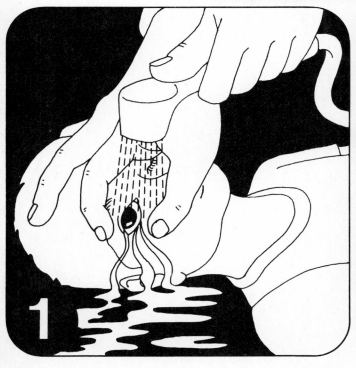

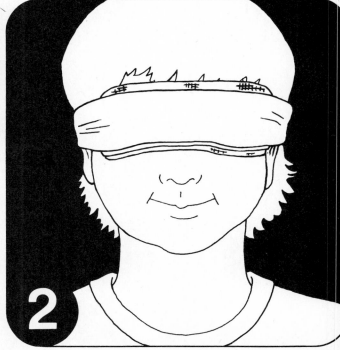

EYE INJURIES: FOREIGN OBJECTS & CHEMICALS

FOREIGN OBJECTS: LOWER EYELID

Remove with a clean handkerchief or cloth.

FOREIGN OBJECTS: UPPER EYELID

1 Clasp the upper lash between your thumb and forefinger, and fold it back over an applicator swab.

2 Have the child look down to expose the upper surface of the eyeball, then wash out the eye with water, letting the water drain down and away from the eye.

CHEMICALS IN THE EYE

1 Holding the eyelid open, flush the eye immediately in gently running water for at least 5 minutes. **Do not** let the water run into the other eye.

2 Apply gauze or a clean cloth, and hold it in place with a loosely fastened bandage that covers both eyes. **Seek medical aid immediately.**

EYE INJURIES:

BLACK EYE

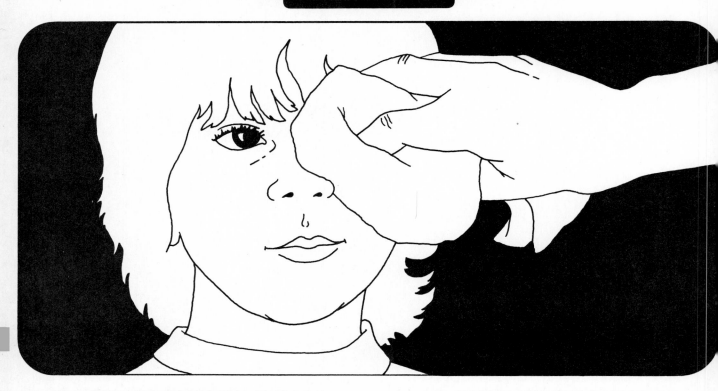

LACERATED EYEBALL

LACERATED EYELID

EYE INJURIES:

IMPORTANT

- **Seek medical aid immediately for a lacerated eyeball or eyelid.**
- **Do not** wash out the eye.
- If you must move the child, use a stretcher. See **TRANSPORTING THE INJURED: STRETCHERS**, page 260.
- For a black eye, consult a doctor to determine if there is a more serious injury.

BLACK EYE

SYMPTOMS

Pain following a blow to the area around the eye. Rapid swelling and dark discoloration of the eyelid or skin around the eye. Discoloration may last 2 to 3 weeks.

To minimize swelling, apply an ice bag covered with a towel to the affected area. If an ice bag isn't available, use ice cubes wrapped in a cloth. **Do not** place ice directly on the skin or eye.

LACERATED EYEBALL

Cover **both** eyes loosely with gauze or a clean cloth. **Do not** apply pressure. Secure the child's hands so he cannot touch his eyes.

LACERATED EYELID

Control the bleeding with a pressure dressing or gentle direct pressure against the lid and bone.

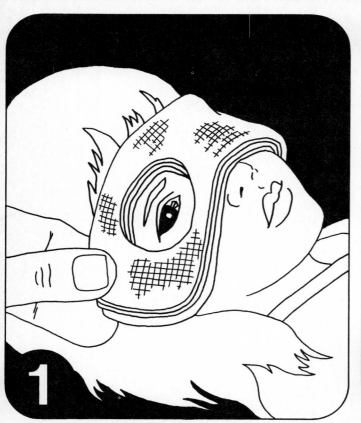

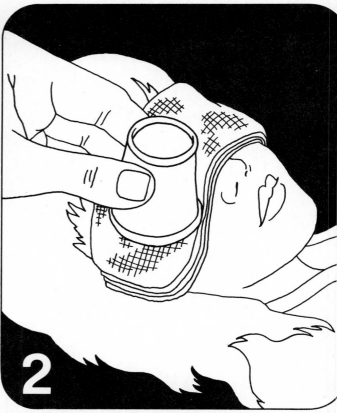

IMPORTANT

- **Seek medical aid immediately.**
- **Do not** try to remove the impaled object.
- **Do not** wash out the eye.
- If you must move the child, use a stretcher. See **TRANSPORTING THE INJURED: STRETCHERS**, page 260.

1 Cut a large hole in the center of a thick dressing, and apply the dressing carefully so it doesn't touch the eye or object.

2 Place a paper cup or cone over the eye. The cup should not touch the eye or object. **Do not** touch the eye itself.

3 Secure the cup in place with a gauze or clean cloth dressing. Bandage both eyes to prevent movement of the injured eye. Keep the child calm and offer reassurance.

FAINTING

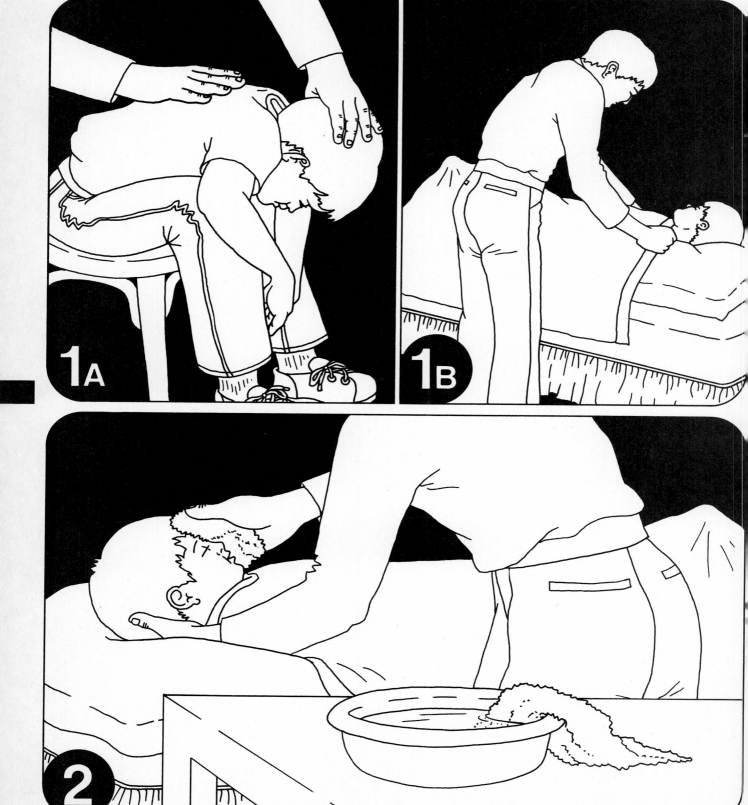

IMPORTANT

- If possible, prevent the child from falling. At the first indication of weakness or faintness, help him sit down.

- **Seek medical aid.** Tell your doctor about all periods of unconsciousness, no matter how brief.

- Watch breathing closely. If necessary, see **BREATHING: ARTIFICIAL RESPIRATION**, pages 134-137.

- **If the child is unconscious**, **do not** give him anything to drink.

- If the child has fallen, check for injuries which may have resulted; see **ASSESSING THE EMERGENCY**, pages 76-79.

SYMPTOMS

Brief, sudden, partial or total loss of consciousness, followed by complete recovery. May occur as a result of remaining in one position for an extended period or from pain, illness, anxiety or other emotional stress. **Early symptoms may include:** Paleness. Sweating. Nausea. Dizziness.

1A If the child is conscious and seated, place his head between his knees. Watch him closely to make sure he doesn't fall.

1B Otherwise, lay him down and elevate his legs 8 to 12 inches. If he vomits, turn his head to the side or roll him onto his side to keep the airway open.

2 Loosen tight clothing and provide good ventilation. Bathe the child's face with cool water. **Do not** permit him to stand or walk until recovery is complete.

FEVER

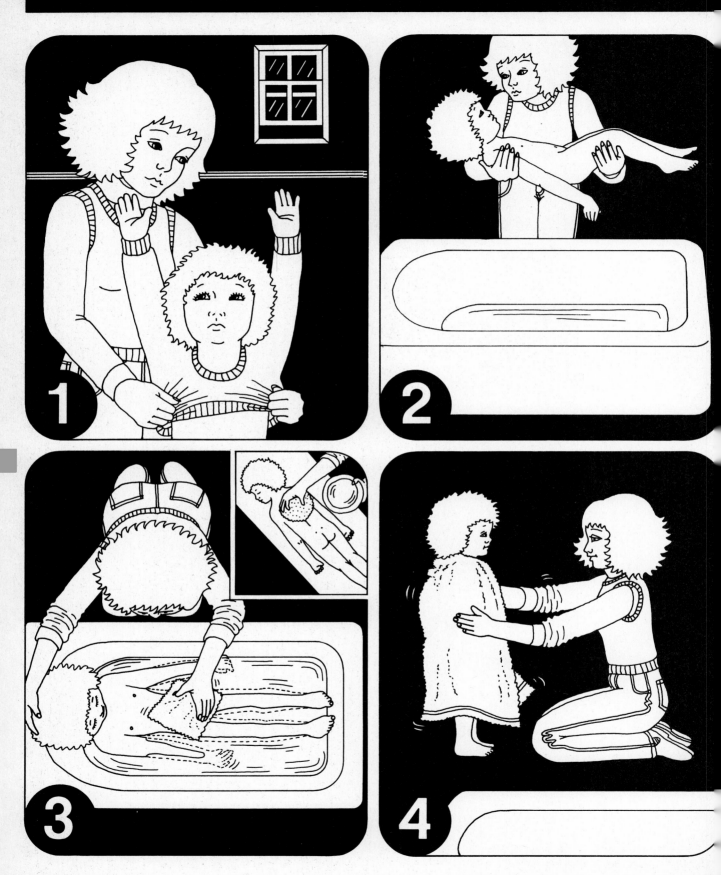

IMPORTANT

- **Call your doctor for any fever.**
- **Do not** use medication, enemas, or alcohol or ice water rubs unless your doctor so advises.
- If the fever is 103°F. (39.4°C.) or higher in a younger child or 102°F. (38.8°C.) in an older child and you can't reach your doctor, begin gently cooling the child as described below.

1 Undress the child in a cool **(not cold)** well-ventilated room. Avoid drafts and chilling.

2 Place the child in a partially filled tub of lukewarm water, keeping most of his body exposed to the air.

3 Sponge his entire body with light, brisk strokes for 15 to 20 minutes. (If a tub isn't handy, use a sponge bath.)

4 Dry the child vigorously. Watch his temperature closely and repeat cooling if necessary.

FROSTBITE

FROSTBITE

IMPORTANT

- **Seek medical aid immediately.**
- **Do not** rub or massage affected area.
- **Do not** apply hot water or strong heat.
- **Do not** break blisters.
- **Do not** give the child anything alcoholic to drink.

SYMPTOMS

Usually affects the fingers, toes, ears, nose or cheeks. The skin looks glossy and white or grayish yellow and is hard to the touch. Blisters may develop. Pain, changing to feeling of intense cold and numbness.

1 Warm the frozen parts against the body.

2 Take the child indoors. Remove clothing restricting circulation. Immerse frozen parts in warm **(not hot)** water, or cover lightly with warm towels or blankets. Discontinue warming when parts become flushed. Raise and lower affected limbs to stimulate circulation. After the child has been warmed, give him warm broth, tea, etc.

3 Keep affected toes or fingers separated with dry gauze or clean cloth.

4 If the child must go to the hospital, bandage affected areas and elevate injured parts.

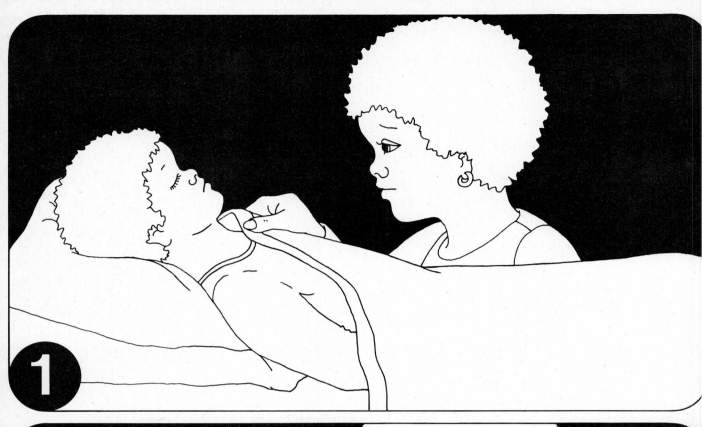

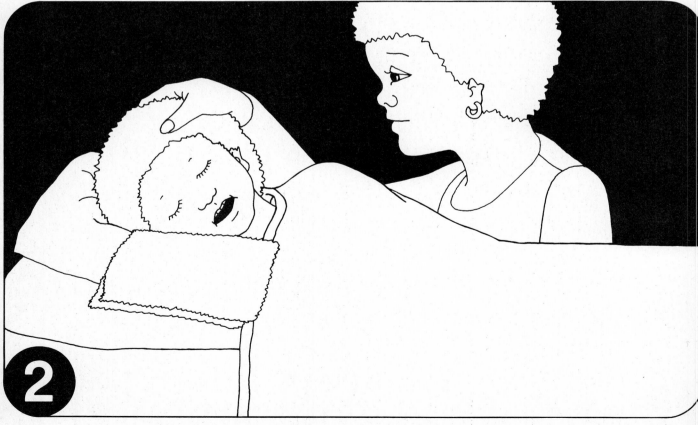

IMPORTANT

- Head injuries may be more severe than they seem. To be safe, **call your doctor immediately**.

- Watch breathing closely. If necessary, see **BREATHING: ARTIFICIAL RESPIRATION**, pages 134-137.

- **Do not** move the child unless absolutely necessary. If you must move him, see **TRANSPORTING THE INJURED**, pages 258-261.

- If the child is unconscious, assume there is a neck injury. See **BACK & NECK INJURIES**, pages 84-85. Note how long he remains unconscious.

- Observe for **SHOCK**, pages 242-245.

SYMPTOMS OF SERIOUS HEAD INJURIES

Unconsciousness. Difficulty breathing. Vomiting. Convulsions. Clear fluid or blood running from ears, nose or mouth. Paralysis of any part of the body. Loss of bowel or bladder control. Unequal pupils. Skull deformity.

1 Keep the child lying down. If there is no sign of neck injury, place a pillow, jacket, etc. under **both** his head and his shoulders, **not** his head alone.

2 Turn him onto his side so fluids may drain from his mouth. **Seek medical aid immediately**.

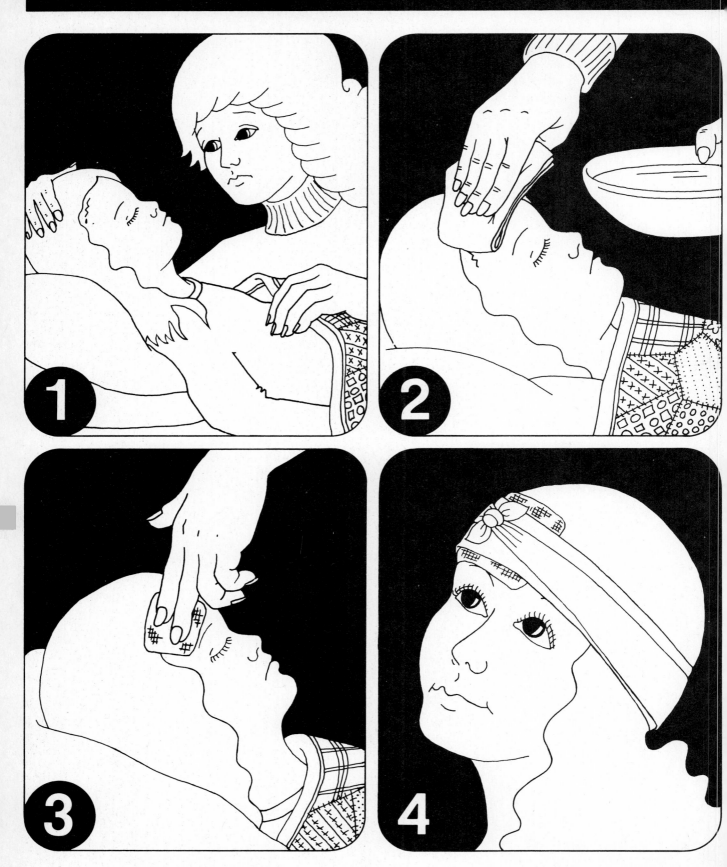

IMPORTANT

- **Seek medical aid immediately.** Head injuries may be more severe than they seem.
- **Do not** attempt to clean deep scalp wounds of foreign matter.
- For serious head wounds, treat for **SHOCK**, pages 242-245.

1 Control bleeding by raising the child's head and shoulders higher than her heart. **Do not** bend her neck.

2 Clean minor head wounds carefully. Wipe **away** from the wound, **not** toward it.

3 Further control bleeding by lightly pressing several layers of gauze or clean cloth on the wound. Avoid heavy pressure.

4 When bleeding is under control, bandage the dressing in place.

CHEEK & SKULL

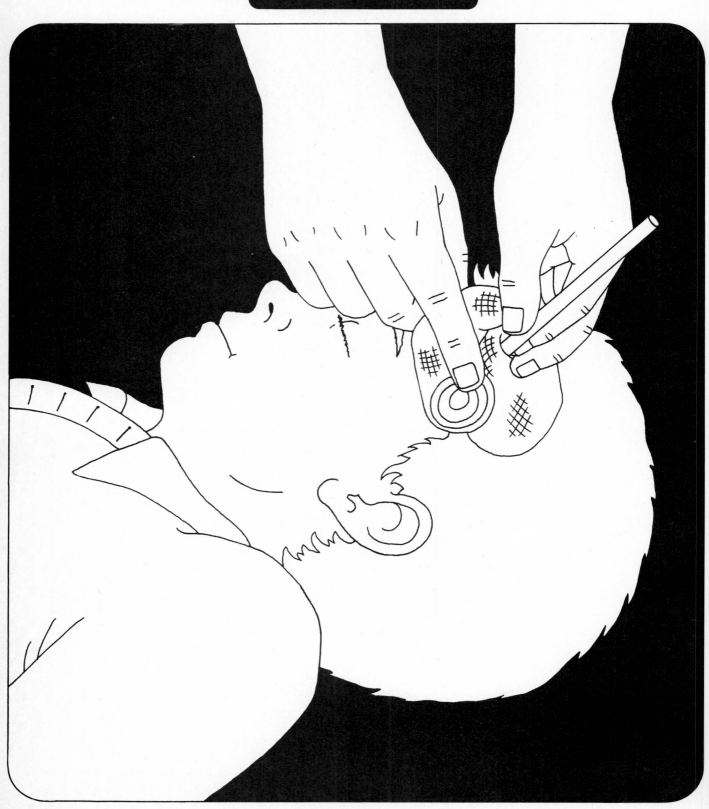

IMPORTANT

- **Seek medical aid immediately.**

CHEEK & SKULL

Do not remove an impaled object from the cheek or skull. See **BLEEDING: CUTS & WOUNDS (IMPALED OBJECTS)**, pages 110-111.

FACE

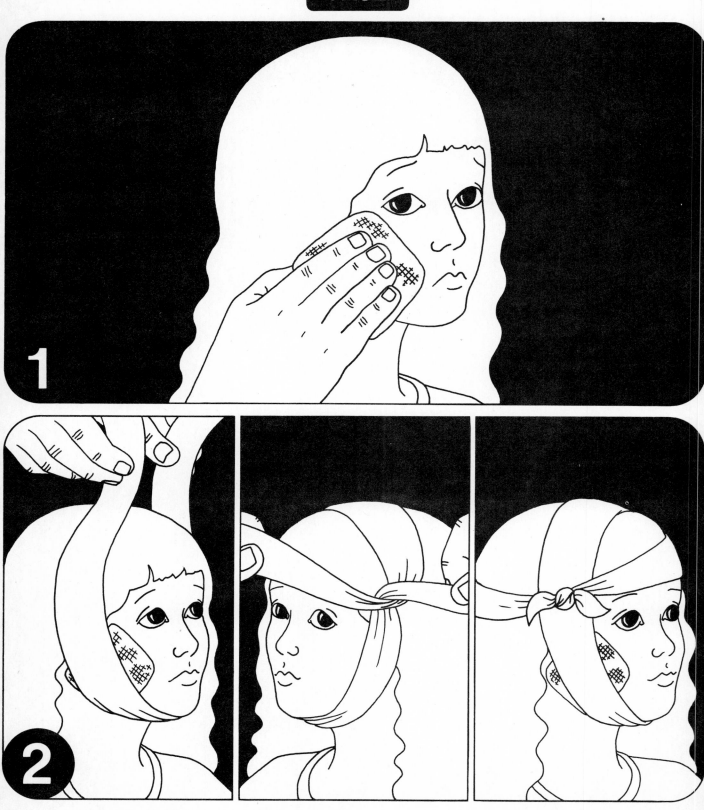

IMPORTANT

- **Seek medical aid.**
- Remove all broken teeth and foreign matter from the child's mouth. Save the teeth for possible replanting.
- Observe for **SHOCK**, pages 242-245.

FACE

1 Raise the head higher than the heart and control bleeding through direct pressure with gauze or a clean cloth.

2 Apply a clean dressing or cloth, and hold it in place with a bandage.

JAW

Seek medical aid immediately. Do not move the jaw.

HEART ATTACK

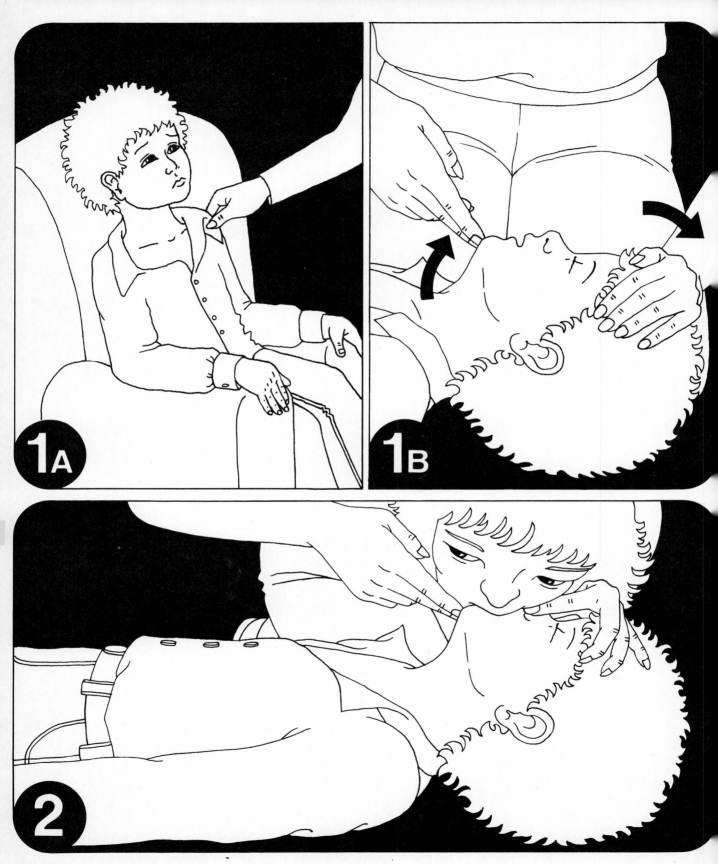

IMPORTANT

- **Send for an ambulance and oxygen immediately.**
- Observe for **SHOCK**, pages 242-245.

SYMPTOMS

Persistent pain at the center of the chest, which may radiate to the shoulders, arms, neck or jaw. Extreme shortness of breath. Anxiety. Pale or bluish lips, skin and fingernails.

1A Place the child in the most comfortable position and loosen his clothing. Provide good ventilation but avoid chilling.

1B **If unconscious**, place him on his back. (To check unconsciousness, call him loudly, tap him on the shoulder or shake him gently.) Open his air passage by using the **head-tilt/chin-lift: For an infant**, see pages 134–135 and follow Step 1. **For a child over 1 year old**, see pages 136–137 and follow Step 1.

2 If necessary, start rescue breathing immediately; see **BREATHING: ARTIFICIAL RESPIRATION**, pages 134–137. If breathing does not resume and there is no pulse, see **HEART FAILURE**, pages 192-207.

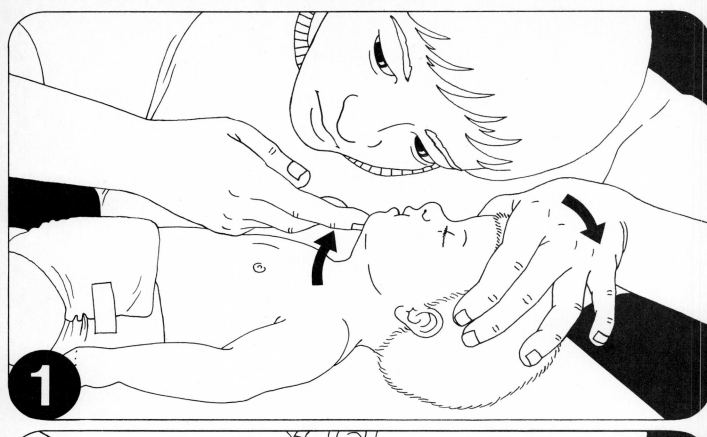

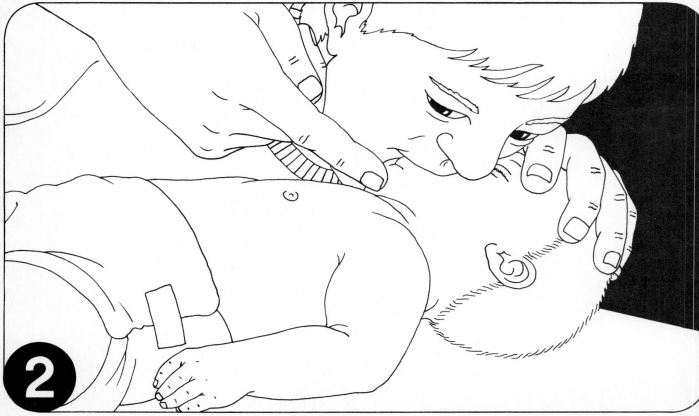

IMPORTANT

- **Send for an ambulance and oxygen immediately.**

- **Because first aid for heart failure is difficult and potentially dangerous, it is best administered by someone who has been fully trained in the procedure. However, if a trained person is not present, you must begin first aid immediately since the alternative is death.**

- **Waste no time, but be certain all symptoms are present before starting first aid.** To check unconsciousness, call the infant loudly, tap him on the shoulder or shake him gently.

SYMPTOMS

Unconsciousness. No breathing. No pulse.

1 Place the infant on his back on a firm surface. Open the air passage by using the **head-tilt/chin-lift:** Place your hand—the one closest to his head—on his forehead. Place 1 or 2 fingers (**not** the thumb) of your other hand under the bony part of his jaw at the chin. Gently tilt his head back to a neutral position by applying gentle backward pressure on his forehead and lifting his chin. **Do not** close the infant's mouth completely. **Check for breathing by looking and listening for air leaving his lungs.**

2 **If breathing does not resume**, put your open mouth over his nose and mouth, forming an airtight seal, and give 2 slow, gentle breaths (1 to 1½ seconds each), allowing the lungs to deflate fully between each breath.

CONTINUED ON NEXT PAGE

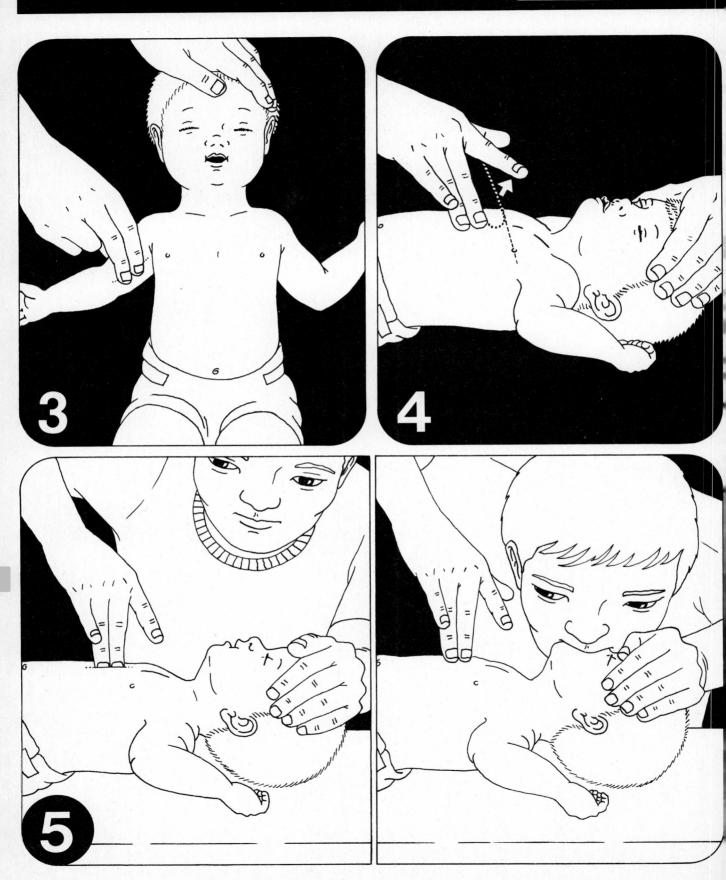

3

4

5

194

CONTINUED

3 Continue to hold the infant's head in a neutral position with your hand on his forehead. With the fingertips of your other hand (**not** your thumb), **check the pulse slowly and carefully** on the inside of the upper arm. **It is extremely important to find the pulse if one is present. Take between 5 and 10 seconds to find it. Do not rush.** It can be easily missed under emergency conditions. **If pulse has started**, see **BREATHING: ARTIFICIAL RESPIRATION**, pages 134–135. **If pulse has not started, then:**

4 Place the pad of your index finger just below the imaginary line between the infant's nipples. Then place the pads of your middle and ring fingers next to the index finger. Now lift your index finger. Your other 2 fingers should be in the correct position for compressions (see illustration 4 on opposite page). **Do not press the lower end of the sternum.** If you feel the tip, move your 2 fingers up towards the infant's head until they are off the tip.

5 Make 5 short, smooth compressions directly downward about ½ to 1 inch, taking about ½ second for each compression (about 100 to 120 per minute). **Do not remove your fingertips between compressions.** Then keeping your fingertips in place, stop and give the infant a slow, gentle breath. Continue the process of 5 compressions and 1 breath. After 10 cycles of 5 compressions and 1 breath, recheck the pulse and breathing for 5 seconds, then recheck every few minutes thereafter. If breathing seems blocked, see **CHOKING**, pages 150–153, then resume first aid. **Recheck all symptoms. Discontinue compressions when the pulse is restored; continue rescue breathing until the infant breathes on his own or professional help arrives.**

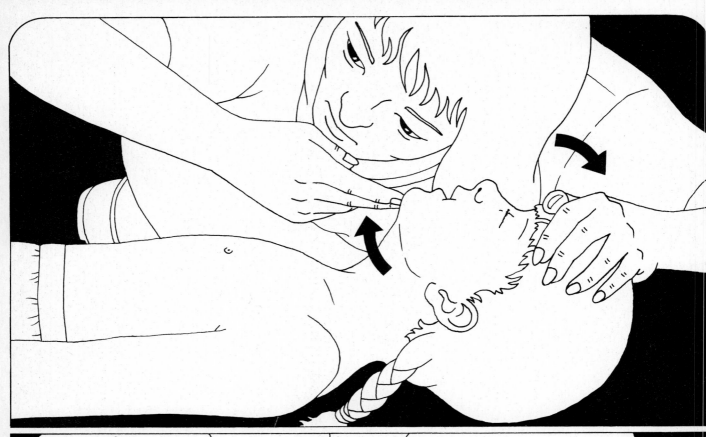

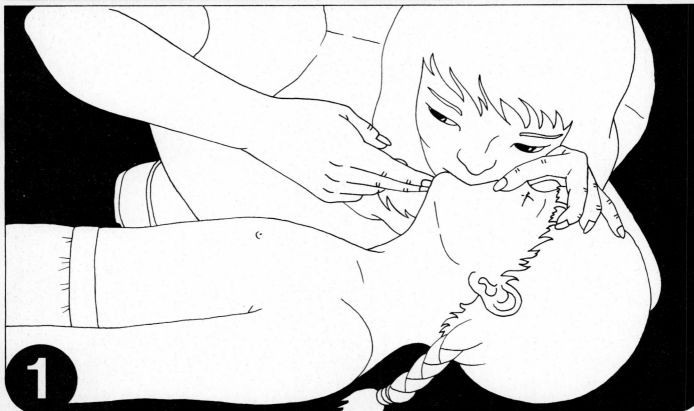

1

IMPORTANT

- **Send for an ambulance and oxygen immediately.**

- **Because first aid for heart failure is difficult and potentially dangerous, it is best administered by someone who has been fully trained in the procedure. However, if a trained person is not present, you must begin first aid immediately since the alternative is death.**

- **Waste no time, but be certain all symptoms are present before starting first aid.** To check unconsciousness, call the child loudly, tap her on the shoulder or shake her gently.

- **If possible, have one person perform rescue breathing and another administer chest compressions. If alone, you will have to do both.**

SYMPTOMS

Unconsciousness. No breathing. No pulse.

1 Place the child on her back on a firm surface. Open the air passage by using the **head-tilt/chin-lift:** Place your hand—the one closest to her head—on her forehead. Place 2 or 3 fingers (but **not** the thumb) of your other hand under the bony part of her jaw at the chin. Gently tilt her head back to a neutral-plus position by applying gentle backward pressure on her forehead and lifting the chin. **Do not** close the child's mouth completely. **Check for breathing by looking and listening for air leaving her lungs. If breathing does not resume:** Pinch her nose closed and put your open mouth over her open mouth, forming an airtight seal. Give 2 slow, gentle breaths (1 to 1½ seconds each), allowing the lungs to deflate fully between each breath.

CONTINUED ON NEXT PAGE

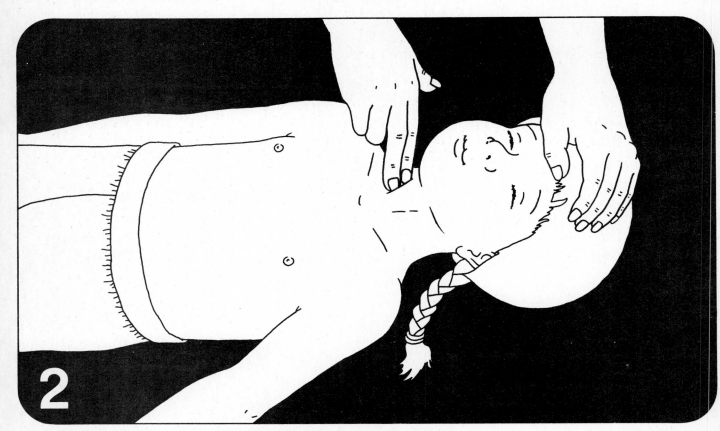

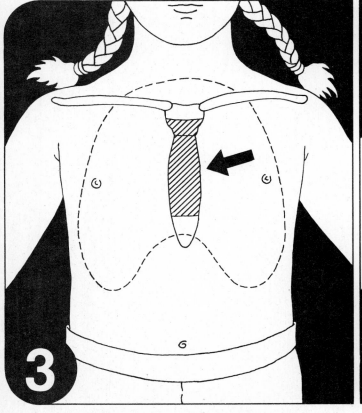

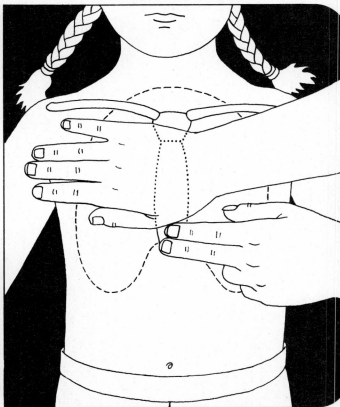

CONTINUED

2 **Check the pulse slowly and carefully** at the large artery of the neck. **It is extremely important to find the pulse if one is present. Take between 5 and 10 seconds to find it. Do not** rush. It is easily missed under emergency conditions. **If pulse has started,** see **BREATHING: ARTIFICIAL RESPIRATION**, pages 136–137. **If pulse has not started, then:**

3 Place the heel of one hand about 2 finger-widths above the tip of the sternum. (**Do not** press the tip.) Your fingertips should be pointing directly across the child's body but not pressing against the ribs.

CONTINUED ON NEXT PAGE

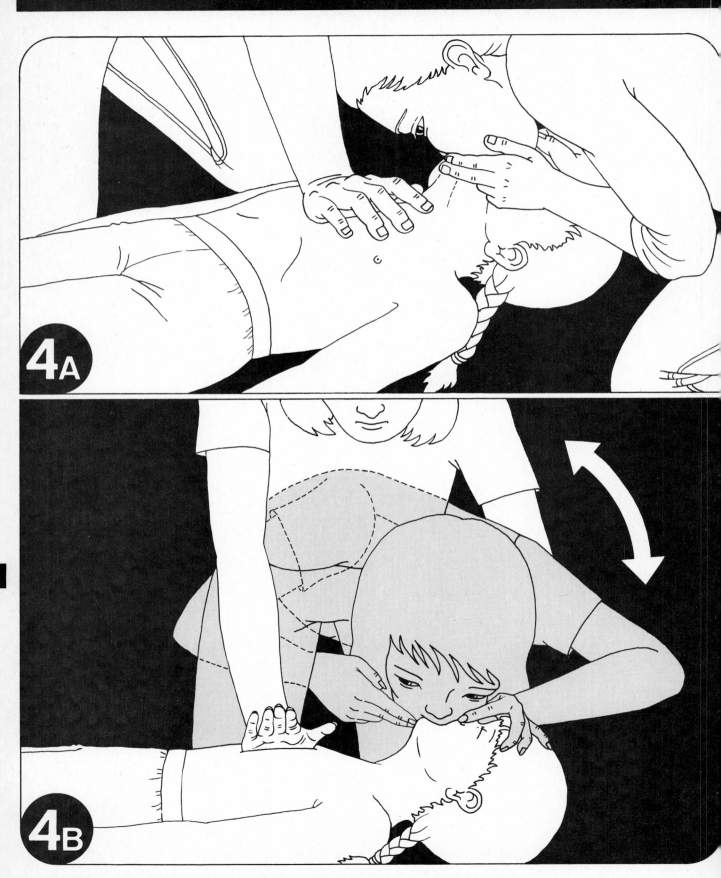

CONTINUED

4A **If you have assistance:** Make 5 short, smooth compressions directly downward about 1 to 1½ inches, taking about ¾ second for each compression (about 80 to 100 per minute). **Do not remove your hand between compressions.** Then keeping your hand in place, stop and have your assistant give the child a slow, gentle breath. Continue the process of 5 compressions and 1 breath. After 10 cycles of 5 compressions and 1 breath, recheck the pulse and breathing for 5 seconds, then recheck every few minutes thereafter. If breathing seems blocked, see **CHOKING**, pages 156–157, then resume first aid. **Recheck all symptoms. Discontinue compressions when the pulse is restored; continue rescue breathing until the child breathes on her own or professional help arrives.**

4B **If you are alone:** Maintain the **head-tilt** with your hand on the child's forehead. Make 5 short, smooth compressions directly downward about 1 to 1½ inches, taking about ¾ second for each compression (about 80 to 100 per minute). **Do not remove your hand between compressions.** Stop after every 5 compressions, remove your hand from her chest and lift her chin. Pinch her nose closed with the hand that is on her forehead and give her a slow, gentle breath. Now re-place the heel of the hand that is under her chin back on her chest. Continue the process of 5 compressions and 1 breath. After 10 cycles of 5 compressions and 1 breath, recheck the pulse and breathing for 5 seconds, then recheck every few minutes thereafter. If breathing seems blocked, see **CHOKING**, pages 156–157, then resume first aid. **Recheck all symptoms. Discontinue compressions when the pulse is restored; continue rescue breathing until the child breathes on her own or professional help arrives.**

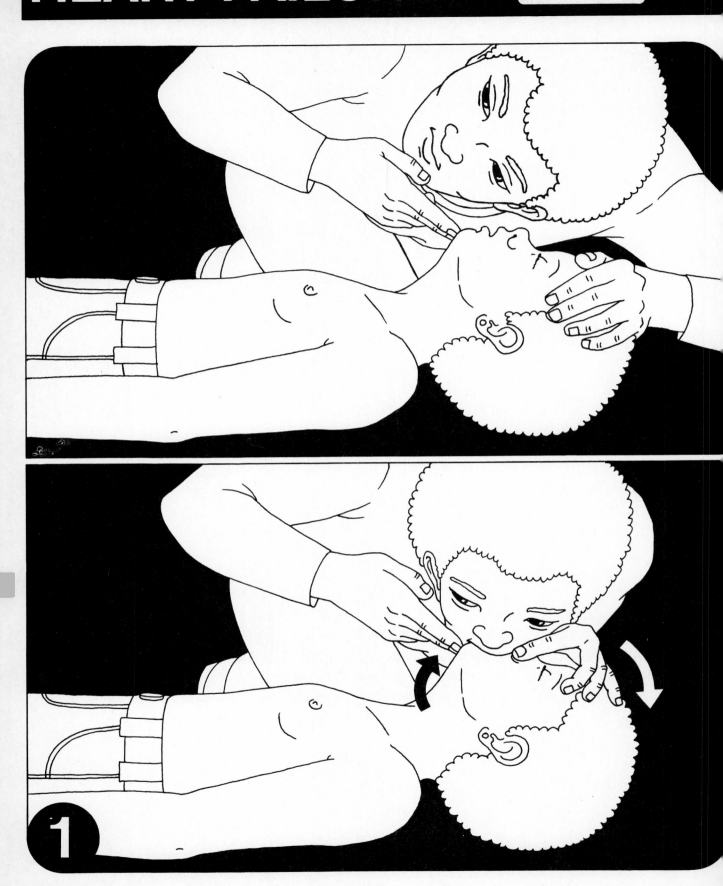

1

IMPORTANT

- **Send for an ambulance and oxygen immediately.**

- **Because first aid for heart failure is difficult and potentially dangerous, it is best administered by someone who has been fully trained in the procedure. However, if a trained person is not present, you must begin first aid immediately since the alternative is death.**

- **Waste no time, but be certain all symptoms are present before starting first aid.** To check unconsciousness, call the child loudly, tap her on the shoulder or shake her gently.

- **If possible, have one person perform rescue breathing and another administer chest compressions. If alone, you will have to do both.**

SYMPTOMS

Unconsciousness. No breathing. No pulse.

1 Place the child on his back on a firm surface. Open the air passage by using the **head-tilt/chin-lift:** Place your hand— the one closest to his head—on his forehead. Place 2 or 3 fingers (but **not** the thumb) of your other hand under the bony part of his jaw at the chin. Gently tilt his head back to a hyper-extended position (with his chin pointing straight up; see illustration 1 opposite page) by applying gentle backward pressure on his forehead and lifting his chin. **Do not** close his mouth completely. **Check for breathing by looking and listening for air leaving his lungs. If breathing does not resume:** Pinch his nose closed and put your open mouth over his open mouth, forming an airtight seal. Give 2 slow, full breaths (1 to 1½ seconds each), allowing the lungs to deflate fully between each breath.

CONTINUED ON NEXT PAGE

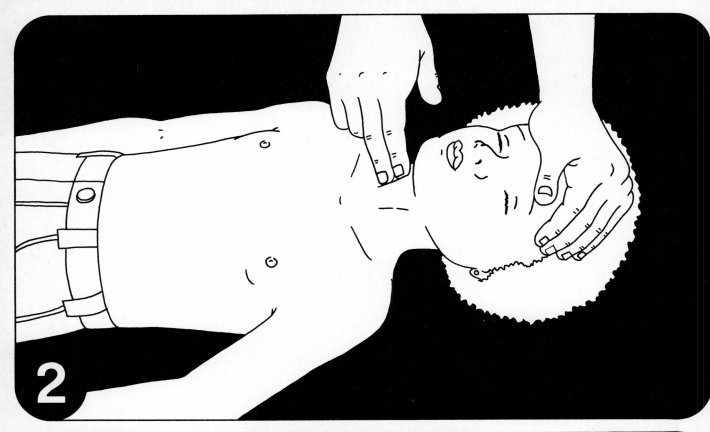

2

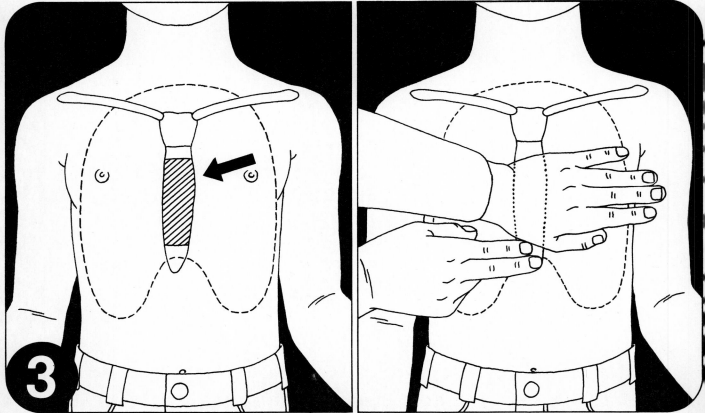

3

CONTINUED

2 **Check the pulse slowly and carefully** at the large artery of the neck. **It is extremely important to find the pulse if one is present. Take between 5 and 10 seconds to find it. Do not** rush. It is easily missed under emergency conditions. **If pulse has started,** see **BREATHING: ARTIFICIAL RESPIRATION**, pages 136–137. **If pulse has not started, then:**

3 Place the heel of one hand about 2 finger-widths above the tip of the sternum. (**Do not** press the tip.) Your fingertips should be pointing directly across the child's body but not pressing against the ribs. Place your other hand on top of the first. Keep your elbows straight and your shoulders directly over your hands.

CONTINUED ON NEXT PAGE

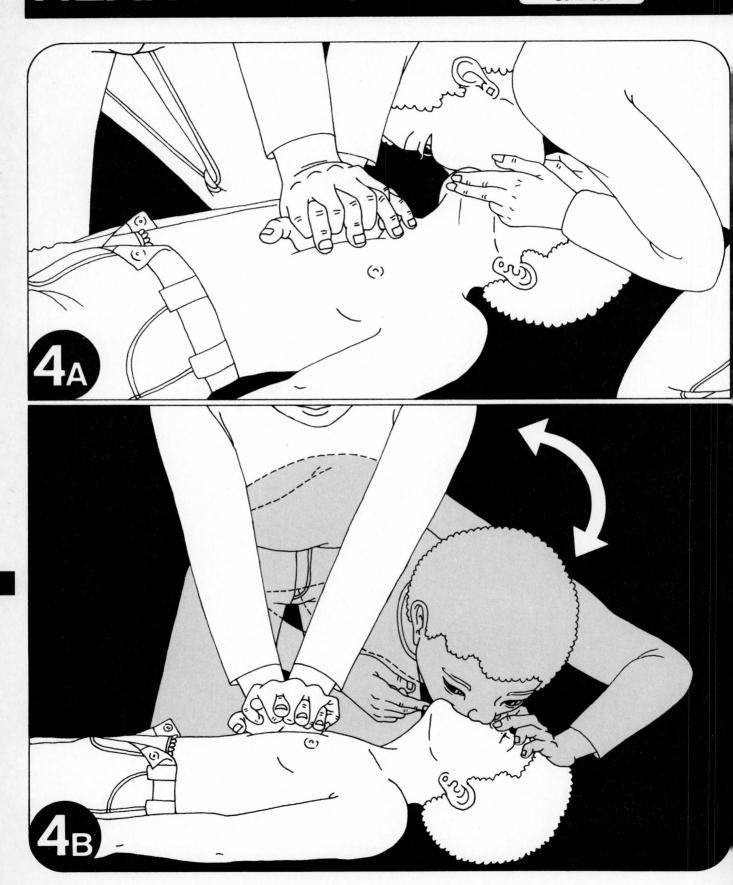

CONTINUED

4A **If you have assistance:** Make 5 smooth compressions directly downward about 1½ to 2 inches, taking about ¾ second for each compression (about 80 to 100 per minute). **Do not remove your hands between compressions.** Then keeping your hands in place, stop and have your assistant take a deep breath and breathe fully into the child's mouth. Continue the process of 5 compressions and 1 breath. After 10 cycles of 5 compressions and 1 breath, recheck the pulse and breathing for 5 seconds, then recheck every few minutes thereafter. If breathing seems blocked, see **CHOKING**, pages 156–157, then resume first aid. **Recheck all symptoms. Discontinue compressions when the pulse is restored; continue rescue breathing until the child breathes on his own or professional help arrives.**

4B **If you are alone:** Place your hands in position described and illustrated in Step 3 (see pages 204–205). Make 15 smooth compressions directly downward about 1½ to 2 inches, taking about ¾ second for each compression (about 80 to 100 per minute). **Do not remove your hands between compressions.** Stop after every 15 compressions, remove your hands from his chest and using the **head-tilt/chin-lift**, give the child 2 slow breaths. Then replace your hands back on his chest. Continue the process of 15 compressions and 2 breaths. After 4 cycles of 15 compressions and 2 breaths, recheck the pulse and breathing for 5 seconds, then recheck every few minutes thereafter. If breathing seems blocked, see **CHOKING**, pages 156–157, then resume first aid. **Recheck all symptoms. Discontinue compressions when the pulse is restored; continue rescue breathing until the child breathes on his own or professional help arrives.**

HEAT CRAMPS

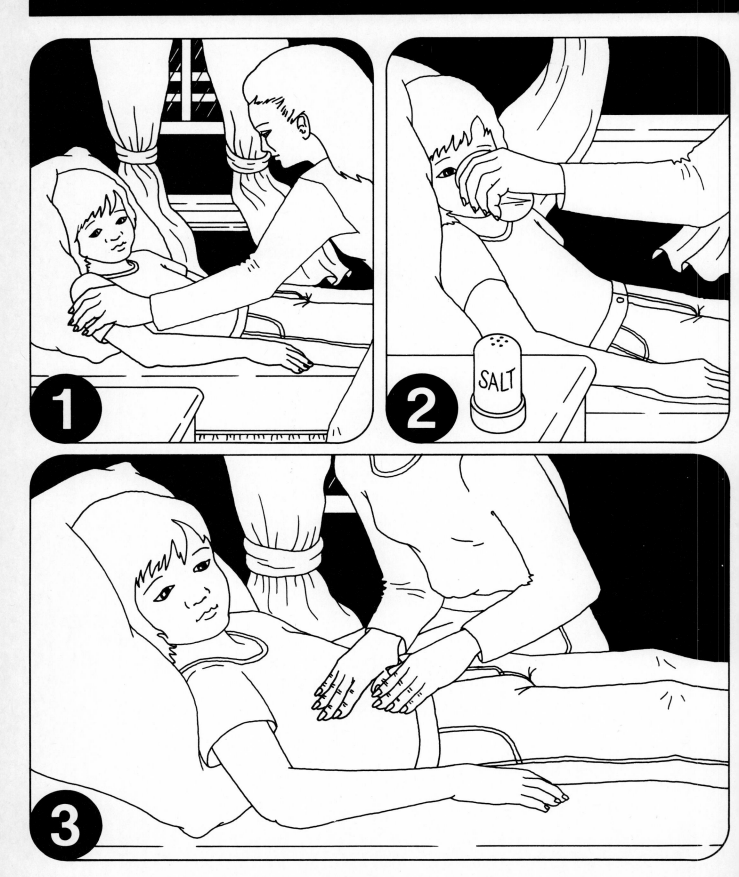

IMPORTANT

- Heat cramps may occur alone or occasionally as one of the early symptoms of sunstroke or heat exhaustion; see **SUNSTROKE (HEAT-STROKE)**, pages 254-255, and **HEAT EXHAUSTION**, pages 210-211.

SYMPTOMS

Sudden onset of severe intermittent muscle pain or spasm following strenuous exertion in high heat and humidity. Often affects the calf, thigh or abdomen, but may be felt elsewhere. **May include:** Pale, moist skin.

1 Take the child out of the heat to a cool, shaded, well-ventilated area.

2 Give her sips of salt water (2 pinches of salt in 8 to 10 ounces of water), ½ glass every 15 minutes for about 1 hour. **Do not** use more than the recommended dosage of salt.

3 To help relieve muscle cramp, apply warm packs, then gently massage the affected area or apply pressure with your hands.

HEAT EXHAUSTION

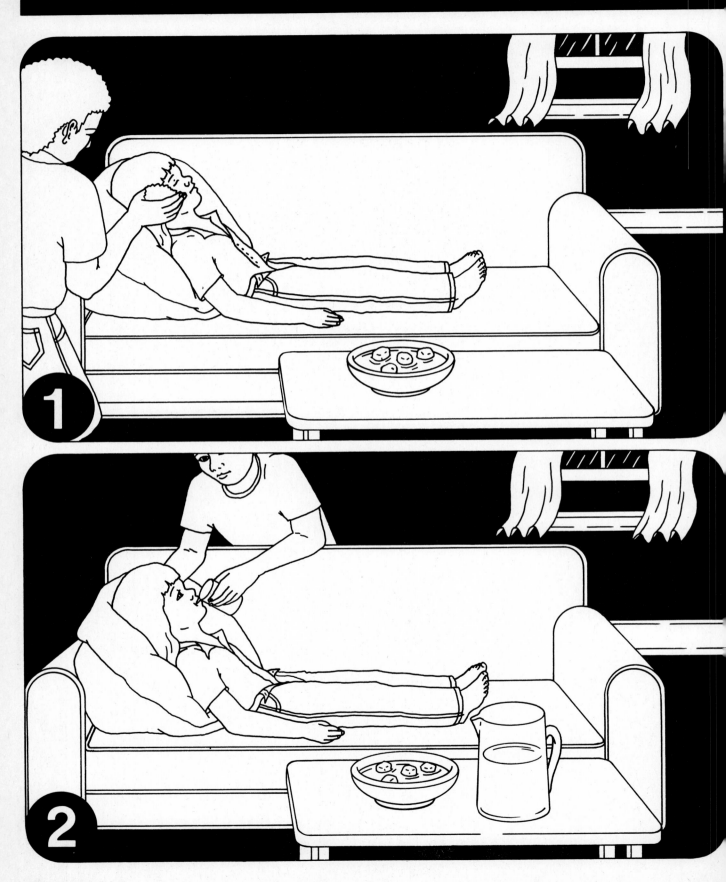

HEAT EXHAUSTION

- **Consult your doctor if the child does not respond to first aid.**

SYMPTOMS

Pale, cold and moist skin. Profuse sweating. Body temperature is about normal. **Early symptoms may also include:** Muscle cramps. Nausea. Fainting.

1 Take the child to a cool, shaded, well-ventilated room. Loosen her clothing and have her lie down. Cool her off with fans, an air-conditioner or cool, moist cloths.

2 If the child is conscious, give her sips of cool water and have her rest. Discontinue water if the child vomits.

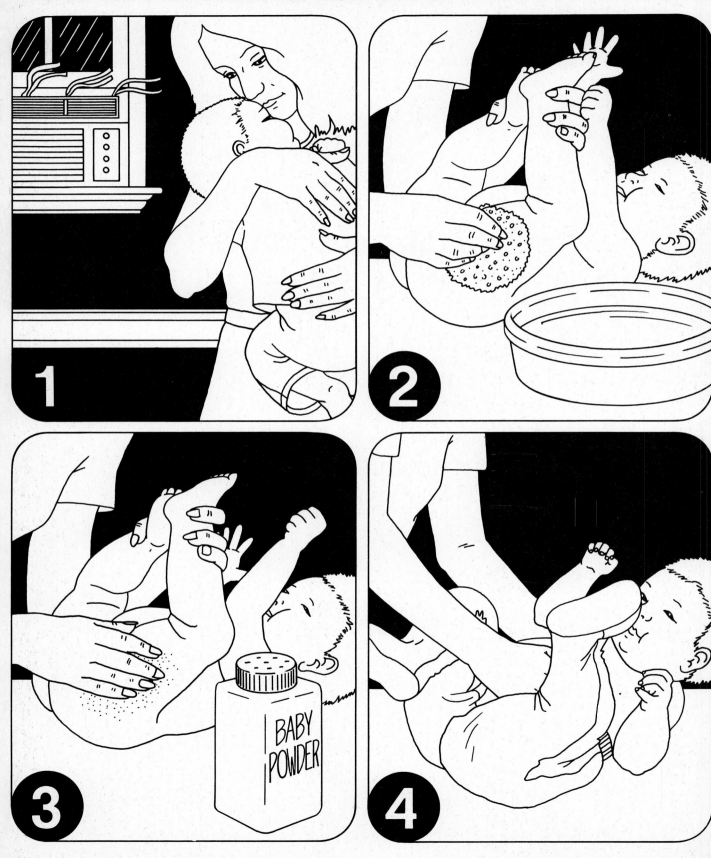

HEAT RASH (PRICKLY HEAT)

- Consult your doctor if the rash persists or worsens.
- Try to keep the child from scratching at the rash.
- May be prevented by wearing light, loose-fitting clothing made of cotton or other absorbent material.

SYMPTOMS

Burning, prickling sensation around the underarm, thigh or groin. May affect other parts of the body. Sometimes accompanied by itching. Usually occurs in high heat and humidity or when a child is overdressed. Progresses to tiny red and pink pinpoints or blisters. The affected area may become inflamed. Commonly affects infants.

1 Take the child to a cool, shaded, well-ventilated or air-conditioned room.

2 Sponge the affected area with cool water. Gently blot dry.

3 Lightly apply baby powder or cornstarch to the affected area to keep it dry.

4 Change damp clothing and try to avoid further sweating.

HYPOGLYCEMIA (LOW BLOOD SUGAR)

IF THE CHILD IS CONSCIOUS

IF THE CHILD IS UNCONSCIOUS

HYPOGLYCEMIA (LOW BLOOD SUGAR)

IMPORTANT

- **If the child is unconscious, seek medical aid immediately.**
- Treat for **SHOCK**, pages 242-245.
- **Do not** administer prescribed insulin.
- **Do not** give the child anything to drink if he is unconscious or has difficulty swallowing.

SYMPTOMS

May affect anyone, though especially common in diabetics who are reacting to an excessive dose of insulin or who have taken a prescribed dose of insulin, then engaged in excessive exercise or have missed a meal. **Sudden appearance of:** Moist, clammy, ashen or pale skin. Profuse cold sweat. **May include:** Hunger. Shallow breathing. Confusion. Trembling hands. Shaking. Anxiety. Weakness. Dizziness. Personality change. **May progress to:** Convulsions. Coma.

IF THE CHILD IS CONSCIOUS

Give him orange juice, soft drinks containing sugar, candy or sugar in any form.

IF THE CHILD IS UNCONSCIOUS

Turn him on his side to keep the airway open and place a pinch of sugar under his tongue. When sugar has dissolved, repeat the dose. Continue small doses of sugar until he regains consciousness.

HYPOTHERMIA (COLD EXPOSURE)

INDOORS

OUTDOORS

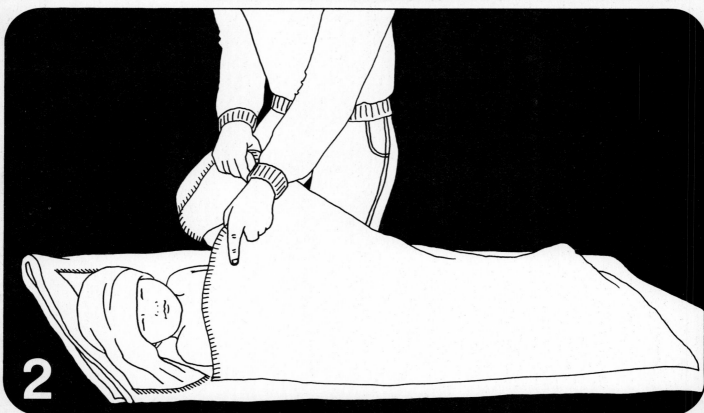

HYPOTHERMIA (COLD EXPOSURE)

IMPORTANT

- **Hypothermia is a life-threatening emergency caused by the lowering of the body core temperature.** It is usually caused by cold or cool air, wind, immersion in water, or wet clothing. Hypothermia may become extremely serious in a matter of minutes or develop slowly over the course of hours or even days.

- If symptoms are present, treat for hypothermia even if the child claims to be fine.

- **Seek medical aid immediately.** A child who has received emergency first aid for hypothermia should be examined by a doctor even if he appears to have recovered fully.

- **Do not** let the child walk or drink anything.

- **Do not** rub the child's body. **Handle him very gently.** Unnecessary manipulation may cause heart failure.

- Watch breathing closely. If it stops, see **BREATHING: ARTIFICIAL RESPIRATION**, pages 134-137.

SYMPTOMS

May include: Persistent or violent shivering. Slow or slurred speech. Personality change. Loss of control over hands. Stumbling. Drowsiness. Impaired reasoning. Confusion. The child may fail to acknowledge symptoms. **In advanced stages:** Muscle spasms and rigidity. Inability to use the arms or legs. Unconsciousness which may mimic death.

In all cases, it is extremely important to reach medical aid as quickly as possible.

1 Gently carry the child out of the wind and cold to a warm place, preferably indoors. If that isn't possible, start a fire and improvise a shelter.

2 Gently remove his wet clothing. (If outdoors, place a folded blanket under him to insulate him from the cold.) Wrap him in a blanket and cover his head with a scarf or the like.

CONTINUED ON NEXT PAGE

217

HYPOTHERMIA (COLD EXPOSURE)

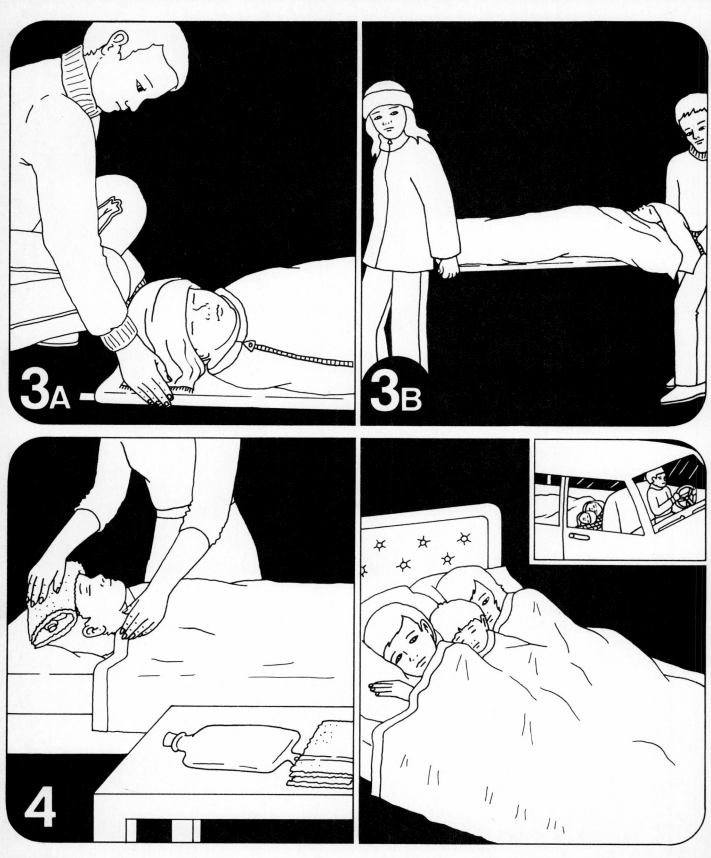

3A

3B

4

CONTINUED

3A **If hypothermia has developed quickly** (as in the case of immersion in cold water): Gently place him in a sleeping bag or several blankets, cover his head, and **transport him to medical aid immediately**; see **TRANSPORTING THE INJURED**, pages 260-261.

3B **If hypothermia has developed slowly over several hours or days** (as in the case of a lost child or the failure of a home heating system): Protect the child from further heat loss by gently wrapping him in a blanket. Loosely cover his head with a scarf or other suitable cloth to conserve heat further and pre-warm the air he breathes. If possible, further insulate the child from wind and cold by placing him in a sleeping bag or wrapping him in a sheet of plastic or plastic garbage bags. (**Do not** cover his face.) **Transport him to medical aid immediately**; see **TRANSPORTING THE INJURED**, pages 260-261.

4 **If travel is delayed or impossible and medical aid cannot reach you, rewarm the child:** Expose him to warm air and apply gentle heat to the head, neck, torso and groin with hot-water bottles wrapped in towels. Or warm his body with your own through skin-to-skin contact. If possible, maximize the warming process by placing him between two people. **It is important that you prevent further heat loss.** If at all feasible, continue skin-to-skin warming or application of gentle heat during travel to medical aid.

MOUTH INJURIES: GUMS, PALATE, TEETH, TONGUE & LIPS

GUMS & PALATE

TEETH

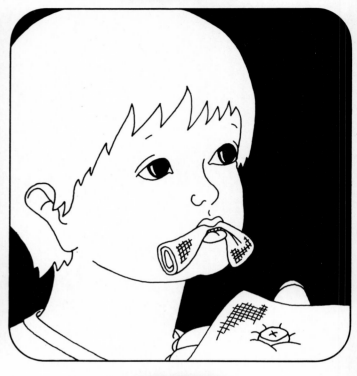

TONGUE

LIPS

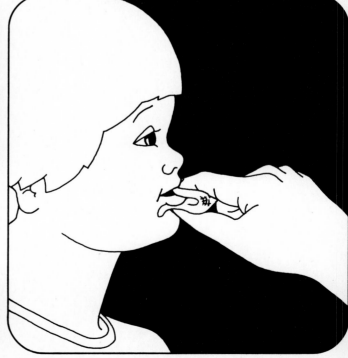

MOUTH INJURIES:

GUMS, PALATE, TEETH, TONGUE & LIPS

IMPORTANT

- Check if there are more serious injuries to the head or neck. If necessary, see **HEAD INJURIES: CLOSED HEAD INJURIES**, pages 182-183, and **BACK & NECK INJURIES**, pages 84-85.
- Clear the mouth of broken teeth. Bring them to the doctor or dentist for possible replanting.
- Lean the child slightly forward so he does not inhale blood.

GUMS & PALATE

Control bleeding by direct pressure.

TEETH

Control bleeding by direct pressure on the tooth socket. Have the child bite down firmly to hold the dressing in place.

TONGUE

Control bleeding by pressing both sides of the tongue. For more severe bleeding, gently pull the tongue and hold it for about 5 minutes.

LIPS

Control bleeding by pressing both sides of the wound.

MUSCLE CRAMP (CHARLEY HORSE)

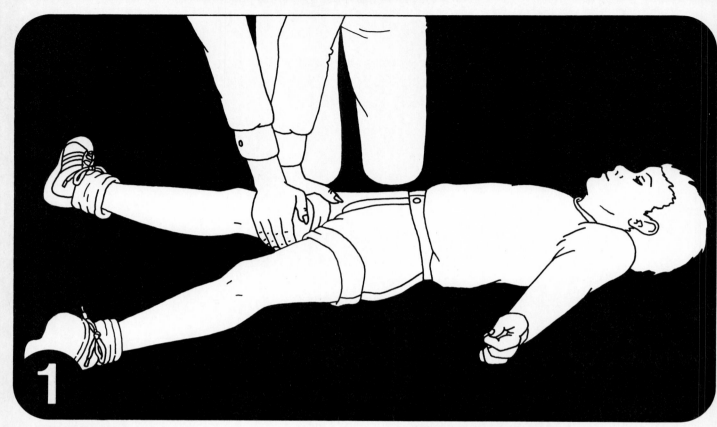

1

2

3

MUSCLE CRAMP (CHARLEY HORSE)

IMPORTANT

- Try to relax the affected area. Tension can worsen the muscle spasm.

SYMPTOMS

Sudden spasm and pain in a muscle, usually the calf or thigh. May worsen with movement and limit use of the affected area. Often occurs following overexertion, injury or exposure to cold or dampness. In severe cases, discomfort may last several days or longer.

1 Stretch the cramped muscle and apply firm pressure to the affected area with your hands until the cramp is relieved.

2 Apply warm wet compresses or a hot-water bottle.

3 Have the child rest the affected part.

NOSE INJURIES:

BROKEN NOSE, FOREIGN OBJECTS, & NOSEBLEED

BROKEN NOSE

FOREIGN OBJECTS

NOSEBLEED

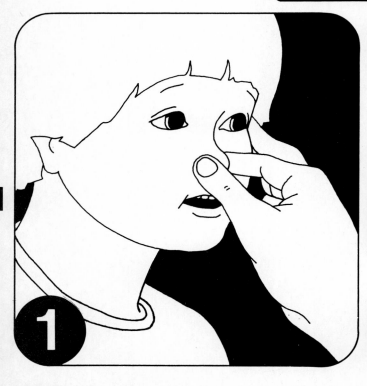

NOSE INJURIES:

BROKEN NOSE

1 Control the bleeding as for **NOSEBLEED**; see below. Gently press cold compresses over the nose. **Do not** splint. **Seek medical aid.**

FOREIGN OBJECTS

1 Tell the child to inhale through his mouth, **not** his nose. Have him blow his nose gently, keeping both nostrils open. If the object does not come out easily, **do not** try to remove it. **Seek medical aid immediately.**

NOSEBLEED

1 Lean the child forward and gently pinch the lower, soft part of the nose for about 5 minutes, then apply cold compresses.

2 If bleeding persists, pack the nostril with absorbent gauze, then pinch the nose closed for about 10 minutes. **Seek medical aid** if bleeding continues.

225

IMPORTANT

- **Call your local Poison Control Center immediately. Also seek medical aid.**

- Save the poison container and a sample of the vomit.

- Watch breathing closely. If necessary, see **BREATHING: ARTIFICIAL RESPIRATION**, pages 134-137.

- **Do not** give the child anything to drink if he is unconscious.

- **Ingredients in products may change over time, and antidotes or counterdoses given on labels may be obsolete or incorrect. Always consult your local Poison Control Center or other professional medical aid. The following treatments are to be used only when emergency medical aid is not available.**

If you cannot reach a Poison Control Center or other medical aid:

- Find the poison swallowed on the list on the opposite page.

- Follow the corresponding treatment on pages 228-229.

- If you don't know what was swallowed, follow Treatment **A**. If there are no burns around the mouth or any petroleum odors, also have the child drink activated charcoal mixed in a glass of water. Determine the proper dosage by consulting the chart below.

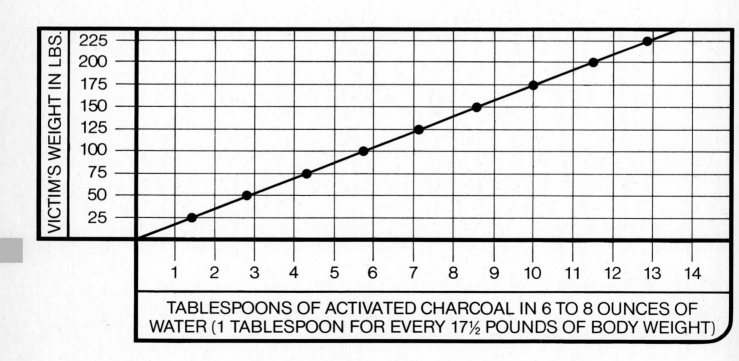

Aspirin or Aspirin Substitutes**B**
Acetone**B**
After Shave Lotion**B**
Alcohol**B**
Antifreeze**B**
Arsenic**B**
Battery Acid**A**
Benzene**B**
Bichloride of Mercury**B**
Bleach**B**
Body Conditioner**B**
Boric Acid**B**
Brush Cleaner**A**
Camphor**B**
Carbon Tetrachloride**B**
Charcoal Lighter**A**
Chlordane**B**
Cologne**B**
Corn Remover**A**
Cosmetics**B**
DDT**B**
Deodorant**B**
Detergent**B**
Dishwasher Granules**A**
Drain Cleaner**A**
Fabric Softeners**B**
Fingernail Polish & Remover**B**
Fireworks**B**
Floor Polish**A**
Fluoride**B**
Furniture Polish**A**
Gasoline**A**
Grease Remover**A**
Gun Cleaner**A**
Hair Dye**B**
Hair Permanent Neutralizer**B**
Hair Preparations**B**
Hydrogen Peroxide**B**

Indelible Markers**B**
Ink (Green & Purple)**B**
Insecticides**B**
Iodine**B**
Kerosene**A**
Lacquer Thinner**A**
Liniment**B**
Lye**A**
Matches (more than 20 wooden matches or 2 matchbooks)**B**
Mercury Salts**B**
Metal Cleaner**A**
Mothballs, Flakes or Cakes**B**
Naphtha**A**
Oil of Wintergreen**B**
Oven Cleaner**A**
Paint (Lead)**B**
Paint Thinner**A**
Perfume**B**
Pesticides**B**
Pine Oil**B**
Quicklime**A**
Rat or Mouse Poison**B**
Roach Poison**B**
Shoe Polish**A**
Strychnine**B**
Suntan Preparations**B**
Toilet Bowl Cleaner**A**
Turpentine**B**
Typewriter Cleaner**A**
Wart Remover**A**
Washing Soda**A**
Wax (Floor or Furniture)**A**
Weed Killer**B**
Wick Deodorizer**B**
Wood Preservative**A**
Zinc Compounds**A**

CONTINUED ON NEXT PAGE

FOR ACID, ALKALI & PETROLEUM POISONING

IMPORTANT

- **Do not** induce vomiting unless instructed to do so by a Poison Control Center or physician.

SYMPTOMS OF ACID & ALKALI POISONING

Burns around the mouth, lips and tongue. Burning sensations in the mouth, throat and stomach. Cramps. Disorientation. Bloody diarrhea.

SYMPTOMS OF PETROLEUM POISONING

Burning irritation. Coughing. Gagging. Coma. May include petroleum product odor on the breath.

1 **If the child is conscious**, give him 1 or 2 glasses of milk to dilute the poison. (If milk isn't available, use water.)

2 Loosen tight clothing and treat for **SHOCK**, pages 242-245.

B **FOR OTHER POISONING**

IMPORTANT

- **Do not** wait for symptoms to develop.

SYMPTOMS

May be intermittent and develop slowly or quickly. **May include:** Nausea. Dizziness. Drowsiness. Slurred speech. Lack of coordination. Cold clammy skin. Thirst. Convulsions. Coma.

1 **If the child is conscious**, give him 1 or 2 glasses of water to dilute the poison.

2 **If he has not vomited**, induce vomiting by giving him syrup of ipecac (2 teaspoons for an infant, 1 tablespoon for a small child, 2 tablespoons for an older child), followed by a glass of water. Keep the child moving. **If he doesn't vomit within 30 minutes**, give him a second dose followed by another glass of water, but **do not** repeat a third time. **If he still hasn't vomited within the next 30 minutes**, try to induce vomiting by placing your finger on the back of his tongue. **Use this method immediately if ipecac isn't available.**

3 When he starts to vomit, make sure his head is between his legs. Hold an infant or small child face down over your knee.

4 When he has finished vomiting, give him activated charcoal mixed in a glass of water. Determine the proper dosage by consulting the chart on page 226.

5 Loosen tight clothing and treat for **SHOCK**, pages 242-245.

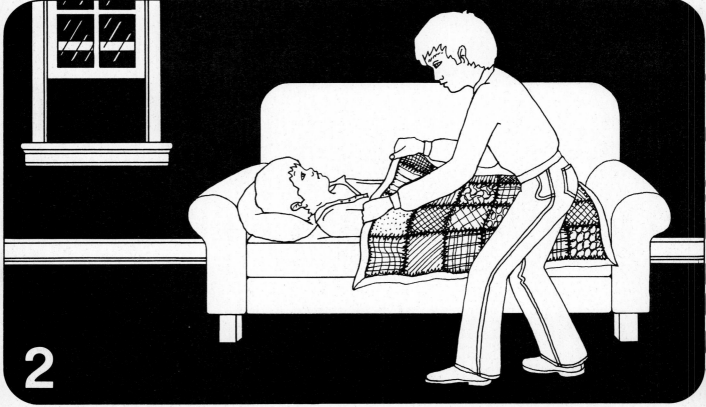

IMPORTANT

- **Seek medical aid and oxygen immediately.**
- **Also call your local Poison Control Center.**
- Watch breathing closely. If necessary, see **BREATHING: ARTIFICIAL RESPIRATION**, pages 134-137.
- If possible, ventilate the area. Open doors and windows, turn on the exhaust fan, etc.

SYMPTOMS

Irritated eyes, nose, throat or lungs. Coughing. Headache. Shortness of breath. Nausea. Dizziness. Convulsions. Unconsciousness. Caused by auto exhaust or chemical fumes from paints, solvents and industrial gases.

1 Remove the child from the source of the poison. Be careful not to inhale the poison yourself.

2 Loosen tight clothing and treat for **SHOCK**, pages 242-245. Keep him from becoming chilled. If the skin is affected by chemical vapor or mist, see **BURNS: CHEMICAL**, pages 138-139.

POISON IVY

POISON OAK

POISON SUMAC

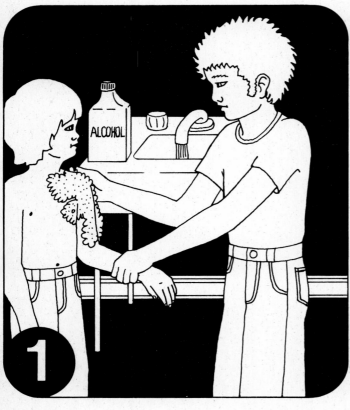

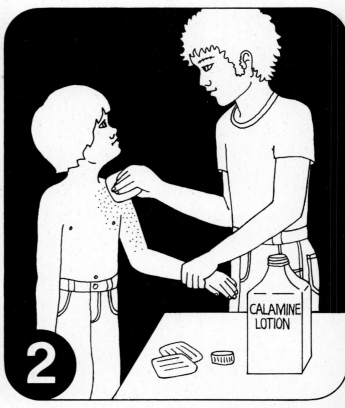

ALCOHOL

CALAMINE LOTION

1

2

IMPORTANT

- **Seek medical aid if there is a severe reaction or the child is highly allergic.**

- Watch breathing closely. If necessary, see **BREATHING: ARTIFICIAL RESPIRATION**, pages 134-137.

- Observe for **SHOCK**, pages 242-245.

SYMPTOMS

Burning and itching. Rash. Blisters. Swelling. Headache. Fever.

1 Remove contaminated clothing. Wash all affected areas thoroughly with soap and water, then apply rubbing alcohol. **Do not** break blisters.

2 Apply calamine lotion to ease the itching. Keep contaminated clothing separate from other laundry and wash thoroughly several times.

POISONING: PLANTS

IMPORTANT

- **Call your local Poison Control Center immediately. Also seek medical aid.**

- Watch breathing closely. If necessary, see **BREATHING: ARTIFICIAL RESPIRATION**, pages 134-137.

- **Do not** give the child anything to drink if he is unconscious.

- If you cannot reach a Poison Control Center or doctor, see **POISONING: SWALLOWED POISONS**, pages 228-229, and follow **Treatment Ⓑ**.

BANEBERRY

SYMPTOMS

Dizziness. Cramps. Vomiting. Headache. Delirium.

BITTERSWEET

SYMPTOMS

Burning sensation in the throat. Nausea. Dizziness. Dilated pupils. Weakness. Convulsions.

CASTOR BEAN

SYMPTOMS

Burning sensations in the mouth and throat. Nausea. Vomiting. Cramps. Stupor. Convulsions.

DAPHNE

SYMPTOMS

Burning sensations in the mouth, throat and stomach. Cramps.

FOXGLOVE

SYMPTOMS

Nausea. Upset stomach. Dizziness. Disorientation.

JIMSON WEED

SYMPTOMS

Extreme thirst. Difficulty speaking. Impaired vision. Rapid heartbeat. Dilated pupils. Delirium. Increased body temperature. Coma.

LARKSPUR (DELPHINIUM)

SYMPTOMS

Tingling in the mouth and on the skin. Upset stomach. Anxiety. Severe depression.

CONTINUED ON NEXT PAGE

LILY-OF-THE-VALLEY

SYMPTOMS

Upset stomach. Dizziness. Vomiting. Disorientation.

MONKSHOOD

SYMPTOMS

Tingling or numbness of the lips and tongue. Excessive salivating. Dizziness. Nausea. Vomiting. Dimmed vision.

NIGHTSHADE

SYMPTOMS

Thirst. Upset stomach. Numbness. Rapid heartbeat.

POISON HEMLOCK

SYMPTOMS

Burning sensations in the mouth and throat. Weakness. Paralysis of the arms and chest. Stupor.

POKEWEED

SYMPTOMS

Burning sensations in the mouth and throat. Nausea. Cramps. Upset stomach. Vomiting. Drowsiness. Impaired vision.

WATER HEMLOCK

SYMPTOMS

Excessive salivating. Foaming at the mouth. Stomach pain. Frenzy. Shivering. Irregular breathing. Delirium. Convulsions. Coma.

YEW

SYMPTOMS

Nausea. Stomach pain. Vomiting. Shivering. Difficulty breathing. Diarrhea.

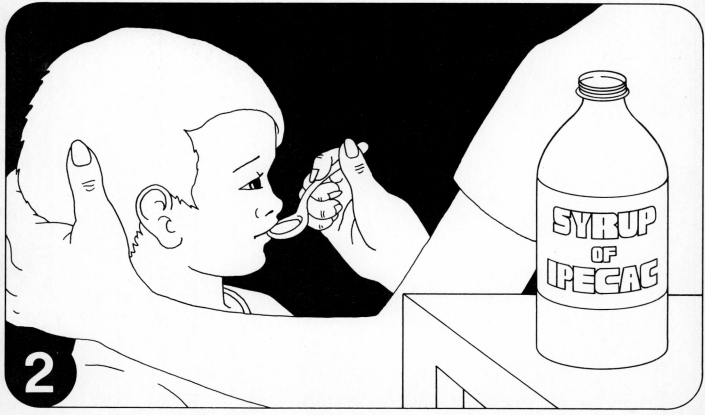

MUSHROOM POISONING

IMPORTANT

- **Call your local Poison Control Center immediately if you know or suspect that a poisonous mushroom has been ingested. Also seek medical aid.**

- **If you cannot reach a Poison Control Center or medical aid, begin treatment immediately. Do not wait for symptoms to develop.**

- Save a sample of the vomit and, if possible, the mushroom.

- **Do not** give the child anything alcoholic to drink.

- **If he is unconscious**, **do not** give him **anything** to drink.

SYMPTOMS

Depending on the mushroom, symptoms may develop rapidly (from minutes to about 2 hours) or slowly (from 6 to 24 hours). **May include:** Profuse salivation or drooling. Tearing of the eyes. Headache. Nausea. Sweating. Tiny pupils. Vomiting. Stomach cramps. Severe diarrhea. Dizziness and confusion. Coma. **In delayed reactions, symptoms may also include:** Passage of little or no urine. After 2 to 3 days, jaundiced (yellowed) skin and eyes.

1 **If the child is conscious**, give him 1 or 2 glasses of water to dilute the poison.

2 **If he has not vomited**, induce vomiting by giving him syrup of ipecac (2 teaspoons for an infant, 1 tablespoon for a small child, 2 tablespoons for an older child), followed by a glass of water. Keep the child moving. **If he doesn't vomit within 30 minutes**, give him a second dose followed by another glass of water, but **do not** repeat a third time. **If he still hasn't vomited within the next 30 minutes**, try to induce vomiting by placing your finger on the back of his tongue. **Use this method immediately if ipecac isn't available.**

CONTINUED ON NEXT PAGE

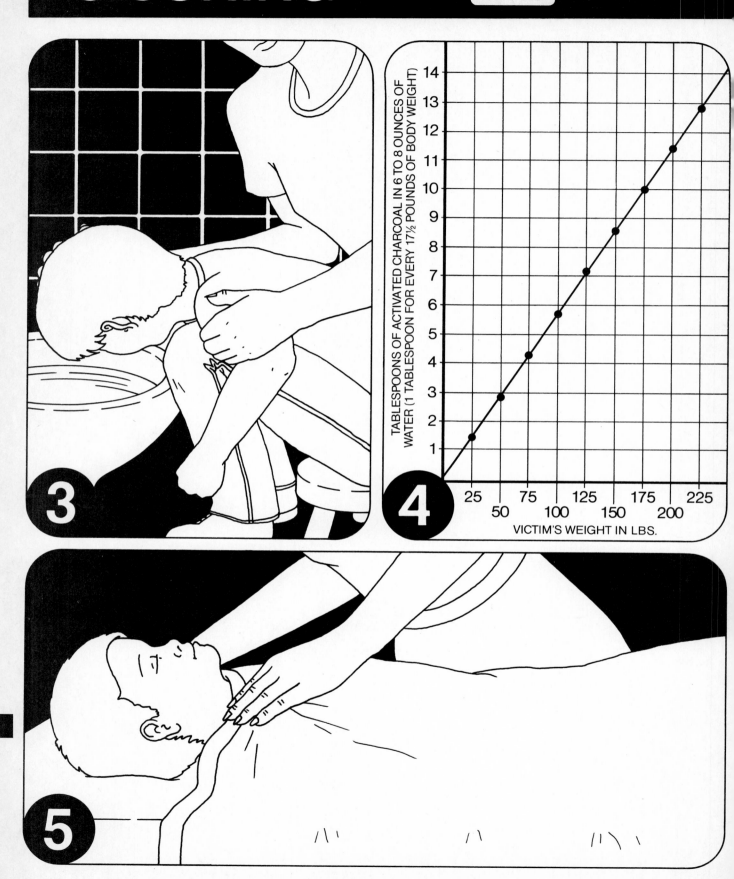

TABLESPOONS OF ACTIVATED CHARCOAL IN 6 TO 8 OUNCES OF WATER (1 TABLESPOON FOR EVERY 17½ POUNDS OF BODY WEIGHT)

VICTIM'S WEIGHT IN LBS.

CONTINUED

3 When he starts to vomit, make sure his head is between his legs. Hold a small child face down over your knee.

4 When he has finished vomiting, have the child drink activated charcoal mixed in a glass of water. Determine the proper dosage by consulting the chart.

5 Loosen tight clothing and treat for **SHOCK**, pages 242-245.

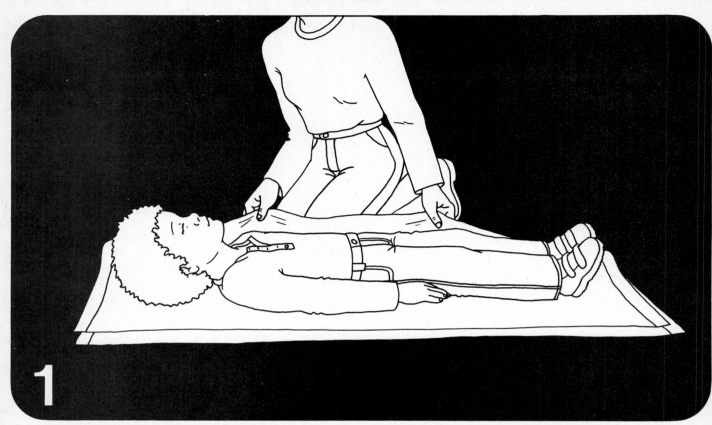

1

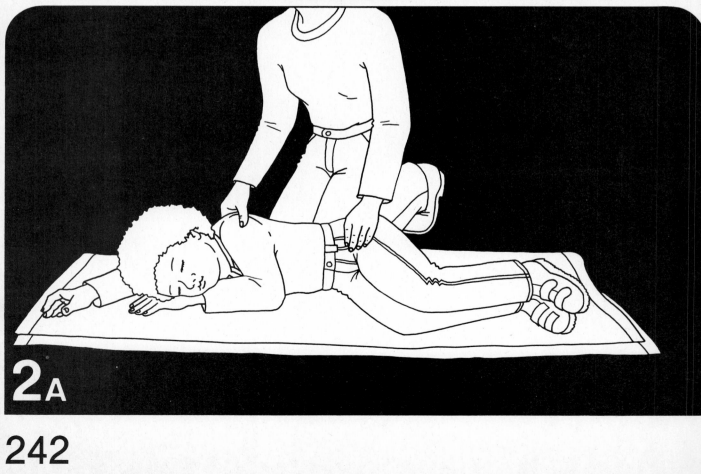

2A

IMPORTANT

- **Always treat a seriously injured child for shock.**
- **Do not** give the child anything to drink.
- **Do not** overheat.
- **Seek medical aid immediately.**

SYMPTOMS

Pale or bluish lips, gums and fingernails. Clammy skin, mottled in color. Weakness. Breathing is weak and shallow or deep but irregular. **May also include:** Anxiety. Apathy. Nausea. Thirst.

1 Lay the child down. Place a blanket under him if he is cold or damp, but **do not** move him if his back or neck is injured.

2A **If he has no back or neck injuries and is unconscious or bleeding heavily from the jaw or lower face**, turn him on his side to keep the airway open. In the case of an open chest injury, turn him onto the injured side.

CONTINUED ON NEXT PAGE

SHOCK

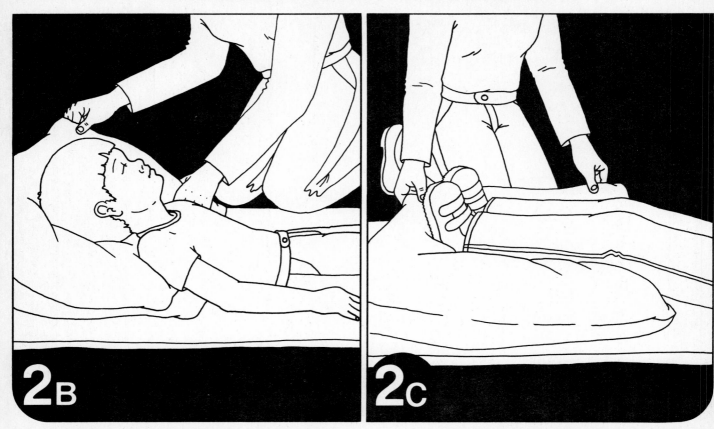

2B

2C

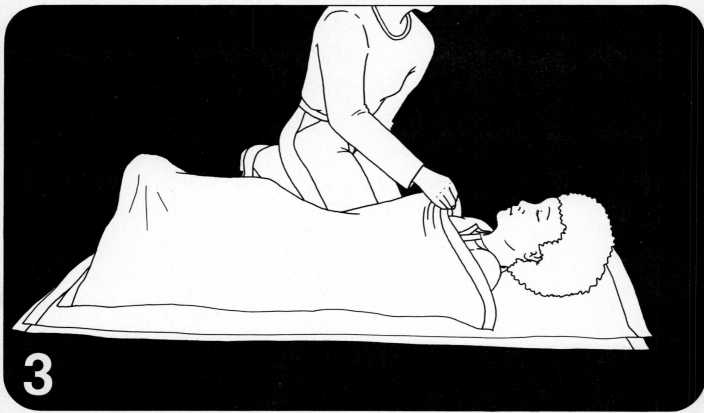

3

CONTINUED

2B **If his head is injured or he has trouble breathing**, elevate his neck and shoulders.

2C **Otherwise**, elevate his legs about 8 to 12 inches, unless that causes pain.

3 Cover the child lightly with a blanket to prevent loss of body heat.

SPLINTERS

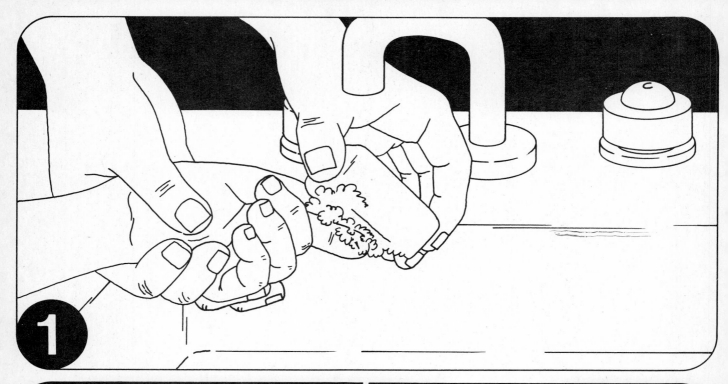

1

2A

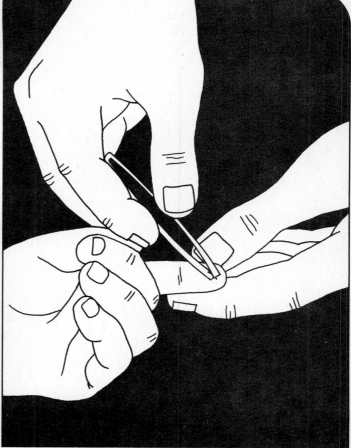

IMPORTANT

- **Seek medical aid if the splinter is deeply embedded beneath the skin or if signs of infection develop after it has been removed.**
- Wash your hands thoroughly before you attempt to remove the splinter.

1 Gently wash the area around the splinter with soap and water.

2A **If the splinter is protruding from the skin**, sterilize a tweezers by holding it over an open flame or soaking it for 10 minutes in rubbing alcohol or boiling water, then gently remove the splinter at the same angle at which it entered.

CONTINUED ON NEXT PAGE

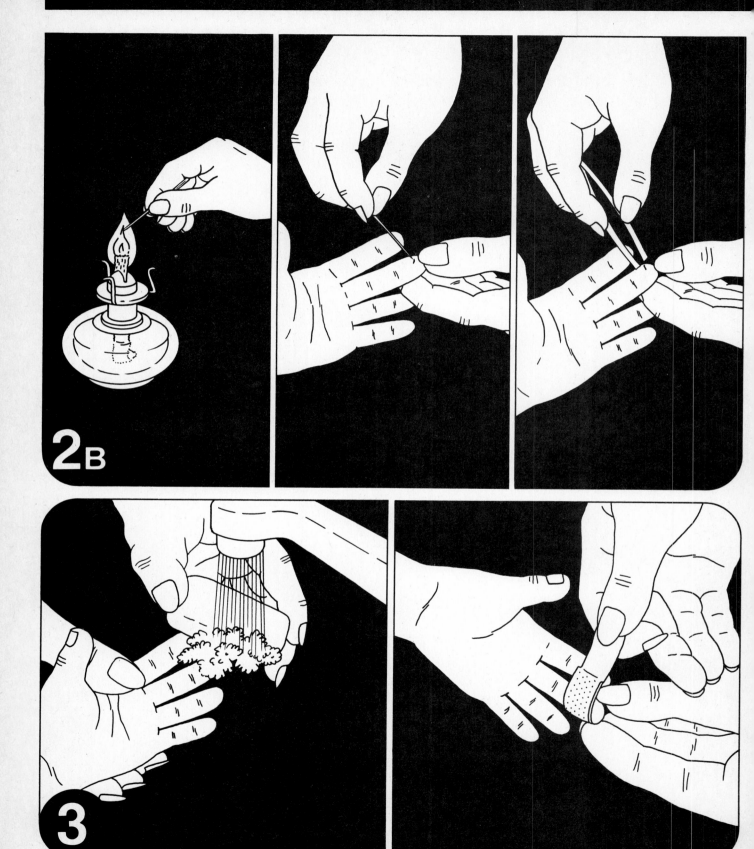

2B

3

CONTINUED

2B **If the splinter is embedded just under the skin**, sterilize a needle by holding it over an open flame or soaking it for 10 minutes in rubbing alcohol or boiling water, then gently loosen the skin around the splinter and remove it with a sterilized tweezers at the same angle at which it entered.

3 Wash the affected area with soap and water, then cover with a bandage.

SPRAINS & STRAINS

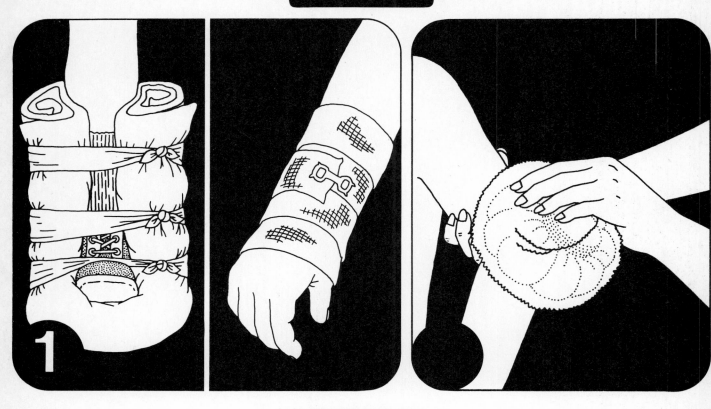

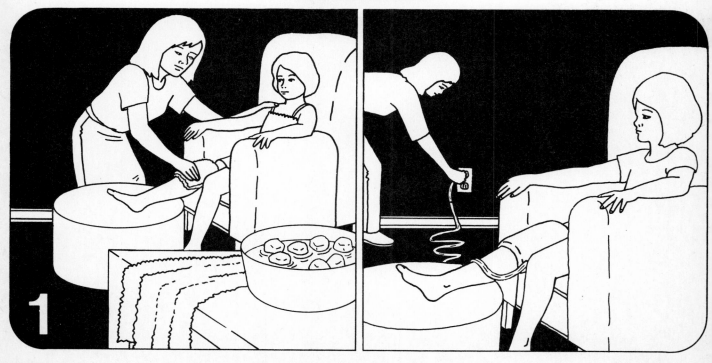

SPRAINS & STRAINS

IMPORTANT

- Keep the child off the injured parts.
- **Do not** pack in ice or immerse in ice water.

SPRAINS

SYMPTOMS

Pain, rapid swelling, tenderness and discoloration of the soft tissue surrounding a joint.

1 Immobilize the injured area with a blanket, splint, pillow, elasticized bandage, etc. **Do not** bandage too tightly; sprains swell.

2 To minimize swelling, elevate sprained elbows, knees or ankles. Apply cold, wet compresses or an ice bag covered with a towel.

STRAINS

SYMPTOMS

Pain caused by stretched or pulled muscles.

1 Rest the injured part. To decrease swelling, apply cold, wet compresses. After 24 hours, apply warm, wet compresses or a heating pad.

STOMACH INJURIES

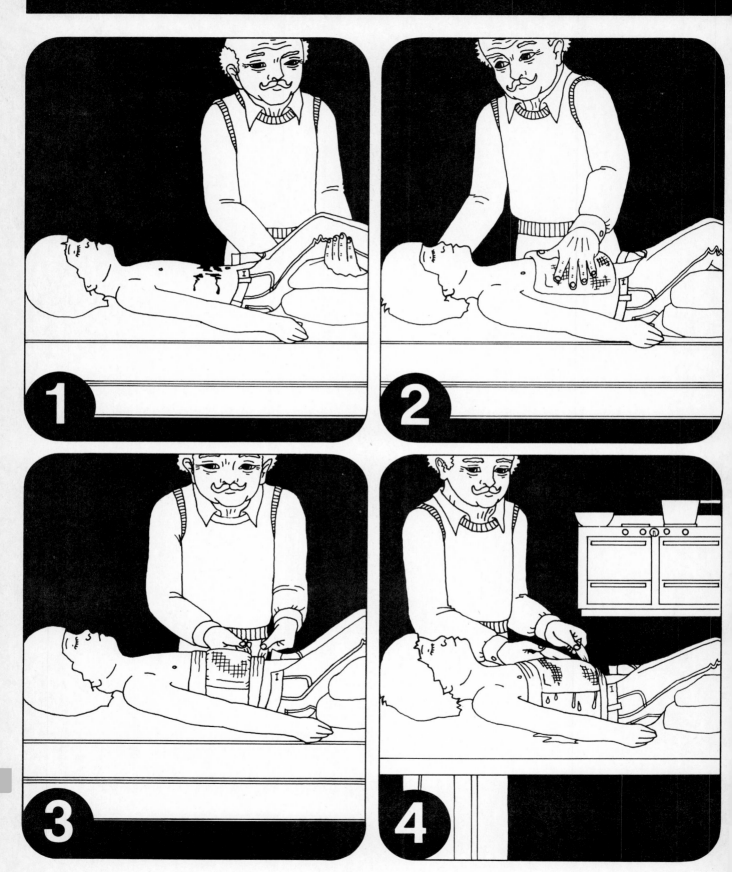

STOMACH INJURIES

IMPORTANT

- **Do not** give the child anything to drink.
- If breathing becomes difficult, elevate the head and shoulders.
- For impaled objects, see **BLEEDING: CUTS & WOUNDS (IMPALED OBJECTS)**, pages 110-111.
- **Seek medical aid immediately.**

1 Relax the stomach muscles by placing the child on his back with a pillow or blanket under his knees.

2 Control bleeding by applying gentle direct pressure on the wound with gauze or a clean cloth.

3 Bandage the dressing firmly in place.

4 If organs or intestines protrude, **do not** attempt to replace them. Cover the area with a clean dressing dampened with sterile or cooled boiled water. Bandage in place firmly but not too tightly. Treat for **SHOCK**, pages 242-245.

SUNSTROKE (HEATSTROKE)

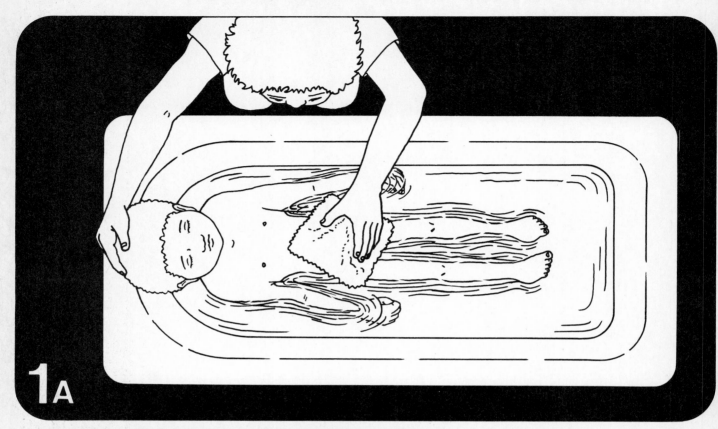

1A

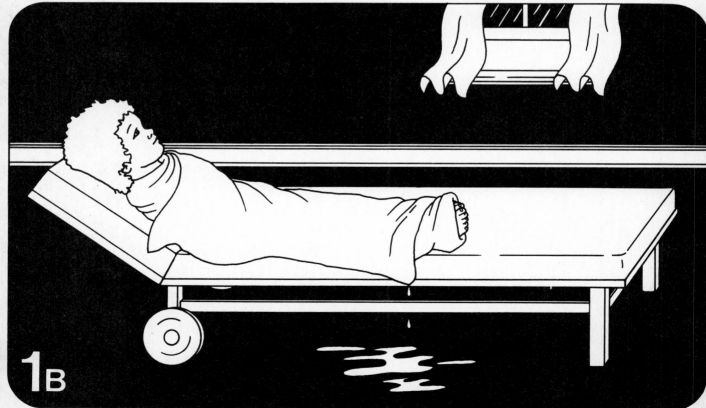

1B

SUNSTROKE (HEATSTROKE)

IMPORTANT

- **Seek medical aid immediately.**
- **Act quickly. Body temperature must be lowered at once.** Recheck temperature every 10 minutes. **Do not** reduce temperature below 101°F. (38.3°C.). Repeat first aid if temperature rises.
- **Do not give stimulants.**
- **Do not** chill.
- Observe for **SHOCK**, pages 242-245.

SYMPTOMS

Red, hot and dry skin. Extremely high temperature. No sweating. Rapid pulse. **May also include:** Disorientation. Unconsciousness.

1A Place the child in a partially filled tub of cool water. Using light, brisk strokes, sponge his entire body until temperature is reduced.

1B Or take the child to a cool, well-ventilated room, and wrap him in wet, cold sheets until temperature is reduced.

TAKING THE PULSE

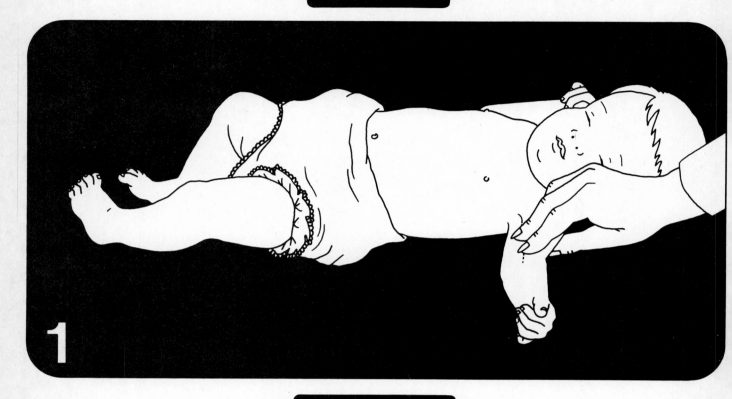

CHILDREN

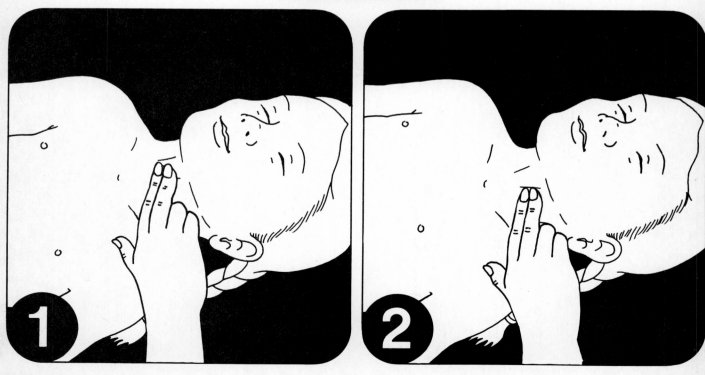

TAKING THE PULSE

IMPORTANT

- In a serious emergency it may be necessary to check the child's pulse to determine whether the heart has stopped beating and emergency first aid for heart failure should therefore begin. In this case, **it is extremely important to find the pulse if one is present since first aid for heart failure is potentially dangerous and should never be performed needlessly**. **Do not** rush. Check the pulse slowly and carefully, taking between 5 and 10 seconds to find it.

- **Do not** use your thumb to check the pulse since its own pulse may be mistaken for that of the child.

- If possible, check the pulse when the child is at rest. The pulse is normally strong and regular. The rate typically rises to reflect increases in activity, body temperature, anxiety, etc. Illness or injury may produce a pulse that is irregular, slow and/or weak.

NORMAL PULSE RATES (AT REST)

Infant: 100 to 130 beats a minute
Small Child: 80 to 100 beats a minute
Older Child: 60 to 90 beats a minute

INFANTS

1 Place the tips of your fingers on the inside of the upper arm.

CHILDREN

1 Place your first two fingers on the child's Adam's apple (about halfway between the chin and the collarbone).

2 Slide your fingers into the groove next to the windpipe on the side nearest you, then press gently.

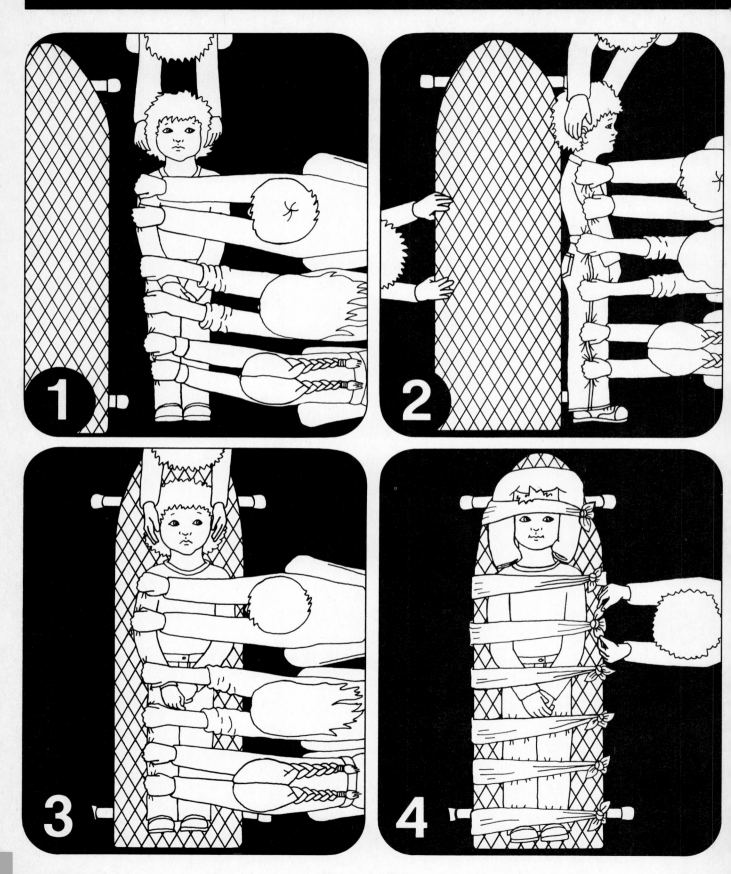

IMPORTANT

- **If the child is seriously injured, call an ambulance immediately. Do not move him unless it is a matter of life or death and no ambulance is available.** It is almost always better to wait for proper equipment and expert help. If you must transport the child, get as much aid as possible.

1 Devise a stretcher out of a sturdy board, door, ironing board, etc.

2 **Do not** twist the child. Move his body as a single unit, keeping his head in line with his spinal column. On a signal from the person holding the head, roll him gently onto his side and place the stretcher next to him.

3 Roll him onto the stretcher carefully without twisting his body or head.

4 Immobilize his head with a rolled blanket or the like. (For spine injuries, also immobilize his torso.) Bind him to the stretcher with bandages, belts, etc.

IMPROVISED STRETCHERS

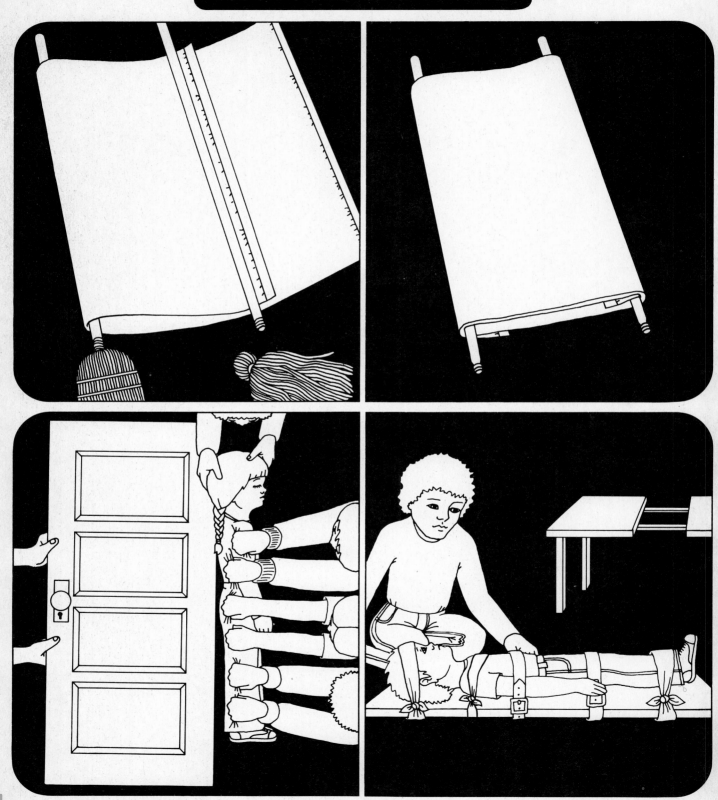

CHAIR CARRY

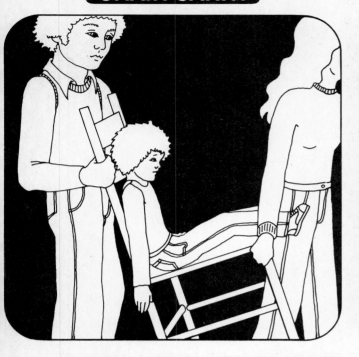

ONE-PERSON LIFT

FIREMAN & PACK-STRAP

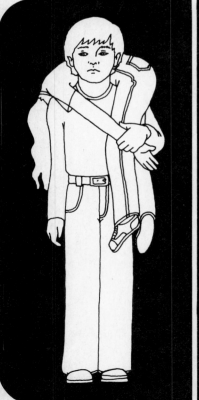
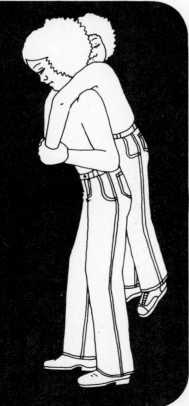

TWO-MAN SEAT

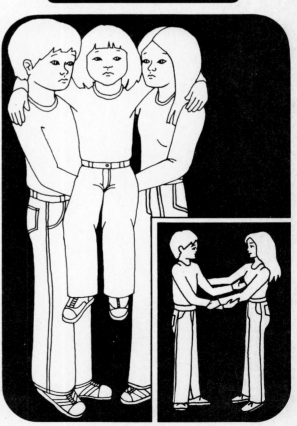

UNCONSCIOUSNESS

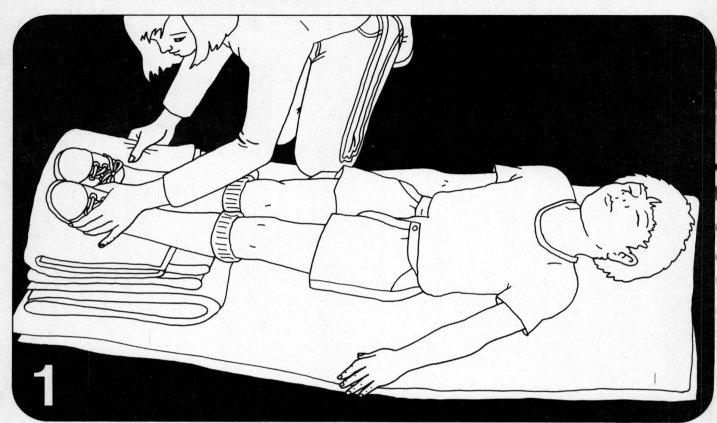

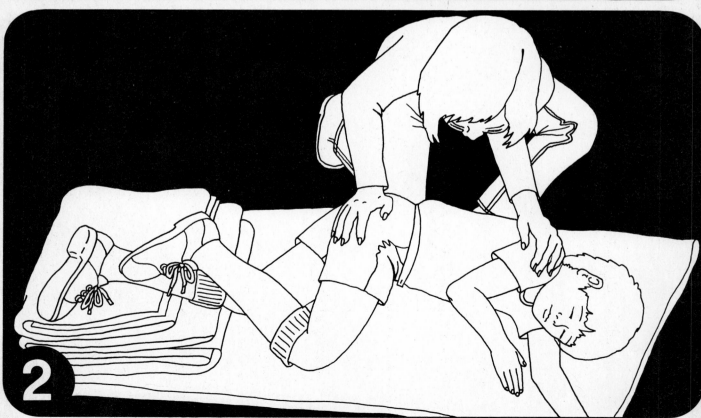

UNCONSCIOUSNESS

IMPORTANT

- **Seek medical aid immediately if the child does not revive when you call him loudly, tap him on the shoulder or shake him gently.** Note how long he remains unconscious and any changes in his state.

- Watch breathing closely. If necessary, see **BREATHING: ARTIFICIAL RESPIRATION**, pages 134-137.

- **Do not** move the child unless absolutely necessary. You may cause further harm. If necessary, see **TRANSPORTING THE INJURED**, pages 258-261.

- **Do not** give him anything to drink.

- If the cause of unconsciousness is not known, check for signs of injury, hidden bleeding, bites or stings, poisons, drugs, etc. Look for emergency medical information tags around the neck or wrist, or a card in the wallet identifying the possible cause. On hot days or following vigorous exercise, the child may be suffering heatstroke or heat exhaustion; see **SUNSTROKE (HEATSTROKE)**, pages 254-255, and **HEAT EX-HAUSTION**, pages 210-211.

SYMPTOMS

Can vary from a brief loss of consciousness, from which the child can be easily roused, to a deep coma. Depending on the cause, the face, gums or inner linings of the eyelids may appear either flushed, white or blue.

1 Keep the child lying down. Loosen restrictive clothing. Provide good ventilation. Elevate his legs 8 to 12 inches.

2 If the child vomits, turn his head to the side or roll him onto his side to keep the airway open and allow fluids to drain.

Emergency Telephone Numbers

This list of emergency numbers should be filled in immediately, then photocopied so you can also post it next to your telephone. Keep the numbers up-to-date. Be sure to show it to your baby-sitter whenever you go out.

RESCUE SQUAD OR EMERGENCY AMBULANCE _____

POISON CONTROL CENTER _____ **POLICE** _____

FIRE DEPARTMENT _____ **HOSPITAL EMERGENCY** _____

TAXI _____ **EMERGENCY SHELTER** _____

PEDIATRICIAN: Name _____ Office _____ Home _____

FAMILY DOCTOR: Name _____ Office _____ Home _____

ALTERNATE DOCTOR: Name _____ Office _____ Home _____

SPECIALIST: TYPE _____ Name _____ Office _____

SPECIALIST: TYPE _____ Name _____ Office _____

DENTIST: Name _____ Office _____ Home _____

NEAREST DRUGSTORE _____ Hours _____ Phone _____

ALL-NIGHT DRUGSTORE _____ Phone _____

FATHER'S PHONE AT WORK _____ **MOTHER'S PHONE AT WORK** _____

OTHER FAMILY MEMBERS' PHONES AT WORK: _____

Name _____ Phone _____

Name _____ Phone _____

NEIGHBORS & FRIENDS:

Name _____ Address _____ Phone _____

Name _____ Address _____ Phone _____

Name _____ Address _____ Phone _____

MISCELLANEOUS NUMBERS:

Name _____ Address _____ Phone _____

Name _____ Address _____ Phone _____

Name _____ Address _____ Phone _____

Name _____ Address _____ Phone _____

COAL SUPPLIER _____ **GAS COMPANY** _____

ELECTRIC COMPANY _____ **OIL COMPANY** _____

FIREWOOD SUPPLIER _____ **WATER DEPARTMENT** _____

OTHER NUMBERS _____